1 SEP 04

# THE
# ROAD TO
# RAINBOW

An Association of the U.S. Army Book

# THE
# ROAD TO
# RAINBOW

## ARMY PLANNING FOR
## GLOBAL WAR,
## 1934–1940

## Henry G. Gole

Naval Institute Press ★ Annapolis, Maryland

Naval Institute Press
291 Wood Road
Annapolis, MD 21402

Library of Congress Cataloging-in-Publication Data
Gole, Henry G., 1933–
The road to rainbow : army planning for global war,
1934–1940 / Henry G. Gole.
p. cm.—(Association of the U.S. Army book)
Includes bibliographical references and index.
ISBN 1-55750-409-1 (hardcover : alk. paper)
1. Military planning—United States—History—20th century.
2. Army War College (U.S.)—History—20th century.
3. Strategy—History—20th century.  I. Title.
II. AUSA Institute of Land Warfare book.
U153 .G65 2002
355'.033573'09043—dc21


2002011447


Printed in the United States of America on acid-free paper

10  09  08  07  06  05  04  03    9  8  7  6  5  4  3  2


First printing

*To Lydia,*
*who was there from*
*before the beginning*
*to after the end.*

# Contents

# Preface

An important document from the Center of Military History files (CMH, Historical Records Section 313-2) sheds light on why the war planning done at the U.S. Army War College has not been given the attention it deserves. A memorandum dated 14 March 1957 from Deputy Chief Historian Louis Morton through Chief Historian Kent Roberts Greenfield to the chief of military history refers to Morton's discovery of "25 footlockers of Course Material in the AWC basement and attic" in Carlisle Barracks, Pennsylvania. Among the footlockers were twenty-three containing curricular materials for the period 1919–40. Morton said that the collection at Carlisle was "probably only second in value to the General Staff [collection] of the period 1919–1941 . . . at the [National] Archives."

Washington Barracks, now Fort Lesley J. McNair, was the home of the Army War College when the college closed its doors in 1940. The footlockers were packed and stored for the duration of the war, presumably in Washington Barracks. The army's joint and combined experiences in World War II convinced the leadership of the need for joint staff training for officers. The National War College—a multiservice institution—was established at Fort McNair. There was no AWC. The Naval War College went about its business, and the newly founded Air Force established the Air War College. The army decided to reopen the AWC and did so at Fort Leavenworth, Kansas, graduating a class in 1951 before moving to Carlisle Barracks. It is unclear whether the footlockers found by Morton made the trip to Leavenworth, but they turned up at AWC in Carlisle Barracks in 1957. The building in which they were found later housed the Military History Institute (MHI).

Morton said that while the Army War College was primarily an educational institution from 1919 to 1940, its students for part of this period "based their studies on the actual war plans developed by the joint and general staffs . . . and did important spade work [for the joint and general staffs]." He scanned the contents of the footlockers, recognized their value, and wanted them for CMH. There is no record, however, that the materials got there. I believe that the curricular materials in the archives of MHI at Carlisle Barracks include the former contents of those footlockers.

The AWC course materials for the period 1919–40 were not available to the researchers and authors of the relevant volumes published before 1957 in the celebrated United States Army in World War II series: Ray S. Cline's *Washington Command Post: The Operations Division* (Washington, D.C.: Office of the Chief of Military History, Department of the Army, 1951); Mark S. Watson's *Chief of Staff: Prewar Plans and Preparations* (Washington, D.C.: Office of the Chief of Military History, Department of the Army, 1950); and Maurice Matloff and Edwin M. Snell, *Strategic Planning for Coalition Warfare, 1941–1942* (Washington, D.C.: Office of the Chief of Military History, Department of the Army, 1953). Had Matloff, Snell, and the other authors of the "Green Books" been aware of the war planning at the college, particularly that portion of the War Plans Period called "Participation with Allies" from 1934 to 1940, they would have known that there was an intermediate stage between the Color Plans and the Rainbow Plans available to them as they wrote. "Participation with Allies" was strategic planning for coalition warfare. In fact, it anticipated the United States fighting as part of an allied coalition against an enemy coalition across two oceans. "Participation with Allies" links the Color Plans to the Rainbow Plans.

Matloff expected significant modifications to his interpretation of prewar plans and preparations by future historians as new sources were inevitably uncovered. In 1953 ("Prewar Military Plans and Preparations, 1939–41," *U.S. Naval Institute Proceedings* 79 [July 1953]: 741–48) he said, "The full story must be sought in the archives of the Service, Inter-Service, and British-American staff agencies, which are still in the very early stages of being mined by professional scholars." He was right.

Matloff gave high marks to the harried American military planners of 1939–41 who raced to prepare the militarily weak United States for a war that by then seemed unavoidable. But in praising the men who designed the Rainbow Plans—which realistically assessed the most likely threats to the United States and outlined the options to address them—he dismissed earlier war planning as simplistic and irrelevant. The essence of the mainstream interpretation of prewar military planning is captured in his description of the Color Plans of the 1920s and 1930s:

> A characteristic of all these plans was their limited scope. Nothing in the way of a global or total war was envisaged. With the exception of ORANGE (signifying Japan), they bore little relation to contemporary developments in international affairs. Central in all was the concept,

in accord with United States national policy, of the defense of the Continental United States and its interests by the United States alone against any foreign threat. (741)

Describing the intense activities of U.S. military planners on the eve of war, Matloff asserted that it was not until 1939–41 that war planning went beyond "the earlier abstract exercises" to take into account "concerted aggression by Germany and Italy in conjunction with action by Japan." He concluded that the Rainbow Plans were the first that envisaged a "possible global war" (743–44).

Matloff had had no reason to alter his views over twenty years later when he repeated, "Limited in scope, the [pre–1939–41] plans envisaged neither global nor total war" ("The American Approach to War, 1919–1945," in *The Theory and Practice of War,* ed. Michael Howard [Bloomington: Indiana University Press, 1975], 213–43). He was probably unaware of Morton's discovery, which would have modified his interpretation of planning before the war.

Matloff's conclusions were more than one man's opinion. They were built upon and represented the views of distinguished colleagues with whom he worked to produce the official army histories so soon after World War II. The interpretation outlined also appears in *Strategic Planning for Coalition Warfare, 1941–1942,* written with Snell. They call it "a product of cooperative effort" (ix). It was an outgrowth of Cline's *Washington Command Post,* which weaves the history of plans and operations into the history of the War Plans Division. (WPD became the Operations Division, OPD, on 23 March 1942.) Cline's book, according to Matloff and Snell, was the basis for their book (x). The authors express their great obligation to colleagues at the Office of the Chief of Military History by name, names that are now permanently associated with the official histories, the "Green Books": Kent Roberts Greenfield, Stetson Conn, Louis Morton, Richard M. Leighton, and Robert W. Coakley, all writers of books in the United States Army in World War II series. Louis Morton (*Strategy and Command: The First Two Years* [Washington, D.C.: Office of the Chief of Military History, Department of the Army, 1962]) used almost the same language as Matloff and Snell in describing the pre-Rainbow Plans: "The early war plans were little more than abstract exercises and bore little relation to actual events" (22). That he could repeat that refrain in 1962 after finding the AWC curricular archives in 1957 suggests that he scanned rather than closely examined the contents of the footlockers.

The historians working at the Office of the Chief of Military History

(OCMH) had far more shared professional interests than is the norm in a history department at a university, where history writing is a solitary business and colleagues pursue diverse interests. They were a military unit working together on a huge project. Working for the army to produce the "Green Books," they had a shared interest in telling the story of the army in the recently ended war—and telling it quickly. Expressing gratitude to colleagues in OCMH was more than a polite convention; it was acknowledgment of collegiality. It is probable that differences in interpretation among the several authors of the official histories were ironed out while the works were in draft stage. The weight of their combined expertise, the thoroughness demonstrated in accomplishing their task, and the speed with which they did their work were impressive. That is why their work has been the accepted wisdom since publication in the early 1950s. They concluded that pre-1939 planning was not very useful to Rainbow planners. Matloff maintained in 1975 that it was the "quickening environment" of 1939–41 that transformed American war planning as American strategic planning "came of age" ("American Approach to War," 229–35).

The Army War College course materials Louis Morton identified four years after Matloff and Snell published *Strategic Planning for Coalition Warfare, 1941–1942* are readily available. It seems that no one has gone through the 1919–40 course materials in detail with war plans specifically in mind, nor has anyone asked if the General Staff or WPD cared what was done at the college. In mining the AWC curricular materials housed in the Military History Institute, particularly the war plans addressing coalition warfare from 1934 to 1940, one finds high-grade nuggets that do in fact modify the way we should understand American war planning between the world wars. To assess the significance of student work at the college, an appreciation of the accepted wisdom on war planning is necessary. American strategic planning may have come of age in 1939–41, but the "spade work" done by students and faculty during the period 1934–40 at the U.S. Army War College was very important to the maturation process. That is the main point of the book you see before you.

# Acknowledgments

Teachers, archivists, colleagues, librarians, and friends helped me to shape this book. Waldo Heinrichs, Jay Luvaas, Ernst L. Presseisen, and Russell F. Weigley read early drafts. Rick Cox showed me how to tap the resources of the National Archives; Dr. Evelyn M. Cherpak, Curator, Naval Historical Collection, Naval War College, Newport, Rhode Island, made research there productive and pleasant. The research payoff for me, however, was in the archives at the U.S. Army Military History Institute, Carlisle Barracks, Pennsylvania, where John J. Slonaker, Richard J. Sommers, David A. Keough, Louise Arnold-Friend, and Pamela A. Cheney showed personal interest in my work and great professional competence as they suggested sources and brought me box after box of interesting stuff bearing on my subject.

I thank the entire staff of the U.S. Army War College Library for years of cheerful support, most particularly Mary Rife, Virginia Shoupe, Jane Gibbish, and James Dorrian.

My prose and math were improved by Mary V. Yates, a first-rate copy editor. I owe a special debt to Roger Cirillo for his encouragement and to Tom Bowers for his keen editorial eye and sage advice.

The Dissertation Fellowship given to me by the U.S. Army Center of Military History helped in a material way. The friendship and expert knowledge that Charles E. Kirkpatrick shared with me helped in ways more important. David Jablonsky took time from his own work to read an early draft and provided sage advice I gladly accepted. Jack Madigan encouraged me, and I miss him.

# Introduction

The image of Japanese bombs falling on innocents at peace in a tropical paradise is seared into American memory. Black smoke still rising from the twisted metal of the mauled battleship fleet is the backdrop to a cascade of memorable events, including President Franklin Delano Roosevelt's call for a declaration of war in his "day of infamy" speech to the U.S. Congress. It was followed by the rapid mobilization of men and materiel to the tune of "Praise the Lord and Pass the Ammunition."

Folk wisdom has it that from a standing start the totally unprepared United States rose from the ashes, rolled up its sleeves, and proceeded to defeat Germany and Japan. Not quite. The United States was not totally unprepared.

It is true that the U.S. Army between the world wars was a third-rate outfit, numbering some 140,000 men for much of the period. In 1932 Peyton March, former army chief of staff, said the United States was militarily "impotent."[1] In 1938 the entire War Department General Staff concurred in a War Plans Division study reporting that the United States had not a single complete division, while Germany had ninety divisions, Italy forty-five, and Japan fifty actively employed on the Chinese mainland alone.[2]

In 1939 the "pitiable"[3] U.S. Army ranked seventeenth in the world in size. It was scattered about in understrength and undertrained formations armed and equipped with World War I hand-me-downs. In his 1941 annual report as chief of staff, George C. Marshall called the army he inherited on 1 September 1939 "ineffective."[4] Doctrine had not kept up with technological developments, Congress and the public were disinclined to become involved in the affairs of others, and the president had to move carefully to avoid getting too far ahead of public opinion.

However, historian Stephen E. Ambrose puts his finger on one aspect of American strengths:

> Franklin Roosevelt's aide Harry Hopkins once told the writer Robert Sherwood that it was a miracle that the United States, which had neglected its Army from 1919 to 1939 in a shameful manner, produced

so large and so brilliant a group of World War II military leaders, competent to deal with complex and unique problems that were as much political as military.[5]

The "miracle" has a secular explanation. The U.S. Army entered the war with a nucleus of professional officers schooled in analytical thinking and keenly aware of the political component of strategic planning. Another component of American readiness for the challenge of total war was the experience of mobilizing people and things for an earlier war of materiel, World War I.

The National Defense Act of 1920 put the War Department's supply bureaus under the newly created position of the assistant secretary of war, who would plan for wartime procurement. In 1922 an Army-Navy Munitions Board was established to coordinate the supply systems of the two services. In 1924 the War Department supply planners established the Army Industrial College. In 1930 the Industrial Mobilization Plan was written, an economic blueprint for war that was updated in 1933, 1936, and 1939. The Protective Mobilization Plan, based on the nation's industrial potential, was drawn up between 1936 and 1939. Starting in 1937–38, Congress authorized "educational orders," small orders awarded to firms without competitive bidding. They were intended to help industry in the transition phase from planning to mobilization as industry acquired the know-how to posture itself for mass production of war materiel. The army tested its munitions designs and procurement plans. The enormous potential was waiting; the systems were in place.[6] What was required was authorization and funding to crank up the industrial base.

When President Roosevelt summoned his principal advisers to the White House on 14 November 1938 to order a massive aircraft construction program (an order that would be reduced as a consequence of military advice recommending a balanced force), effective rearming of the army and air forces began. The commander in chief authorized specific preparations and committed to getting the money from Congress to pay for them.[7] It would take some two years from presidential decision to concrete results, but the nation had three years before bombs fell on Pearl Harbor. By then other vigorous steps, including the first peacetime conscription of Americans, had been taken. Bellicose acts by the Japanese, Italians, and Germans created an atmosphere of good versus evil, a morality play resulting in a crusade, the kind of war to which Americans respond with enthusiasm.

The army schools system was key in preparing those who would lead the crusade. The army was resource poor in an isolationist country, but it invested its limited resources and energy in education, training, studies, and planning.

Thomas T. Handy, one of those important but low-profile professionals probably known only to keen students of the U.S. Army in World War II, spent the war years running the Operations Division, serving as George C. Marshall's deputy chief of staff, and later earning four stars. Asked how well the Army War College prepared officers for the later challenges of World War II leadership, Handy responded, "General McNair used to call those guys, the ones that had gone through the War College, the Ph.D.s of the Army. Anything that came up, there was some guy who just knew a hell of a lot about it. It was the one place where you could sit down and think."[8]

They did a lot of thinking in Handy's student year at the Army War College (AWC). His class of 1935 wrestled with the prospect of the United States and allies fighting simultaneously a German-led coalition and Japan. It produced a detailed and prescient war plan that was a big step toward the Rainbow options and the strategy to fight World War II. Details are discussed in the chapters that follow, but note that as early as 1935 Handy's class (1) decided for the defeat of Germany first, while appreciating that (2) "it will not suffice that our assistance be limited to money and supplies and it has been decided to send an expeditionary force to Europe," and that (3) "it is essential that a strong naval force be stationed in the Pacific." (See chapter 5.)

Handy did some more thinking at the Naval War College (class of 1936) before he joined the War Plans Division of the General Staff in 1936. He provided unprecedented continuity in the War Plans Division/Operations Division from 1936 to 1944 (except for June 1940 to June 1941, when he was with troops).

The very first war planning at the Army War College contemplated war with Germany and Japan in 1904. Concern that Germany might find its place in the sun in the Western Hemisphere, challenging the Monroe Doctrine, produced some saber rattling in the United States and Germany.[9] Japan's victory over Russia in 1905 drew the attention of American war planners as it became evident that Japan was near America's newly acquired Pacific possessions and the United States was far away. So when the century was new and navalism and neocolonialism were in the air, three aspiring Pacific powers emerged in the war plans: the United States (designated in the plans as Blue), Germany (Black), and Japan (Orange).

Planning for war at the Army War College—indeed, at the War Plans

Division of the War Department General Staff, at the Naval War College, and in joint committees—was constant, even when no enemy was visible on the horizon. Orange is the most famous of the Color Plans, war plans identifying a potential foe of the United States, usually in a one-on-one war. War with Japan was a concern, even an obsession, of the U.S. Navy beginning in 1907. From 1919 to 1940 Orange was regularly revised in Washington by army and navy war planners in the respective services and in the Joint Army and Navy Board (Joint Board) and Joint Planning Committee. It was also the centerpiece of the curriculum at the Naval War College in Newport, Rhode Island. Year after year faculty and students planned and "fought" the war with Japan. So rehearsed was the U.S. Navy for war with Japan that historian Michael Vlahos refers to it in the subtitle of his book as "the American mission."[10] The "mission" was essentially how to address Japanese local superiority—a good navy close to the Philippines, and possession and probable Japanese fortification of the mandated Caroline, Mariana, and Marshall Islands that sat on American lines of communication—in the political context of naval reductions and a freeze on fortifications imposed by the Washington Naval Treaty, all of this in an era of low military budgets and a general attitude of U.S. pacifism, isolationism, and antimilitarism.

The Color Plans developed annually at the Army War College included Orange. Even in the absence of any serious concern for immediate military threats to the United States for much of the interwar period, plans were prudently oriented to the cardinal directions, primarily for training in the method and format employed by the War Plans Division of the War Department. Green addressed Mexico, usually proceeding from instability endangering Americans in border states or from foreign intervention in Mexico to collect debts. Crimson, Canada, was premised on the proposition that it is prudent to have a plan for a long and unguarded frontier. Similarly, if planners were to exercise their skills in defending the Atlantic coast, Red, Great Britain, had to be cast as foe, however far-fetched the notion, then or since. To flesh out a land and sea threat to the northeastern region of the United States, the college created a Red-Crimson coalition. Similarly, a worst-case scenario combined two of the world's great naval powers, Red-Orange, in a contest with Blue. The implausibility of Red, Red-Crimson, and Red-Orange in the context of the 1930s caused historians to regard pre–World War II war planning as abstract exercises that "bore little relation to contemporary developments in international affairs."[11]

Mainstream interpretation of the Color Plans in the interwar period is that they failed to imagine total war, did not take contemporary international affairs into account, and did not consider the possibility that the United

States would fight as a member of a coalition. Except for Orange, it is alleged, realistic prewar military planning began in 1939, perhaps in 1938. That is not correct.

Close examination of the Army War College curricular files maintained at the Military History Institute, particularly "Planning for War"—and most particularly planning involving "Participation with Allies"—reveals systematic planning for coalition warfare versus Japan in 1934 and versus Germany and Japan in 1935, 1936, and 1937, and for hemispheric defense with Latin American allies in 1938, 1939, and 1940. The files provide evidence of a previously missed connection between AWC work and the Rainbow options. A two-ocean war was considered early on, as was consideration of the need to defeat Germany first in a war with Germany and Japan.

It is generally known that the Army War College trained carefully selected future leaders, but it also prepared the nation to fight and win a global war by anticipating many of the twists and turns of World War II strategy. Moreover, the degree to which the college worked closely with the War Department General Staff (WDGS), most particularly with the War Plans Division (WPD), has not been appreciated.

The arrival of Maj. Gen. George S. Simonds as AWC commandant in 1932 brought a new realism and sophistication to war planning at the college. Simonds (AWC 1920) had been assistant commandant at the college from 1922 to 1924 and later was chief of the War Plans Division of the War Department General Staff. He was the military adviser to the American delegation at the arms limitation conference in Geneva when appointed commandant.

In 1934 Simonds introduced "Participation with Allies" to AWC war planning, an innovation that resulted in friendly-coalition-versus-enemy-coalition and two-theater thinking at the college. He also created a War Plans Division at the college in 1935. It consisted of six officers, including two naval officers and an Air Corps officer, thus ensuring what later military jargon would call "jointness." Simonds wanted his officers to think at the national level. The college WPD ensured that student work was in the same form used at the War Plans Division of the War Department General Staff, preparing students for assignment to the kinds of tasks with which he was familiar. AWC work also reflected the "real-world" dynamics of the mid-1930s, particularly "Participation with Allies" with its attention to Japan and the "Nazi Coalition," work that led to the Rainbow options. After his assignment to the college from 1932 to 1935, Simonds served as deputy chief of staff under Douglas MacArthur. His successor as AWC commandant, Malin Craig, continued "Participation with Allies" at the college until he succeeded

MacArthur as chief of staff of the army. Both Simonds and Craig continued to task the college from their lofty positions at the top of the army. The college was tightly wired to the General Staff and did plans and projects of special interest to the staff, including the chief of staff.

We need to make distinctions between War Department plans and those done at the college, but these distinctions should not be overdrawn. The former were produced by the responsible agencies, the War Plans Divisions of the army and navy, and approved by the service secretaries after a filtering and coordinating process through joint committees. The plans at the college allowed for creativity inhibited only by lack of imagination. They were not "approved." They were discussed openly by the entire class and faculty after an oral report by the committee that had written the plan. It will be shown that many projects and much of the college war planning were done at the specific requests of the various assistant chiefs of staff of the War Department General Staff. Finally, when the college closed its doors in 1940, both faculty and newly minted graduates went to work for WPD.

Part I of the book is context. Chapter 1 is a sketch of the America in which professional officers operated in the period between the world wars. Chapter 2 shows that from its founding, the Army War College was charged with doing the strategic thinking for the army. The continuity of fundamental considerations regarding American security in 1904–7 and in the 1930s is striking, as are service preferences. Chapter 3 illuminates plans and the planning process at the college and in the General Staff among colleagues a trolley-ride apart in the Washington, D.C., of the period.

Part II examines year-by-year planning for coalition war from 1934 to 1937 at the college under the rubric "Participation with Allies." The United States and its allies consider ways to fight Japan and a German-led coalition sequentially and simultaneously.

Part III examines the plans worked out at the college under "Participation with Allies" from 1938 to 1940, when the War Plans Division of WDGS turned its attention to defense of the Western Hemisphere. Purple (Brazil) and Orange loom large as the real-world situation focuses college efforts on the establishment of a secure base and mobilization for the projection of U.S. power abroad.

Part IV is a summing up. It ties planning at the college to planning at WDGS, particularly during the transition to war, and it describes the cohesion of the professional soldiers, the brain of the army, who made the segue from school to War College Group (WCG), a planning element under WPD, WDGS, and then to Ground Force Headquarters.

Military historians will probably note with some interest the previously overlooked transition from Color Plans to Rainbow. Their attention is invited to the preface, which explains why relevant Army War College curricular materials from the 1930s were not included in the "Green Books," the official histories that make up the celebrated United States Army in World War II series. Military planners for the contingencies of the twenty-first century not yet apparent might benefit from the insights provided by those who wrestled with strategic planning on the eve of a great war. Finally, plans for "Participation with Allies" and the evolution of a successful strategy may interest the general reader whose fascination with World War II continues and whose respect for the thoughtful professional soldiers of the 1930s will be enhanced.

# Part I

# CONTEXT

# 1

★ ★ ★

# American Military Preparedness between the World Wars

Today the Peace Treaty was ratified at Paris; the War is over.
A terrible era begins for Europe, like the gathering of clouds
before a storm, and it will end in an explosion probably
still more terrible than that of the World War.
**—COUNT HARRY KESSLER,** 10 JANUARY 1920

This diary entry of German diplomat and sophisticate Harry Kessler is the antithesis of the American perspective of 1920.[1] Ratification of the peace treaty was a burst of sunshine, even without America's signature. To Americans the defeat of Germany and the exhaustion of the European powers suggested the end of wars, at least wars of interest to the United States, for a long time. Traditional rejection of a large standing army in peacetime conspired with American political attitudes until the late 1930s to ensure that defense budgets would be severely reduced. For most of the interwar period a small army was considered adequate. In the event of war, thanks to broad oceans and weak neighbors there would be time to mobilize America's enormous industrial and demographic resources. The United States would then crush its enemies. A few statistics illustrate the pattern.

Expenditures of the War Department were $9 billion in 1919 and some $50 billion in 1945. But from 1922 through 1935, expenditures remained less than $500 million per year.

The strength of the active army was 2.5 million in 1918 and would exceed 8 million in 1945. For most of the 1920s and until 1935, army strength was about 140,000. From 1936 until 1940, strength would climb steadily to 270,000. In 1941 almost 1.5 million men wore U.S. Army uniforms.

Navy expenditures were $2 billion in 1919, reaching $30 billion in 1945, but for most of the interwar period annual expenditures were $400 million.

There were steady increases from 1936 on, and in 1941 expenditures were again $2 billion. Navy and Marine Corps personnel strengths parallel army strengths from the end of World War I. They bottom out to some eighty thousand for the navy and seventeen thousand for the marines in the 1920s and early 1930s before turning upward in 1936 to peak in 1945, for the navy at three million and for the marines at five hundred thousand.[2]

Soldiers of the period, out of discipline and a scrupulous loyalty to the principle of civilian authority, became mute once the president or the Congress decided on the budget or the size of the army. The situation for the navy improved after the inauguration of Roosevelt, himself a former assistant secretary of the navy, as naval appropriations increased. It would have been reassuring to the admirals to have had the ships sooner, but the late start meant that many of the navy's ships incorporated the latest technology when it counted: in war. As a matter of perverse fact, America's armed forces would go to war with the most modern arms and equipment precisely because of the late start.

Familiar milestones mark the retreat to isolationism after the adventure of the Great War, among them economic depression, disillusionment, and the absence of a clear danger to American security. Army leadership had to consider the possibility of war in the future, but it was not evident which part of the army's past should shape its future, the long years as a frontier army or the brief European intervention. The former suggested a force structure emphasizing mobility for small wars of maneuver, while the latter suggested weight and power suitable for large wars and the massive application of power. Without a clearly defined enemy and in the absence of a perceived threat to national security, neither the purpose nor kind of an army was apparent to the public or to military planners. The army remained ambivalent on this key issue in World War II, when it was shown to be seriously undergunned in battles with German tanks despite having decided upon the massive application of power that has been called "the American way of war."[3]

Following the armistice in 1918, the American expeditionary force returned to the United States for swift demobilization, except for a fifteen-thousand-man occupation contingent in Germany that was phased out by January 1923 and an expedition of some fifteen thousand U.S. troops active in Russia until 1920. When the army troops pulled out of Germany and Russia, the Marine Corps provided most of the small overseas garrisons and conducted the foreign military expeditions required by the United States, particularly in the Caribbean region. Exceptions were one thousand army troops in Tientsin, China, from 1912 until 1938 and another one thousand men sent to Shanghai for five months in 1932. Army garrisons were routinely maintained in Panama, Hawaii, and the Philippine Islands, but, considering the Great Power status of the United States, relatively few American troops served abroad.

The prestige of the army was not enhanced when the Regular Army was called upon in the summer of 1932 to disperse a gathering of veterans encamped in Washington, "Bonus Marchers" seeking payment of a promised bonus for military service in World War I. Some six hundred troops—including Dwight D. Eisenhower and George S. Patton, Jr.—and some tanks, all under the personal leadership of Chief of Staff Gen. Douglas MacArthur, settled the situation without firing, but the use of military force against civilian war veterans damaged the image of the army.

On the other hand, the army burnished its image in emergencies—in hurricanes and floods, for example—and the Corps of Engineers in its work in harbors and rivers to improve navigation and control floods. The Air Corps flew the mail for several months in 1934, but there were fatal accidents; the army had not prepared for the task, and unnecessary risks were taken to advertise aviation. The most significant nonmilitary function of the army in the 1930s, however, was a consequence of the Great Depression.

In 1933 President Roosevelt directed the army to organize and supervise large numbers of jobless men into what became the Civilian Conservation Corps (CCC). Although the army was explicitly ordered not to make the CCC a military project, the mobilization of over three hundred thousand men was a useful experience. The emergency experiment produced long-term benefits, but the army was initially not pleased with the short-term costs.

About three thousand officers and many noncommissioned officers, taken from tactical units, were committed to the CCC project, rendering tactical units ineffective as military training simply stopped. As if to prove that every cloud has a silver lining, a War Department solution to the problem at hand in the middle of 1934 contributed to the solution to some larger problems of military readiness. The War Department called some ninety-three hundred reserve officers to active duty so that the regulars could return to their units. This windfall of officers was not counted against army strength. Many reservists called up for duty with the CCC remained on active duty until the United States entered World War II in 1941, available and more ready than they would have been had it been necessary to call them from their civilian jobs. Experience in the mobilization of large numbers of men, training of reserve officers, and a disciplined routine for hundreds of thousands of young Americans were unintended benefits of the CCC program.[4]

If they thought about it at all, Congress and the American people pinned their hopes for security on war-weariness around the world and disarmament. The National Defense Act of 1920 authorized army strength, but actual strength depended on the amount of money appropriated annually by Congress. The Congress, not at all sure that the U.S. military involvement in World War I had been a good idea, was disinclined to spend much on defense. Appropriations in the interwar period generally amounted to about one-half of what full implementation of the National Defense Act would cost. Half-funding resulted in half-strength. The navy, the first line of defense, was not lavishly funded, but it fared better than the army. There was an assumption that in the eleventh hour before a catastrophe the United States would be able to fill the ranks of the army, but it was understood that it takes a long time to build a modern warship.

The act of 1920 also added three new branches to the army: the Air Service, the Chemical Warfare Service, and a Finance Department. Aviation and chemical warfare emerged from combat experiences in France; the establishment of a separate Finance Department reflected the army's efforts to adopt modern management techniques being developed in the civilian sector.

The Tank Corps, which briefly enjoyed an independent function, was put in the infantry, suggesting doctrinal uncertainty as well as fiscal constraints. Some military planners saw the tank as a mobile machine gun, others saw it as an assault gun, and still others were worried about keeping tanks fueled and operating, if they were used in great numbers. The army could not, in any event, afford to buy many tanks.

For twenty years ground units managed with the weapons and equipment left over from World War I. It was rare for large formations to train together, since units were skeletonized and widely dispersed to a number of posts whose military utility had ended with the close of the nineteenth century. Many senior U.S. commanders in World War II experienced prewar troop command at levels no higher than battalion or company. The best opportunities to command fully manned and larger formations were to be found in Hawaii, the Philippines, and Panama, and in the school system, where school troops gave student-officers the chance to experiment in the presence of their peers. That so many senior officers commanded tens and hundreds of thousands of soldiers with distinction during World War II is a tribute to those officers and to the military school system. Professionals expecting modest careers nevertheless prepared themselves for what in fact happened: a world war requiring professional American soldiers and sailors to command at the highest levels. Command at the lower levels in war would fall to citizen soldiers whose desire to serve and to lead had to compensate for hasty training or that obtained on a part-time basis.

After World War I there were a great number of trained officers and men. Few chose to remain in the Enlisted Reserve Corps, but a number of officers continued training as members of the Officer Reserve Corps through extension courses and in short tours of active duty. Training was generally haphazard, but the Reserve Officers Training Corps (ROTC) course at the colleges was encouraging. The ROTC men provided junior leadership at a time of mass conscription in the early 1940s.

The National Defense Act of 1920 contemplated a National Guard of 436,000, but that figure was trimmed by fiscal constraints to about 180,000. Nevertheless, the guard was the largest component of the U.S. Army. Each year members drilled in their armories forty-eight times and spent fifteen days training in the field. The guard relieved the regular force of most requirements regarding domestic emergencies in the states and was also available to be integrated into the active forces as the need arose. In the years between the wars the War Department spent about 10 percent of its military budget on the National Guard, detailed regular officers as instructors and advisers, and provided large quantities of materiel, mostly of World War I vintage. When war approached, there was an orderly mobilization of guard and reserve units and individuals into the active army. These reserve and guard programs were, along with the regulars, the nucleus of what would become an army of more than eight million men and women.

Low pay, often boring duty, and slow promotions characterized the career of the regular. It took about thirteen years to go from first lieutenant to captain, and some captains remained in grade for seventeen years. Many talented men left the service; others stagnated. When war came, it was necessary to weed out from both the active force and the reserve components those who were unfit for the stress of combat, making room at the top for gifted officers in the transition to war as they never could have advanced in peacetime.

Recruiting quality enlisted men for the navy and for aviation between the wars was no problem, and quality was high. But the army had a recruiting problem in the 1920s. The Great Depression solved the problem, and conscription was imposed in 1940.

The U.S. armed forces in World War II consisted mostly of citizen soldiers: conscripts, reservists, and, after the Japanese attack, patriotic volunteers. Leadership, after some pruning of deadwood, consisted of dedicated and competent professionals who had carefully reflected on war for many years. The best among them had taken advantage of the service schools, as much to be with kindred souls as to absorb the curriculum. In the small army it was possible for an officer to know all of his year group, all officers of his branch, and many others, particularly those with whom he attended professional schools. George S. Patton, Dwight D. Eisenhower, and Omar N. Bradley, for example, had known one another for years before World War II. Similarly, in the navy those who became household names in the course of the war in the Pacific had established their reputations among peers in the small interwar navy.

Army officers were keenly aware of the profound political and technological changes that would make a return to a frontier army mentality impossible. Denied troops and hardware, the best among the officers carefully studied the art of war at all levels. The U.S. Military Academy and the ROTC provided initial schooling for officers, and branch schools trained both officers and men of the Regular Army and the citizen soldiers of the reserves. Extension courses augmented those attended by residents. The capstone of the army schools consisted of the oldest, at Fort Leavenworth, Kansas, known from 1928 as the Command and General Staff College; the Army War College in Washington; and, after 1924, the Army Industrial College, whose establishment highlighted the importance of industrial mobilization and logistics in modern war and the need to educate officers both as modern managers of resources and as leaders of men.

The Naval War College in Newport, Rhode Island, educated officers generally at the level of the courses at Leavenworth and in Washington. The war colleges exchanged faculty and students. A senior commander or a captain of the navy was normally on the faculty of the Army War College, and Capt. William F. Halsey—"Bull" Halsey of Pacific battles fame—attended the Army War College as a student (AWC 1934) after he completed the Newport course of instruction (NWC 1933). Marines selected for advanced schooling attended the school at Newport, but there were usually two senior marines in each class of the Army War College from 1920 to 1940.

President Woodrow Wilson insisted that the League of Nations was central to peacemaking in 1919, but his country never joined that organization. Senate resistance to U.S. membership caused Wilson to say that the United States had retreated into sullen and selfish isolation. The United States withdrew from foreign entanglements and invested hope in universal disarmament.

The debts stemming from World War I promoted an anti-American feeling in Europe and isolationism in the United States. From a European perspective, U.S. insistence upon repayment of war loans and loans made to relieve suffering in an economically dislocated Europe seemed petty. Practical American bookkeeping contrasted sharply with idealistic American verbiage. The United States joined the war late, suffered relatively light casualties, left Europe as quickly as it had arrived, attained Great Power status, uttered sanctimonious pronouncements, and then insisted on its pound of flesh. Indeed, the remark of President Coolidge regarding the debt—"They hired the money, didn't they?"—contrasted sharply with the lofty principles enunciated just a few years earlier as Wilson was cheered in the streets of Europe as the savior of Western civilization.

Americans saw the issue of war debts differently. The New World had pulled the Old World's chestnuts out of the fire only to find the Europeans prepared to renege on their just and legal obligations as they reverted to their bad old habits. As the 1920s became the 1930s, it seemed to Americans that incorrigible Europeans and duplicitous Japanese continued to play the old power game, endangering world peace. George Washington's admonitions about foreign entanglements seemed applicable to Americans prepared to regard Europeans as ingrates, nudging the United States toward isolationism. The war debts issue was complicated by the extraordinarily large indemnities and reparations imposed on Germany by the victors in the Treaty of Versailles. Byzantine arrangements found Germany propped up by the United States so that it could make payments to nations that would, in turn, make payments to the United States. The treaty was another reason to distance the United States from bickering Europeans. Europe, however, was just one of the regional concerns of the United States.

President Warren G. Harding invited the principal powers to attend the Washington Armament Conference, held from November 1921 to February 1922, to consider naval disarmament and Pacific and Far East issues. In addition to scrapping ships already built or in construction, it was agreed to fix the tonnage of capital ships (defined as those displacing 10,000 tons or mounting guns larger than 8 inches) at a ratio of 5 (U.S.): 5 (Britain): 3 (Japan): 1.67 (France): 1.67 (Italy). The parties also agreed to a ten-year naval holiday during which no new capital ships were to be built.

The United States was signatory to treaties restricting the use of submarines in war, outlawing poison gas, and guaranteeing China's independence and territorial rights. The United States, Britain, Japan, and France agreed to respect each other's rights in the Pacific and to consult in the event of "aggressive action" in that region. The U.S. Senate ratified the treaties, stating that there was no commitment to armed force, no obligation to join in any defense, guarding legislative power to declare war and resisting automatic U.S. involvement in war.

Further attempts to control arms and outlaw war were made, with mixed results. President Calvin Coolidge called for a conference on naval disarmament in 1927 in Geneva (June–August). France and Italy refused to attend, the United States and Britain were unable to agree on cruiser restrictions, and the conference adjourned without accomplishment. But the impulse to find a way to peace was strong, even utopian. Memories of the war in the trenches that had cost Europe a generation of young men were still fresh. A series of French-American conversations between March and August of 1928 resulted in the Kellogg-Briand Pact. The initial bilateral treaty to outlaw war was eventually signed by sixty-two nations but, lacking means of enforcement, is another victory of hope over experience.

In 1930, at the initiative of Britain's prime minister, J. Ramsay MacDonald, another naval conference was attended by the five naval powers in London. France refused Italy's demands for parity, and neither of those countries signed important provisions of the treaty. The United States, Britain, and Japan agreed to limit cruisers, but the British needed an escape clause that would permit them to start construction should France or Italy threaten Britain's traditional policy of maintaining a fleet equal to any two European navies. Britain and the United States contended that the concerns and responsibilities of a world power differed from those of a regional power, such as Italy or Japan. Hence the 10 (United State and Britain): 6 (Japan) ratio in capital ships and the 10:7 ratio in other types. Japan resented the relegation to second-class status. France, as an Atlantic and a Mediterranean power, could not accept Italy's claim to parity, since Italy was a naval power only in the Mediterranean. The U.S. Senate, however, approved the London Treaty, which would expire on 31 December 1936.

The League of Nations continued its disarmament efforts, and the United States, not a member, participated in the general disarmament conference in Geneva in 1932, proposing the abolition of all offensive armaments. When the conference failed to adopt the proposal, the disarmament movement wound down and was effectively dead by 1936. Germany withdrew from the league in 1933, the year in which Japan announced its intention to leave in 1935. Japan also withdrew from the London Naval Conference of 1935–36. In 1935 Italy waged war in Ethiopia. In 1936 Germany remilitarized the Rhineland in violation of the Treaty of Versailles, and civil war came to Spain. In 1937 Japan was on the march in China.

The naval limitation movement between 1922 and 1936 resulted in a gradual improvement in Anglo-American relations. Shared interests in confronting aggression in Europe and in Asia and shared cultural values contributed to the close relationship that characterized the Anglo-American alliance during World War II.

The U.S. Navy saw its mission as providing America's first line of defense and had no doubt about its purpose: it would sooner or later fight Japan. Officers at the Naval War College annually war-gamed Orange, war with Japan. Mainstream naval thinking in the interwar period focused on capital ships, battleships slugging it out in decisive fleet actions like Trafalgar, Tsushima, and the recent—if less conclusive—Jutland. The strategic scenario was correctly anticipated, but neither planners nor aviators predicted that battles in the Pacific would routinely be fought by battle fleets that neither saw nor engaged one another with their big guns.

The potential of land-based and ship-borne aircraft as scouts was recognized early: the airplane would find the enemy fleet, and naval gunfire would fight it. But the rapid evolution of aircraft from the fragile frame of World War I to light metal construction and powerful engines, permitting heavier payloads, led to dive-bombing techniques and aircraft launching torpedoes. The navy had to decide how to apportion its limited funding to build and train surface combatants, submarines, amphibious forces, logistical support, and naval aviation.

The navy indicated the importance of aviation by establishing its Bureau of Aeronautics (BuAer) in 1921 and by qualifying senior officers as pilots or aerial observers. Among the latter were William F. Halsey and Ernest J. King, who became famous during the Pacific War, and William A. Moffett, who as chief of BuAer reduced resistance to naval aviation by saying that it would go to sea on the back of the fleet. This formulation had the advantage both of being true and of appeasing surface fleet admirals dubious about a challenge to naval tradition. The Morrow Board, appointed by President Coolidge to review aviation in 1926, provided a five-year plan to build one thousand planes and to organize a Naval Air Reserve. By the mid-1930s the fast carrier task force was taking shape and finding acceptance in the navy. It is ironic that an era of American isolationism and pacifism ushered in the fast carrier task force that has allowed the United States mastery of the seas for over a half-century. Another anomaly that worked to the long-term advantage of the United States was the failure to fortify U.S. Pacific bases in the period between their acquisition in 1898 and the war with Japan. The lack of forward bases resulted in the development of replenishment-at-sea techniques, giving the U.S. Navy great operating range and making it an incomparable force into the twenty-first century.

After World War I the U.S. Navy refocused on the Pacific, where the victors confronted one another. British forces were thinly spread around the world as Britain attempted to maintain its empire while honoring European commitments. Japan, the dominant regional power since 1905, seized the German colonies in the Marshalls, the Carolines, and the Marianas during World War I (they became mandates from the League of Nations in 1920), thus putting Japan astride the U.S. route to China and the Philippines. U.S. bases on Guam, Midway, Wake, and the Philippines, hostage to forward Japanese airfields and fleet operating bases, would be taken by the Japanese early in World War II. The U.S. bases were not fortified. The Five-Power Treaty of 1922 prohibited the fortification of bases in the Pacific, but it was generally believed that Japan was secretly fortifying its bases in violation of the treaty. When the treaty lapsed in the mid-1930s, Congress was not disposed to invest in the construction of bases. Fortifying bases would provoke Japan, and, mired in the depression, Congress preferred to spend money closer to home.[5]

Since Japan was capable of overwhelming U.S. garrisons in the Pacific in the early days of war, the Marine Corps commandant began planning for a force of six thousand to eight thousand men on the West Coast, prepared to deploy rapidly for a campaign in the Marshall and Caroline Islands to secure naval bases for the fleet. Unlike the army, the Marine Corps had a clear mission early in the interwar period.

The defeat of the British at Gallipoli in 1915 convinced many military professionals that the inherent strength of defenders in prepared fortifications with modern firepower made amphibious assault a risky proposition, perhaps an exercise in futility. Despite the risks, the prognosis for the course of war in the Pacific demanded at least careful analysis and tentative plans to seize bases in the Pacific to support the fleet. The marines were so successful in developing all aspects of amphibious warfare that combat assault on beaches became synonymous with the Marine Corps. The pieces of this complex form of war were slow in coming together.

Commandant John A. Lejeune assigned Maj. Earl H. Ellis the task of fitting a Marine Corps role into the navy's Plan Orange. By early 1921 Ellis had produced several drafts of "Advanced Base Force Operations in Micronesia," Operations Plan 712. Ship-to-shore movement by waves of assault craft under the cover of massive naval gunfire and tactical air support to penetrate beach defenses characterized the concept. But much more than a concept was needed. People, equipment, and rehearsals were required to coordinate the many parts of an effective amphibious assault, but the costs stopped exercises from 1926 until 1934.

In 1933 the amphibious assault force was named the Fleet Marine Force (FMF). From 1934 until 1941 the FMF conducted fleet landing exercises, providing practical experience that would validate the soundness of the concept in place since 1921. Ships' boats required near-acrobatic stunts by combat-loaded marines to get ashore. The boats were replaced by the innovation of New Orleans boat designer Andrew Higgins: a shallow-draft, flat bow for landing and retracting, and a protected propeller. Addition of a bow ramp for troop disembarkation produced the basic LCVP (landing craft, vehicle, personnel) of World War II fame. Larger variations would transport tanks, artillery, and other heavy gear over the beach. A tracked landing vehicle mounting guns was developed, providing a kind of amphibian tank for the initial shock and firepower essential early in an assault over the beach. Despite the progress in the Marine Corps, the General Board (the navy's equivalent to the army's General Staff) assessed the navy's readiness for war in 1939 in a pessimistic report listing "critical deficiencies."[6]

On the eve of war, President Roosevelt knew that the United States would either be drawn into war or risk standing alone in a world dominated by militaristic Germany and Japan. He also knew that his country wanted peace. He had to be circumspect in making preparations he regarded as prudent without provoking either domestic or foreign enemies. His unprecedented election to a third term by a wide margin in November 1940 showed his sure sense of the mood of the American people.

At the beginning of 1939 a public campaign of limited American preparedness was begun. Concerned that potential European foes might establish air bases in the Western Hemisphere, the policy of "hemispheric defense" replaced the narrower concept of the "strategic triangle" (Alaska-Hawaii-Panama). The presence of large numbers of Germans and Italians in South America—and their economic influence, particularly in the aviation industry—was noted by American war planners. They were also concerned that others would eventually develop bombers like the American B-17, an aircraft capable of carrying heavy payloads across the Atlantic. Defense of the hemisphere became the sine qua non of each of the five options provided in the Rainbow Plans drafted by the army and navy to supersede the individual Color Plans. After France fell, twenty-one nations of the Western Hemisphere signed the Act of Havana (30 July 1940), proclaiming collective security to keep Germany out of the hemisphere. The following month, the United States and Canada established the Joint Board of Defense.

President Roosevelt declared a limited national emergency on 8 September 1939, after the shooting war in Europe had begun on 1 September with the German invasion of Poland. The Regular Army increased enlisted strength to 227,000 and the National Guard to 235,000, while in April 1940, 70,000 troops took part in the first corps and army training maneuvers ever held in the United States. These maneuvers revealed a number of weaknesses and deficiencies to be corrected in training in the time remaining before the United States was engaged in a major land war.

In response to Hitler's victories from Norway to France in the spring of 1940 and during the Battle of Britain that followed, the first peacetime conscription in the United States was introduced. The Selective Service Act of 16 September 1940 required men between the ages of twenty-one and thirty-six to register and provided for the training of 1.2 million troops and 800,000 reservists for one year.

A two-ocean naval program was announced to address the simultaneous threats of Japan in the Pacific and Germany and Italy in the Atlantic, a particularly ominous prospect should Britain be defeated. In the last six months of 1940 there was a doubling of the active army, and by mid-1941, 1.5 million men were serving. An Armored Force was established in July 1940, and a new General Headquarters assumed responsibility for training in the same month. Later, antiaircraft and tank destroyer commands were established in the continental United States and trained under the control of General Headquarters. Even the considerable resources of "the arsenal of democracy" were strained. Hard decisions had to be made regarding the distribution of U.S. weapons and equipment to training and combat units— and to Britain and later to the Soviet Union and China to prevent their defeat by the Axis powers.

Two days after the invasion of Poland, in one of his "fireside chats," President Roosevelt publicly revealed his attitude: "This nation will remain a neutral nation, but I cannot ask that every American remain neutral in thought as well." The Neutrality Act of 1937 was modified on 4 November 1939, to permit "cash and carry" export of arms and munitions, an action clearly favoring maritime Britain. After the fall of France in June 1940, Germany dominated Europe. On 2 September 1940 the United States obtained naval and air bases from Britain in British Guiana, Antigua, Trinidad, St. Lucia, Jamaica, the Bahamas, Bermuda, and Newfoundland on a ninety-nine-year lease in exchange for fifty overage U.S. destroyers desperately needed by Britain. Germany, Italy, and Japan could only regard this as an unfriendly act by the United States.

The Lend-Lease Act, signed by Roosevelt on 11 March 1941, removed all pretense of neutrality, authorizing the president to transfer, lease, sell, or exchange war materials to "any country whose defense the President deems vital to the defense of the United States." Congressional and public opinion hoped for peace, but analysis of public opinion polls and voting records indicates a gradual acceptance of the need for the United States to rearm and to help Britain. The vote for Lend-Lease, for example, was 60 to 31 in the Senate and 317 to 71 in the House.

The nation's defense policy broadened from one of hemispheric defense to an undeclared participation in the war. By the time American and British military representatives met for staff conversations concluded in Washington at the end of March 1941, the American military had already decided that Germany was a greater threat than Japan. If it came to war in the Atlantic and Pacific at the same time, the United States would defeat Germany first, a concept explicit in Rainbow 5, the strategy that would guide American and British conduct in the war.

In April 1941 the U.S. Navy was directed by President Roosevelt to patrol the western half of the Atlantic Ocean as the British did the same in the east. In May, Roosevelt proclaimed an unlimited national emergency. The United States assumed responsibility to develop and operate military air routes across the Atlantic via Greenland in the north and Brazil in the south, and the president directed the army and navy to prepare an expeditionary force to be sent to the Azores to block possible German movement into the South Atlantic.

In June, Hitler attacked his Soviet ally, and U.S. Army troops landed in Greenland to protect it from German attack while building air bases there to facilitate the ferrying of aircraft from North America to Britain. In July, U.S. troops relieved British troops securing Iceland, and in August, Roosevelt met with British prime minister Winston Churchill in Newfoundland to draft and proclaim the Atlantic Charter, outlining the terms of a just peace. October saw the U.S. Navy escorting convoys in the North Atlantic, while in November, American merchant ships were armed and permitted in combat zones, producing an undeclared war between the United States and Germany.[7]

The incremental steps toward war in the Atlantic were accompanied by a deterioration of Japanese-American relations. Japanese aggression in China antagonized American public opinion, long paternalistic regarding China, and the United States warned Japan not to take European possessions in Asia and the Pacific made vulnerable in 1940 when Germany conquered and occupied Western Europe. Economic sanctions imposed by the United States in an effort to influence Japanese policy had the opposite effect when Japan decided on war rather than accepting what it regarded as yet another humiliation imposed by non-Asians. Japan failed to see how the United States could take the proprietary stance expressed in the Monroe Doctrine while denying Japan an analogous stance in its part of the world. In July 1941, Japan sent troops into French Indochina. The United States retaliated by curtailing oil shipments to Japan, freezing Japanese assets in the United States, and reinforcing the U.S. garrison in the Philippines.

Japan's strategic decision to take the rich resources of Southeast Asia—rather than cooperating with Germany to defeat the Soviet Union on the Asian mainland—meant that the Japanese could not ignore the flank exposed to the Americans in the Philippines. The same logic convinced them to launch the strike aimed at destroying the U.S. fleet in Hawaii, despite the known risks that resource-poor Japan would take in a contest with a very large and rich United States.

To interpret the condition of the American military between the wars as a hibernation from which it was jarred by the Japanese attack on Pearl Harbor on 7 December 1941 would be an exaggeration. The nation had other legitimate concerns and inhibitions, but its military leadership was prepared to use the abundant national resources rationally as they became available during the transition to war at the end of the 1930s and in the early 1940s. In fact, the army of 1,643,477 at the end of 1941 marked the first time the nation had gone to war with a large army already in uniform, conscription in place, and an industrial base already making the changes necessary for war production. The nation's armed forces were prepared to defend the Western Hemisphere against invasion even as the Japanese attacked Pearl Harbor. Time was required to develop the forces that would be sent thousands of miles across the oceans to fight Germany and Japan.

Army planners fully expected American material and human resources to overwhelm any foe or combination of foes. It was only necessary to manage the transition to war in a manner that avoided the temptation to do everything at once.

After the attack on Pearl Harbor, a mobilized United States focused on winning the war. Capable leadership, sound service doctrines and war plans, unmatched industrial capacity, and enthusiastic public support transformed the United States from isolationism to superpower status. But first a strategic problem had to be solved, a problem that had arisen when the twentieth century was new.

# 2

★ ★ ★

# The Army War College, Strategic Continuity, and Service Preferences

You are brought together to do the thinking for the Army.
**—ELIHU ROOT**, 1908

Secretary of War Elihu Root in 1899 intended the Army War College to be a small General Staff "at least until a reluctant Congress formally approved a War Department General Staff." The college was established by General Orders on 27 November 1901, with senior War Department officers appointed to it in 1902. They functioned for the first thirteen months exclusively as General Staff officers before there was a General Staff. With the establishment of a General Staff in 1903, the Army War College began to function as the Third Division of this staff, "the thinking and planning part of the new General Staff."[1] The college was to be "a body of officers linked by a community of interest for the consideration of common problems, and charged with the special duty of assisting the Chief of Staff and the other divisions of the General Staff in preparing plans for the nation's defense." Tasker H. Bliss, the first president of the Army War College, was determined that mature officers, the "students," would "learn things by doing things." This applicatory theory of learning remained the basic educational concept of the college until 1940, "whatever the apparent academic character of the course that evolved."[2] Both Bliss and Root noted that the Naval War College (founded in 1884) functioned as a working group for the navy's brain, the General Board.[3] The founders had something of the kind in mind for the Army War College.

The first "class" consisted of eight officers, including Capt. John J. Pershing, forty-four years of age. It arrived on 1 November 1904 to complete a "course" by 30 June 1905, but the course "was General Staff work pure and simple." The "permanent personnel" of the Army War College (later called faculty) were assisted by the "temporary personnel" (later called students). Together they comprised the Third Division, later renamed the War College Division of the General Staff. Secretary Root at the dedication of the AWC building in 1908 told the college community, "You are brought together to do the thinking for the Army." In brief, up to World War I, "all activities were geared to the needs of the General Staff."[4]

The college suspended operations from May 1917 until September 1919, when it reopened as the General Staff College. It was redesignated the Army War College in 1921, and the mission changed. The college took on more of the character of a school and less that of an operating element of the General Staff. One lingering tie to the staff remained: in the event of mobilization, the work of the college would be suspended, and its staff would be used to buttress a General Headquarters directing wartime field operations. That was done in 1940.

The 1921 curriculum reflected the new organization of the War Department, consisting of War Plans and Command courses as well as courses pertaining to G-1 (personnel), G-2 (intelligence), G-3 (training and operations), G-4 (logistics), and the Office of the Assistant Secretary of War (industrial mobilization). The ten-month academic year was divided into roughly equal periods called Informative, or Preparation for War, and Command and War Plans, or Conduct of War. The methods used and level of instruction resembled graduate education at civilian universities as it was conducted at that time. Individual work, initiative, originality, and reporting out to colleagues in seminar—called committees or work groups at the Army War College—were supplemented by a speaker program that brought expert opinion to the college from academe, industry, journalism, and the military.

Scrupulous efforts encouraged creative individual solutions; there were no hard-and-fast "school solutions." The assumption was that the Leavenworth courses had prepared students in technical military methods and tactics up to and including corps command. It was proper at Leavenworth to accept the principles and doctrines laid down by the faculty, but at AWC the process was best characterized as a full and free discussion of the subject supported by reasonable premises.

The mission was to prepare officers to command echelons above corps; to examine political, economic, and social matters as they affect the conduct of war; to prepare officers for duty in the War Department General Staff and in the Office of the Assistant Secretary of War; to train officers for joint operations of the army and navy; and to instruct in the strategy, tactics, and logistics of large operations with special reference to the world war.

Between 1920 and 1940 annual class size was about eighty-five. Usually some seventy-nine army and six navy and Marine Corps students attended. The Army and Naval War Colleges regularly exchanged graduates to attend the other service's school. Approximately three-fourths of the army officers were of the combat arms, but all branches were represented each year. Army students were in the grade of captain or higher and were graduates of the Command and General Staff course at Leavenworth. The average age of AWC graduates was 45.4 years. The faculty numbered sixteen to eighteen, including two naval officers. Between 1921 and 1933 a number of National Guard and Organized Reserve Corps officers attended a part of the course, for example the G-1/mobilization course or the G-2 or G-4 course. When the United States entered World War II, 259 of the 305 army generals (84.9 percent) were AWC graduates, and by 1946 some 859 AWC graduates wore stars.

Historian Stetson Conn observes that after World War I "there was no such intimate relationship between the course at the Army War College and current General Staff business as there had been to 1917." Reducing the intimate official relationship broadened perspective and tended "to exempt College work and thinking from the prevalent isolationism of the times." Students could and did look into issues and problems that were "anathema to official plans and policies," but the intent was always to use students "for immediate staff purposes in the event of threatened war or mobilization."[5] That is precisely what happened in 1939 and 1940, when the college was used by the staff to serve immediate needs.

Relations between the Army War College and the General Staff from 1919 to 1940 were very close, with the college enjoying the best of two worlds. It accepted tasks, including war planning, from the staff, subject always to the approval of powerful AWC commandants, and it assigned to students tasks that were "anathema to official plans and policies." As a consequence, consideration of strategic options by the political and military leadership in 1939–41 had the benefit of prior AWC consideration of war with a German-Japanese-Italian coalition and defense of the Western Hemisphere with the United States a member of a friendly coalition.

Connecting the violation of the Monroe Doctrine to a simultaneous threat to the Philippines, a real-world consideration in the late 1930s, takes us full circle to the earliest strategic considerations of military planners as the United States stepped onto the world stage as a major player after the Spanish-American War. The newly established General Staff began war planning by considering how the United States might react to a threat to the recently acquired Pacific islands and a simultaneous violation of the Monroe Doctrine. A brief visit to 1904 shows the beginning of some remarkable continuities in both the substance of war planning and the process to 1940.

In a letter dated 22 April 1904, Army Chief of Staff Lt. Gen. Adna R. Chaffee recommended to Secretary of War William Howard Taft that the newly created Joint Army and Navy Board be tasked to "agree upon a series of practical problems (taking them in the order of their assumed importance) which involve cooperation of the services, and for the execution of which in a time of emergency the two Staffs will be responsible." Chaffee went on to say that what he had in mind was not academic work "but practical general staff problems, the details of which should be worked out by the permanent personnel of the two War Colleges in cooperation to be then passed upon by the General Staff of the Army and the General Board of the Navy." If the Joint Board of the Army and Navy concurred, it could recommend action to the secretaries of war and the navy. Signature by the two secretaries would make approved war plans of the "practical problems."[6] Chaffee and Taft had discussed the action previously, for on the same day Taft wrote a note to Chaffee saying, "[I] think it very desirable that the Joint Board, representing as it does the Genl staffs of the two services, should agree upon a series of practical general staff problems."[7] The president of the Joint Board, Adm. George Dewey, directed Adm. Henry C. Taylor and Gen. Tasker H. Bliss "to prepare and submit each" a paper to get the subject of war planning before the board for its study.[8]

What the founding fathers of systematic war planning had in mind was a shakedown cruise to test the system and the several recently established planning organizations: the Joint Board and the Army General Staff (1903), the Army War College (1901), and the General Board of the Navy (1900).[9] Essentially the planning process begun in 1904 was the planning process of 1940, with some fine-tuning along the way. The ever-reflective Tasker Bliss, president of the Army War College from 1903 to 1905 and again in 1909—and lecturer at the first Naval War College class of 1885—produced a twenty-one-page paper in 1904. His tour of the horizon, analysis, and conclusion set the war-planning agenda for the next thirty-five years.[10]

Bliss assumed that enforcement of the Monroe Doctrine would be the most probable cause of wars in which the United States might be involved. He pointed out that the war with Spain in 1898 was brought about by our only foreign policy, the Monroe Doctrine, and noted that other countries might also take a proprietary interest in their regions of the world:

> The Monroe Doctrine grew out of and was an expression of our policy to remain isolated from the rest of the world. Its application in 1898 left our isolation in one direction untouched while it completely destroyed it in the other. There is no doubt that this will result in due time in the formulation of a second line of foreign policy; we shall then have one policy based on contact with, and another based on isolation from the rest of the world. We may yet find ourselves fighting for our Monroe Doctrine on one side of the world and against somebody else's Monroe Doctrine on the other side of the world. However, that time has not yet come.[11]

The War College president ("commandant" from 1919 onward) believed that possessing the Philippines would "undoubtedly" involve the United States in war with a European nation in the short run, and possibly with an Asiatic power one day. He considered the Philippines "more likely to be a vulnerable object of the enemy's attack rather than a base for aggressive movements of ours upon the Asiatic mainland."[12] Bliss considered violation of our Monroe Doctrine by a power whose real purpose might be to grab the Philippines (which we could not defend); he regarded British aggression against the United States as unlikely (since British possessions in the Western Hemisphere were hostages); he regarded U.S. interventions in Latin America as likely (to keep European powers from intervening); and he thought it unlikely that three European countries would ever "come against us" (because rival interests closer to home would prevent that). Anticipating concerns of future war planners for hemispheric defense, particularly concerns about Italian and German penetration of South America, Bliss thought it unlikely that Europeans in South America would call upon the motherlands they had escaped to intervene in this hemisphere. Even if Argentina or Brazil became entirely Germanized or Italianized, he thought that they would still rely on the United States for aid to protect them "from political aggression by the motherland precisely as now they would expect our protection against Spain or Portugal, were the latter in a position to seriously threaten such aggression."[13] As we shall see, American war planners returning to this issue in 1938–41 were less sanguine.[14]

Bliss concluded his 1904 tour of the horizon by suggesting that "progressive study" be undertaken by the army and navy staffs, in this order:

1. The United States intervenes in a South American country, Venezuela for example, to assist the government in ousting a foreign power supporting insurgents. The theaters of war in this scenario are the Caribbean Sea and the Philippine Archipelago.
2. The United States confronts a coalition of two European powers, excluding England.
3. Assume England as an intervening power alone and in coalition (presumably with Canada).
4. Assume intervention by the United States in Mexico, "with other foreign complication" (presumably a European power collecting debts from Mexico).[15]

It is noteworthy that Bliss included the Western Hemisphere and the Philippines in the war plan he assigned first priority in 1904. The Joint Board directive to the Joint Planning Committee in 1939 said, "Make exploratory studies and estimates as to the various practicable courses of action open to the military and naval forces of the United States in the event of (a) violation of the Monroe Doctrine by one or more of the Fascist Powers, and (b) a simultaneous attempt to extend Japanese influence in the Philippines."[16] This 1939 directive resulted in a combination of Purple (plans for a corps-size expedition to Brazil) and Orange (war with Japan).

Second priority was assigned by Bliss to a coalition of two European powers, excluding England. It is not clear who would be the other power, but one would be Germany. Antipathy between Germany and the United States dated from the Samoan crisis of 1889 and from the unpleasant experience Dewey had had with the German fleet in Manila Bay while still conducting operations against the Spanish fleet in 1898.[17] Both Germany and the United States, in an era of superheated nationalism that found them latecomers in the scramble for colonies, were for a while deadly serious in planning for war against one another. However, it soon became clear to strategists in both countries that Germany could hardly turn its back on its European rivals for an adventure in *Weltpolitik* in the Western Hemisphere in the early years of the twentieth century.

Meanwhile, feelings toward Japan cooled as it dawned on American strategists that Japanese victory over the Russians made Japan a rival in the western Pacific. Orange (Japan) became more ominous than Black (Germany), particularly at the Naval War College, where planning for war with

Japan began in 1906. By 1907 the potential foes were "Japs." By the end of the 1930s they had become an "inevitable enemy."[18]

When it came to actual war between Germany and America in 1917, it would not be a war in which the German fleet had to be turned back by a U.S. fleet in the Caribbean. Imagining a Trafalgar-like battle between German and U.S. fleets in the vicinity of Puerto Rico in 1904 may seem fantastic, but it was no more fantastic than imagining the United States mobilizing several million men and sending more than a million to France to fight Germany. In any event, in 1904 Germany was regarded as a likely enemy; after 1906 Japan was regarded as the most likely enemy.

Bliss's third priority assumed war with England (Red) alone, or with an English-Canadian (Red-Crimson) coalition. War with England became increasingly improbable with every passing year, but Red was exercised regularly from 1905 to 1940. Only by assuming that England was the foe could planners rationalize a study in the American North or in the North Atlantic requiring a maximum effort by the U.S. Army and the U.S. Navy, the object of the exercise. Intervention by the United States in Mexico (Green) was also regularly exercised, and concern for German and Italian penetration in South America in the late 1930s would result in planning a U.S. intervention in Brazil (Purple).

Bliss recommended a variety of problems requiring a range of efforts to be examined by the War Colleges and the Joint Board. Intervention in Mexico was the simplest proposition. The army could manage that alone, probably from a standing start. In 1904 defense of the Caribbean against a European power might be managed, depending on the enemy, but simultaneous defense in the Caribbean and in the Philippine Archipelago was probably beyond the reach of the U.S. Army and Navy, unless the foe should once again be Spain. Military officers would find it necessary to stretch their imaginations as they contemplated how they could win a war with two European powers simultaneously, or a war with England and Canada. That was the idea of the "practical problems": to stretch the best of military minds.

The navy also responded to the call for "a series of practical general staff problems." Rear Adm. Henry C. Taylor's 10 June 1904 memorandum to the Joint Board stated that "our conceptions of the future wars should be kept constantly modified by the rapidly shifting conditions," not the least "the rapid development of our country." In a review of recent history, Taylor noted that before the war with Spain, England had been regarded as the chief threat to U.S. security. In the course of the 1898 war, however, German ambitions in the Caribbean, in Colombia, and in Venezuela had become clear, and memories of German-American competition in the Pacific were fresh. It was also noted that the French had begun "vigorously to improve the fortifications at Martinique." American victory in the war with Spain had discouraged possible opponents, and "respect for the Monroe Doctrine was increased." Yet Germany desired "to see how far she could go in testing the Monroe Doctrine." Taylor was suspicious of "an attempt by Germany, in coalition with one or more European powers, to gain permanent foothold upon the South American continent." But the navy in 1904 already had its eyes fixed on the Pacific. The admiral concluded that "the sacredness of the Monroe Doctrine [would] drop to second in the national mind, and our trade relations with Eastern Asia assume first place, and become the primal cause of war." In his mind, trade with China was "the ultimate objective."[19]

The siren call of the Pacific expanse was irresistible to American sailors. The prospect of China trade—and the concomitant requirement for a great blue-water fleet—apparently fascinated the U.S. Navy as hemispheric defense did not. Taylor's seven recommendations for war planning provide the naval *Weltanschauung* of 1904. The first priority takes us to the Pacific. The second priority takes us to the Pacific. The third defends against violation of the Monroe Doctrine, but it too requires the U.S. Asiatic Fleet, U.S. Marines, and troops from the Philippines to conduct offensive operations across the Pacific. Priorities four to seven are in the Western Hemisphere. This preference of the navy for a Pacific strategy is evident in all war planning from 1904 to the eve of World War II.

This excursion to the world of war planning in 1904 shows several continuities. First, the same cards were shuffled and reshuffled as U.S. war planners responded to the American geopolitical situation by examining threats to American security in the Pacific, in the Atlantic, and in the Western Hemisphere in 1904 and in 1939. Second, the planning process remained essentially unchanged over time as political authority (usually the two service secretaries and sometimes the president) worked with the army chief of staff and the chief of naval operations (the latter position being established in 1915). The service chiefs, their deputies, and their chiefs of war planning constituted the Joint Board. Initiatives could flow from the military to civilian authorities or from the civilians to the military, but approval of the plans rested squarely with civil authority. The Joint Board typically referred problems to the Joint Planning Committee (JPC), chaired by the chief war planners of both services, for JPC analysis and recommendations back to the

Joint Board. The members of the JPC turned to experts on the army and navy staffs for advice and technical information. Up to World War I, the Army War College was the army war-planning agency. Between the world wars the War Plans Division of the War Department General Staff performed that function.

It will be shown that the Army War College never ceased war planning and was particularly useful to the General Staff and the War Plans Division both in war planning and in conducting various individual and group studies for the General Staff. Finally, the U.S. Navy's tilt toward the Pacific is a constant. The predisposition to link the navy to U.S. trade interests in the Pacific basin was already manifest in the Taylor memo to the Joint Board on 10 June 1904. The navy's fixation on defeating Orange became an all-consuming "American mission."[20] Whether the chief antagonist of the United States was Germany or Japan, the U.S. fleet would be found in Asian waters.[21]

The army was considerably less focused on a single possibility for war in the future. Orange, Green, and Red (and sometimes Crimson for Canada) war plans were maintained in the War Plans Division and were exercised annually at the Army War College in the period between the world wars. It was only when Japan, Germany, and Italy emerged in the 1930s as the likely enemies of the United States that the army focused on those opponents, but even then planning for Green and Red continued in order to cover all possibilities—North, South, East, and West—and to provide General Staff officer training.

Finally, there were variables as well as continuities. As Admiral Taylor pointed out, before the war with Spain, Britain had been regarded as the most likely foe. But German and American interests collided in the Pacific. German interests in the Western Hemisphere concerned the United States, and the Monroe Doctrine irritated Kaiser Wilhelm II.[22] After its successful war with Russia, Japan shared with Germany the distinction of American suspicion, and war plans featuring Orange soon outstripped plans to fight Black. In an unexpected turn of events, it was the United States that sent its forces overseas to fight Germans. Then, recoiling from World War I, the United States sought means other than war to resolve international disputes. Nevertheless, planning for Orange, Green, and Red went on almost reflexively. It will be shown that beginning in 1934, with "Participation with Allies," creative planning for coalition warfare was conducted at the U.S. Army War College. Those plans were known to the General Staff. In fact, at times it was difficult to distinguish between college planning and General

Staff planning as the college in 1938 and 1939 approached its metamorphosis to General Headquarters in 1940. The student work of 1934 to 1937 is impressive in its grasp of international affairs and in anticipating what actually happened in the Pacific and in Europe in the course of World War II. That work at the college illustrates the transition from the Color Plans to Rainbow planning.

# 3

# Plans and Planning

*The actual preparation of war plans had been given more prominence than any other feature of the course.*
**—GEORGE S. SIMONDS,**
ASSISTANT COMMANDANT, ARMY WAR COLLEGE, 1923

War planning is a complex and dynamic process.[1] Strategic thinking during the interwar period was shaped not just by documents signed by the secretaries of war and the navy as approved plans, but also by planning exercises conducted at military schools, tutorials with senior officers, and private study and reflection among the best of the officer corps. Perhaps the greatest contribution of the army school system was providing time and a venue in which thinking soldiers could exchange ideas while removed from the day-to-day routine of troop duty in a skeletal force at some remote post. The Army War College encouraged reflection and originality.

This is not to denigrate the importance of approved plans. Among other things, approved plans triggered supporting plans, such as those concerned with manpower and industrial mobilization, training, concentration, and transportation—all developed in detail at subordinate headquarters throughout the chain of command both in the United States and in overseas possessions. But there were not many approved or final plans in the interwar period, and of those that did exist, only Orange was important and realistic. Green (Mexico) was an annoyance. Few planners or policymakers lost sleep worrying about the threat from the other bank of the Rio Grande in the 1930s. Red (England) was an unlikely foe in the 1930s, but it provided the rationale for an exercise in Atlantic warfare and defense of the East Coast, the kind of mental gymnastics and manipulation of data that might prove useful if the foe turned out to be *any* European power. But the official plans prepared by the General Staff were wooden and unimaginative compared with the war planning at the Army War College. Succeeding chapters will outline the realistic and comprehensive plans worked out at the college and illustrate the staff's familiarity with them.

The discovery of inadequacies in war planning by the General Staff did not have to await post–World War II analysis. Shortcomings were noted by the army leadership in the decade before the United States entered the war. Persistent equipment shortages created an atmosphere that was not conducive to imaginative planning. Gen. Douglas MacArthur expressed concern about equipment shortages in his annual report as chief of staff in 1933, but shortages continued.[2] Planners were forced to look past the puny army in which they served to a mass army that would function on the grand scale. This meant that the planners of the 1930s had to do their work on the basis of hypotheses. One hypothesis was that the threat would match the means available to address it. Focusing on the frontier with Mexico was a form of addressing a challenge that could be handled by the modest U.S. Army without massive mobilization. Or planners could assume away the personnel and equipment shortages and plan for a big war, like Red or Orange. They could ignore contemporary realities and assume that the nation would provide the means in extremis. Alternatively, one could plan on the basis of probabilities derived from analysis of current international relations, but that approach had the disadvantage of projecting today's threat into the future.

As his parting shot in 1939, outgoing Chief of Staff Malin Craig repeated MacArthur's point when he said that equipment shortages affected planning as well as training and all other aspects of military readiness: "The problem encountered on my entry into office [2 October 1935] was the lack of realism in military war plans." He went on to explain that planners worked with paper units, "conjectural supply," and "a disregard of the time element which forms the main pillar of any planning structure." Lamenting that "time is the only thing that may be irrevocably lost," Craig concluded that "sums appropriated this year will not be fully transformed into military power for two years."[3] He might have added that a clear statement of national security policy from the political leadership is always sought by military planners, who need to know the ends desired in order that the ways and means to those ends may be found. However, political authority usually—and prudently—preserves all options until the eleventh hour before turning loose the dogs of war.

## The Army War College as Think Tank

For imaginative planning during his tenure as chief of staff of the army, Craig often turned to the Army War College, where he had served as commandant immediately before becoming chief of staff. Both Craig and George S. Simonds, his predecessor as AWC commandant and a former chief of the War Plans Division of the War Department General Staff, maintained the nexus between AWC and WPD. The intent was to exercise not only approved plans, planners, and the planning process, but also to raise the what-if questions that stretch minds. The most imaginative what-if questions—those about waging war as a member of a coalition fighting an enemy coalition—were addressed at AWC between 1934 and 1940. Often what-ifs were neither raised nor addressed by the undermanned and overworked War Plans Division until the eve of war. The General Staff, and particularly WPD, had its hands full with the day-to-day problems that crowd out reflection and contemplation. Despite admonitions to stay out of the day-to-day business of running an army, the army's General Staff drifted too often from policy to operations. That was as true in the 1930s as it usually is, but in the interwar period the problem was compounded because the General Staff lacked the number of officers needed to do what was expected of it. The War Plans Division was spread thin.

In the entire period from 21 September 1921 to 31 December 1940, only ninety-two officers served in the War Plans Division of the General Staff.[4] At any given time, eleven or twelve officers were assigned to WPD, most of them majors and lieutenant colonels. They were very busy men. Among the division's responsibilities were these:

The chief of WPD was a member of the Joint Board.

The executive officer collaborated with the State Department regarding international conferences and other international subjects.

The five officers of the Operations Section were responsible for (higher than army level) joint plans; strategic plans; organization and mobilization problems affecting war plans; joint exercises; maneuvers, command post exercises, terrain exercises, and staff rides; exercises involving tests of war plans; unit mobilization plans and establishment of the General Headquarters (GHQ) that would direct the army in war; and special studies of broad problems of national defense.

The five officers of the Supply and Projects Section were responsible for defense projects of Overseas Departments and defense plans based thereon; harbor defense projects; antiaircraft defense; strategic highway projects; supply problems affecting war plans; budgetary matters; and special studies of broad problems of national defense.

In addition to the above, four officers of WPD were members of the Joint Planning Committee to work on joint army and navy plans; joint army and navy exercises; and other matters pertaining to national defense and involving action of the Joint Board.

One member of WPD served as a member of the Aeronautical Board.[5]

That was a tall order for a dozen men. WPD needed data from all divisions of the General Staff, as well as data from line units and supply branches, so that plans could be coordinated for the army. WPD also provided the officers who dealt directly and routinely with other governmental departments and agencies as the army's representative. Further, the officers of WPD were the nucleus of the General Headquarters to be established on the approach of war. Gen. George V. Strong did not exaggerate when he said in 1939, "There is not an activity of the War Department . . . that does not tie in with the work of the [War Plans] Division."[6]

The pace had not eased by the time of Dwight D. Eisenhower's assignment to WPD (which would become OPD, the Operations Division, in March 1942). A 6 February 1942 entry in his diary observed, "The General Staff is all to be cut down, except the WPD, which now has all joint and combined work (a terrible job), all plans and all operations so far as active theaters are concerned. We need help!" On 8 March he wrote, "What a headache this combined stuff is." (Eisenhower's nice-guy image concealed the acerbity of his private observations. Richard K. Sutherland is a "bootlicker" [23 January 1942]. "One thing that might help win this war is to get someone to shoot [Adm. Ernest J.] King." "[Adm. Harold R.] Stark was just a nice old lady" [10 March 1942]. The British also drew Ike's fire: "Their practice of war is dilatory" [5 January 1942].)[7] Eisenhower had probably been alerted to the problems inherent in coalition warfare by his mentor, Maj. Gen. Fox Connor, who told the AWC class of 1934, "Dealing with an enemy is a simple and straightforward matter when contrasted with securing close cooperation with an ally. I would rather fight an alliance than a single nation and an alliance of three than an alliance of two enemies."[8]

Effective 9 March 1942, help came in the form of the Marshall reorganization of the War Department General Staff (an event no doubt in Eisenhower's mind when he made his diary entry of the previous day). To streamline the decision-making process, G-1 and G-3 were reduced by 75 percent and G-4 by 90 percent of their personnel, while the War Plans Division became a much expanded Operations Division. The Operations Division became General Marshall's operating command post, enabling him to concentrate on the larger issues of the war.[9] Fewer people reported directly to him, and they were expected to identify a problem and its solution in short desk-side briefings for the boss.

But until the Marshall reorganization in 1942, the busy War Plans Division did the formal planning that resulted in the approved plans. Increasingly at the end of the 1930s, the staff farmed out work requiring sustained and independent evaluation, much as the Department of Defense would later tap the resources of research institutions, so-called think tanks. It is probably in the nature of things that official plans will be more conservative than those worked out at colleges and research institutes. Bureaucracies tend to change slowly in the absence of dramatic interventions. Colleges and think tanks do not execute war plans. They are happily irresponsible in the sense of being free to dare, to challenge. Their task is to think.

The imaginative reflections on coalition warfare at the Army War College from 1934 to 1940 would be most useful to military and political leadership on the eve of war. Communications between the college and the War Plans Division regarding plans and other projects illustrate the degree to which WPD and the rest of the General Staff used the brainpower of the students at AWC.

The work produced by the students, staff, and faculty beginning in 1934 at the Army War College anticipated the very conditions faced by the United States in 1939–41. The student plans worked out each year at the college—and Orange, war-gamed so assiduously for more than thirty years at the Naval War College in Newport—existed on paper in precisely the format used by army and navy planning staffs. Moreover, student work was known to General Staff war planners. Students were routinely assigned projects—including war plans—requested by the various divisions of the General Staff.

Each year several graduates of each AWC class were assigned to the War Plans Division and to other key positions on the General Staff. The classes of the 1930s were heavily represented in WPD.[10] It is important to know that all AWC graduates were aware of all the war plans developed by their classmates in the academic year they shared. All war plans developed by student committees were presented at mandatory conferences at the end of the War Plans Period of the course. The mandatory conferences were attended by all students and many faculty members, including the commandant. Moreover, officers assigned to WPD/OPD also had access to correspondence between the college and WPD, as well as to the WPD files. The rationale and substance of AWC war planning were known to WPD.

The Army and Naval War Colleges exchanged students and faculty. The officers exchanged routinely completed the course at their own service college first. For example, Capt. William F. Halsey was a student at the Naval War College in 1933 and at the Army War College in 1934. As a consequence, the carefully selected graduates of both services, those most likely to be involved in joint planning, were familiar with the war plans done at both colleges, and they knew the culture of the "other service."[11]

From 1934 to 1940, at least one AWC student committee each year produced a war plan called "Participation with Allies." These plans addressed the scenario of the United States as a member of a friendly coalition fighting an enemy coalition or coalitions, including hemispheric defense, a two-ocean war, and a commitment to defeat "Germany first."

## Evolution from Color to Rainbow Plans

The unifying feature of student plans at the Army War College from 1934 through 1937 was the idea of the United States fighting as a part of a coalition: against Japan in 1934, against a "Nazi Confederation" in 1935, against the "Central Coalition" in 1936, and against Japan and Germany in 1937. The AWC plans for 1938, 1939, and 1940 returned focus to the Western Hemisphere for more modest tasks after four years of bold planning for coalition warfare in Europe and in the Pacific. The plans reflect boldness when the prospect of war was remote, caution when war was imminent.

The introduction of "Participation with Allies" into the War Plans portion of the course at the Army War College in 1934 brought a new realism to war planning.[12] The 1934 coalition of Blue (United States), Pink (Russia), Red (Britain), and Yellow (China) confronted Orange (Japan) and Carnation (Manchukuo or Manchuria).[13] The student committee presentation on 21 April 1934 was followed by a critique conducted by students and faculty in a question-and-answer period. The question-and-answer sessions following student presentations are particularly useful. They are spontaneous, frank, and sometimes amusing. Faculty and peer review provide the "why" as well as the "what" of the presentation. The entire AWC community attended the oral reports of each student committee and joined the discussion following the presentation. At times participants are named, adding human interest, as the then-unknown middle-grade officers will be recognized as the American military luminaries of World War II and the Cold War, but sometimes the recorder fails to identify speakers.

The old Color Plans, pitting the United States alone against a single foe, were continued because they served the primary teaching purpose of the college: to train student planners in the methods of the War Plans Division and the War Department General Staff. Students were organized into fifteen-man committees, and each addressed one scenario in the spectrum of wars ranging from a simple expedition into Mexico to a coalition conflict with Japan and a "Nazi Coalition." Once a foe was identified, the student officers collected information and went through the entire process involved in designing war plans. Several of the Color Plans—Green, Orange, and Crimson—had become standard at the college, but they were new to each class. Furthermore, the faculty would work in some new wrinkles each year to make the scenarios realistic.

War planning at the Army War College was taken seriously. Assistant Commandant George S. Simonds pointed out concerning the 1922–23 curriculum that "the actual preparation of war plans had been given more prominence than any other feature of the course."[14] The class of 1925 was told that "all work done is preliminary to and preparatory for the preparation of actual war plans."[15] Emphasis on war planning in the AWC course continued to 1940, when the college suspended courses.[16]

The Green (Mexico) and Crimson (Canada) war scenarios were played every year because it was prudent to have plans on file to cover war with contiguous foreign powers, however improbable hostilities with our immediate neighbors might have been in the 1930s. Hemispheric concerns usually were expressed by reference to the Monroe Doctrine.

Orange was also played each year. From 1906 onward, war planners recognized that conflict between the United States and Japan was one of the more likely wars of the future. It was assumed that American interests in China and presence in the Philippines put the United States on a collision course with Japan. Indeed, the U.S. Navy regarded war with Japan as inevitable. The Army and Navy War Colleges both presented Orange as a scenario in which the navy played the major role while the army played a supporting role in securing naval bases in the Pacific.[17]

Red (Britain) was played frequently because it filled a pedagogical need. Red was the only enemy assumed capable of projecting power to America's

Atlantic backyard and, with the cooperation of Canada, to the American northern frontier. Intentions aside, only Red-Crimson was capable of seriously threatening the American Northeast. If students were to plan for the defense of the East Coast, they had to willingly suspend reality in the 1930s and permit our probable friends to wear the villain's cape.

Red allied with Orange was the most dangerous combination that the United States could face, and those responsible for training planners were drawn to the worst case. The college provided the following rationale for Red-Orange planning in 1919: "Great Britain and Japan had emerged from the World War dominant in their respective continents and within their own spheres of influence . . . [and] while there was no threat of hostilities with either of them, a coalition of these two nations against the United States would be a cause of greater embarrassment than would be any other bi-power combination then possible."[18] At the time this "embarrassment" was being considered, the Anglo-Japanese alliance of 1902 had not yet lapsed. By the 1930s war between the United States and Great Britain was unlikely, but Red, Orange, or Red-Orange allowed U.S. officers to think through a big war "in which both the Army and the Navy had important roles to play."[19]

Until Germany, Italy, and Japan demonstrated a willingness to use military force in the 1930s, one had to stretch one's imagination to find a direct military threat to the United States. Nevertheless, prudence dictated that soldiers think about possible wars in the Pacific, in the Atlantic, and in the hemisphere. Not many causes could have convinced the American people that war was necessary, but among them were violations of the Monroe Doctrine, concern for the security of our overseas possessions, and perhaps our China policy.[20] War was a remote possibility. If it came, the United States would have sufficient time to mobilize to meet the challenge. That is why army strength from 1925 to 1935 ranged from 134,000 to 138,000.[21] Thus, it seemed appropriate in planning to assign the lion's share of Orange to the first line of defense, the U.S. Navy, and the dominant role in the hemisphere, for the little wars that might be anticipated there, to the U.S. Army. From time to time domestic crises, such as the Red Scare, would produce a plan to combat domestic disorder (Plan White). The need to give equal billing and major tasks to the army and the navy would bring back Red-Crimson or Red-Orange, but the old reliables at the Army War College remained Orange, Green, and Red.

Planning meant research, requiring students to document the economic, political, psychological, and military strengths and weaknesses of friend and foe in an Information Period that preceded the War Plans Period. Industrial and manpower mobilization, concentration, and transportation schemes were worked out in great detail. Strategies were designed. The techniques and even the standard forms used were those used in the War Department. Students in committees played the roles of G-1, G-2, G-3, and G-4, the Office of the Assistant Secretary of War, and the War Plans Division. They prepared staff studies and memoranda just the way it was done at the General Staff for which the student officers were being prepared. (See appendix F for the war-planning process. See appendixes B and C for assignments of AWC graduates 1934–40 to Washington in 1940 and 1941.)

The classes were instructed during the orientation periods not to make too much of the probability of war with any particular country. (One suspects that this was a response to student grumbling about why the college did Red planning.) International affairs are characterized by surprises; today's friend is tomorrow's foe. Students were encouraged to work the problem provided and not to fight the problem. Work at the college reflected work at the General Staff—until 1934. Beginning with that year, there was a freedom and flexibility of thought in the school that was not matched at the shorthanded War Plans Division of the War Department General Staff engaged in the day-to-day issues of the real world. Until events forced what became the famous Rainbow Plans, the college did the creative thinking while the staff barely had time to think at all. When the staff turned to the Rainbow Plans at the end of the decade, much of the creative thinking of the students—and many of the students of the 1930s themselves—would be found in the middle of the Rainbow planning process.

War planning at the Army War College from 1934 onward showed a great deal of imagination as the college and students carefully monitored contemporary developments in international affairs and considered coalition warfare on a global scale.[22] Between 1934 and 1940 the student planners kept one eye on the region assigned for study by the faculty and one eye on the other side of the world where events raised doubts in their minds as to the location of the greater threat to the United States. Curricular archives reveal that while focusing on events in Asia, for example, student planners kept one eye on developments in Europe. Conversely, while planning for a European war, Japan's impending clash with the United States, Britain, and the Soviet Union remained a pressing concern. There was a general sense that one might easily fall into the trap of committing forces or other resources to the wrong theater or to the wrong war. As U.S. involvement in war moved from remote possibility at the beginning of the 1930s to high probability at the end of that decade, the plans became more conservative. Plans that took planners in 1934–37 to Manchukuo and the Rhineland were scaled back to hemispheric defense for the most fundamental reasons. The modest resources immediately available to the nation, and especially to the nation's third-rate army, suggested modest, short-term strategies, at least initially. Defense of the Alaska-Hawaii-Panama strategic triangle and then the Western Hemisphere was about all the United States could manage until American potential was realized.

What follows is a year-by-year summary of some of the student plans developed at the college from 1934 to 1940. The Color Plans continued to be updated, but only Orange, Purple (Brazil), and plans to fight Germany will be discussed in some detail to show how they evolved into coalition schemes. The centerpiece of this summary is "Participation with Allies," planning that dealt with coalition warfare on two fronts and, ultimately, the decision to defeat "Germany first." Increasingly, sophisticated reflections about world war characterize the transition from Color to Rainbow Plans. The major considerations of the Rainbow planners are visible in the 1934–40 AWC "Participation with Allies" plans.

# Part II

# PARTICIPATION
# WITH ALLIES AND
# TWO-FRONT
# WAR

# 4

★ ★ ★

# 1934

## War with Japan

In the first place the Navy cannot win a war.
The war has to be decided on land.
**—WILLIAM F. HALSEY**, AWC, 1934

In the very first scenario studied at the Army War College under "Participation with Allies," a coalition of Blue (United States), Pink (Russia), Red (Britain), and Yellow (China) confronted Orange (Japan) and Carnation (Manchukuo or Manchuria). Lt. Col. U. S. Grant III, class of 1934, was the chairman of the committee appointed by the AWC faculty.[1] In his dual role as army chief of staff and president of the Joint Board, he had the task of preparing a memorandum of instruction for the Blue representative to the Inter-Allied War Council, covering the following points: the conduct and objectives of the war, the extent of U.S. military participation, and the extent of allied participation. It was apparent from the beginning that the task of the AWC students was to work at the highest level of national security policymaking. This was not an exercise limited to military operations.

As part of the maneuvering prior to the 1935 Naval Conference, a high-profile debate among British, American, and Japanese top admirals took place in the pages of *Foreign Affairs*. This debate, lasting from 1931 to 1935, was part of the backdrop to the students' deliberations as they began their planning of the mandatory memoranda of instruction to the applicable U.S. representatives.[2] To prepare such a memorandum was an innovative way to begin the planning process, though perhaps just a bit legalistic. The reason for this formal approach to strategy was part Karl von Clausewitz and part cost accountant. Establishing the political objectives of a war in a dispassionate manner was in keeping with the teaching of the great philosopher of war. Wars were fought for political purposes. Sorting out those purposes as early on as possible was certainly desirable, but determining the extent of allied participation was also shorthand for ascertaining as early as possible who was going to pay for the war. The successors to Calvin Coolidge would want to know who had hired the money and what the conditions of the hiring had been. One lesson of the Great War was that the United States could not be too careful in dealing with allies who had a tendency to forget favors rendered. The country bumpkins were determined not to buy the bridge from European city slickers—again.

Col. Jonathan M. Wainwright led the group that worked out the American concept of operations and the guidance to the American delegation. Lt. Col. Dawson Olmstead's subcommittee determined allied political and military objectives and designed the organization intended to bring about allied cooperation. Maj. Philip R. Faymonville and colleagues assessed enemy aims, how Orange would conduct war, and how Orange would react to Blue plans.[3] This estimate of the enemy situation became the G-2 annex to Blue's plan.

Capt. William F. Halsey, USN, was asked to do an estimate of the allied situation, determine each ally's supply and transportation requirements, determine the allied military and naval forces available in the theater of operations, and present consolidated allied plans to his colleagues. Halsey had played Orange as a student at the Naval War College before graduating in 1933 and was aware of current naval views regarding war with Japan, among them the expectation that the Japanese would attack without a declaration of war, as they had in 1904 to begin the war with Russia; the assumption that the Philippines would be lost early in the war; and the concern that Japan had secretly and illegally fortified the mandated islands in the Pacific and might have secret sea, air, and submarine bases there. Those considerations, confirmed in the previous year at the Naval War College, allowed Halsey to explain why a bold stroke to reinforce the Philippines was unacceptable: it would risk the U.S. fleet. A deliberate strategy of establishing bases in the Pacific was required. In addition to the professional education of individual officers, the purpose of the exchange of officers between the senior service schools was to bring the latest views of the other service to the colleges and to foster army-navy cooperation. Halsey did that well.

The scenario was also intelligently conceived. The backdrop to the scenario was the actual international situation in 1933–34, except that Pink and Orange were fighting. In the scenario, Orange had violated Blue neutrality in an incident invented by the Army War College that looks very much like the actual incident of 12 December 1937 in which Japanese planes bombed the U.S. river gunboat *Panay,* killing two and wounding thirty Americans. Analyses of current events, friendly and enemy capabilities, and estimates of military, political, economic, and sociopsychological factors were real. They were also "joint" in the sense that Halsey clearly influenced his army "shipmates" to decide upon a strategy much like the one the students at the Naval War College had chosen in 1933. The question-and-answer period following the presentation by the 1934 committee is a fair summary of what Halsey's classmates at the Naval War College had concluded the previous year after playing the 1933 Plan Orange. Earlier it had been thought that Blue was sufficiently superior to Orange to permit the fleet to go to the Philippines without delay en route.[4]

The situation presented to the AWC students was that Pink and Orange had come to blows without a declaration of war. Blue attempted to get the disputing parties to an international body for arbitration, but the committee, attentive to contemporary international events, concluded that "Orange would probably refuse to take part in, or would withdraw from this conference. . . . This action would be similar to the manner in which Orange withdrew from the League of Nations as a result of the Manchurian affair."[5] (In the real world, Japan announced its withdrawal from the league on 27 May 1933.) Therefore, the interested parties (prospective allies) agreed to a conference "to settle the terms on which they would deter the war and to decide on the contribution each would promise for its prosecution." This conference evolved into a "permanent Inter-Allied War Council." Following a plausible scenario, Blue, Red, Pink, and Yellow ultimately declared war on Orange and Carnation (Manchukuo, the puppet state created by Japan on 18 February 1932).

The committee immediately noted that the theater of operations was in Japan's backyard, far from the United States. From New York it was about thirteen thousand miles to Manila via the Atlantic and the Pacific. From San Francisco to Manila via Hawaii was about seven thousand miles. Orange was a mere four hundred to six hundred miles from any port between Vladivostok and Shanghai. The distance to the U.S. naval base in the Philippines was significant. So was the failure of the United States in all the years since 1898 to fortify a port in the Philippines. That meant that the United States would almost certainly be denied a base in the region shortly after the initiation of hostilities with Japan. It was assumed that Japan would enjoy local superiority and seize the Philippines at the war's outset. Knowledgeable army and navy officers had been warning of this eventuality for some thirty years.

As early as 1907 the Joint Board had identified the need for an initial "defensive attitude until reinforcements could be sent," and Maj. Gen. Leonard Wood highlighted the absolute need for sea control if troops were to hold the islands. In 1919 Capt. Harry E. Yarnell, a navy planner, predicted the loss of the Philippines and the capture of our forces there. Capt. Dudley W. Knox pointed out at the Washington Conference of 1921–22 that the United States had given up "all chances of defending the Philippines." In 1933 Stanley D. Embick called the early dispatch of our fleet to Philippine waters "an act of madness," and in 1935 he strongly recommended initial defense from the Alaska-Hawaii-Panama triangle "in such a manner that will promise success instead of national disaster." But initial loss of the Philippines was probably news to some army officers in 1934.[6]

The committee seriously considered two strategic options. One was a risky bold stroke requiring the U.S. fleet to cover great distances to confront the Japanese fleet in decisive battle close to Japan. But the absence of a fortified base in the western Pacific meant that the United States would not be able to repair damaged ships in the region, while the Japanese could. Damaged American ships would have to return to Hawaii, under escort, further reducing the combat power of the striking U.S. fleet. The committee expected that the Japanese would adopt a defensive strategy by meeting the approaching U.S. fleet with light forces at some distance from the home islands. These light forces would include submarines, torpedo boats, destroyers, cruisers, naval air forces, and mining operations. An inner line of Japanese capital ships would avoid combat in the initial stage of the operation. The Japanese intent would be to cause attrition in the U.S. fleet so that by the time the great Trafalgar-like sea battle took place between the opposing capital ships, primarily battleships, the forces would be roughly equal.

The alternative U.S. option would be to seize bases en route to the Far East as the fleet conducted a much slower and more deliberate strategy. This course of action was safer, but it would take much longer and require a greater effort by land forces. Fortunately for the United States, in the context of this scenario the British fleet would take much of the pressure off the Americans. However, even with the combined naval power of the two fleets available to them, the allies were cautious—too cautious in the opinion of those uninitiated to naval combat, the distances involved, and Pacific strategies.

Halsey was specifically asked during the question-and-answer session why so many land forces were needed, why the operation took so long when the friendly coalition enjoyed clear naval superiority (which, of course, it did not), and why the combined British and U.S. fleets could not secure command of the Yellow Sea and the Sea of Japan much earlier. "In the first place the Navy cannot win a war," he stated in a response that would be as relevant for 1942–45 as it was for 1934. "The war has to be decided on land." No doubt that pronouncement got Halsey the attention of his army classmates and the faculty. He went on to say that the allied fleet could force its way into the Yellow Sea, but it was not at all clear that it would want to go into the Sea of Japan. He said that the Straits of Tsushima, scene of a naval battle between the Japanese and Russians in their war of 1904–5, were narrow, permitting the Japanese to bring land-based artillery, mines, and land-based aircraft to bear on friendly forces. If you are caught in that trap, he concluded, "you have lost the war right then and there because you can do nothing with your land forces with that fleet gone."[7]

Wrestling with great issues in a tour of the horizon, the committee's discussion, analysis, and search for concrete solutions reveal a combination of naiveté and sophistication. The United States was always assumed to be on the side of the angels, a dispassionate arbiter in an avaricious world. Blue is prepared to grant the Philippines their independence but wants to prevent Russia and Japan from dominating Asia and to ensure China's integrity. Britain would like to see Japanese military capability reduced. Russia has internal problems. China wants Japan out of China, out of the "lost province" (Manchuria), and out of Korea. Coalitions, it was asserted, are of two types: in one type, one of the allies dominates, as Germany did in the recent war; in the other, the coalition is cooperative, as with the Allies of the same war. The United States finds itself in a cooperative alliance in 1934. The material needs and the possible falling out of allies are taken into account.

China is so ridden with fundamental problems that it is an uncertain ally in need of material and financial assistance and military advice at the higher echelons. The United States or Britain (or both) will be the provider. Russia also requires material and financial aid. The United States is the likely provider.[8] Russia and Britain may become involved in war in Europe; Russia's internal stability is tenuous; Britain has continuing clashes of interest with its dominions; Britain and Russia have longstanding differences in Asia and in Persia; Britain and America are in many ways competitors. One would not expect Britain to continue cooperating in a war with Japan when and if Russia becomes a greater threat to British interests. Unanticipated surprises will emerge as they did in 1914, when Italy deserted the Triple Alliance, and in 1917, when Russia made a separate peace with Germany.

Considerations like these prompted the committee to emphasize close coordination among the allies and the early establishment of the Inter-Allied War Council. The students wanted everything on the table in plain sight.

Reading between the lines, one senses that there was at least as much concern for explaining U.S. official actions to the American public as there was for winning the war.

Students did not take their task of presenting the purpose of the war lightly. They were firm and clear in asserting that the United States would not be committed to war if peaceful solutions were available, or if American purposes could be accomplished by just material support. The seriousness they attached to the problem of cooperation and commitment anticipated the American-British conversations before the United States entered World War II. In 1934, as reflected in student analyses, neither the United States nor Britain was eager for war.

The planners showed a realistic appreciation of public opinion and an understanding of American history, traditions, and institutions. Their ruminations foreshadowed the contentious peacetime conscription of 1940 and the cautious course the president had to follow in dealing with the public, the press, and the Congress as the country edged toward war. The officers seem to have discovered the new scientific public opinion polling and were fascinated by it.[9]

The committee also made every effort to benefit from what the Great War experience had taught about cooperation among allies. The postwar disillusionment with the war was in part due to the lofty hopes that were dashed as nations returned to uninspired and petty politics. This time early agreement on realistic objectives and means would make the process more businesslike. The committee sought explicit war aims, conditions of war termination, promises of contribution to the common effort, and a mechanism to ensure close cooperation. "America's Part in the Supreme War Council during the World War" is listed in the bibliography of the committee report. World War I was much with the planners in 1934.[10] It should be recalled that they were a mere sixteen years removed from that conflict. Evident is the craving for a future without surprises, the desire to manage war the way one manages any other business, and the belief that reasonable men could draw up a binding contract for the conduct of war. Their concerns reflect awareness of the great events of the recent past: world war, peacemaking, internationalism, and economic depression. They realized that the citizens of a democracy would demand a strict accounting of how and why the United States had been led into another war.

Six members of the committee took the trouble to produce a thoughtful minority report. They made two significant points: a punitive peace is a bad idea in principle, and a crushed Japan would invite the Soviet Union to dominate the region. In their words, a total defeat of Japan "would not produce a satisfactory settlement of the Far Eastern question and would be inconsistent with the best interests of both Blue and Red." The students drew their own lessons from what by 1934 had come to be called a Carthaginian peace, a reference to the vindictive terms of the Treaty of Versailles, and they demonstrated a sophisticated Realpolitik in suggesting that what was needed was a peace that would

> not lay before Pink an irresistible temptation to adopt herself the policy, heretofore pursued by Orange, of establishing a dominion over China. . . . Whatever indignation we may feel at the ambition of Orange and at the lack of consideration of others' rights and international usage with which she is trying to satisfy that ambition, we should not enter a war the outcome of which may turn, even in the event of victory, in a direction inconsistent with our own best interests. . . . Reasonable foresight, therefore, seems to demand that Blue and Red leaders ask themselves whether a domination of Northern China by Pink (Russia) will not be more injurious to their interests than the domination now threatened by Orange.[11]

The minority report pointed out that only Pink rivaled Blue in raw materials and overall potential. It was clearly not in the United States' interest for Pink to dominate Manchuria. The minority report was clearly as concerned with the Soviet Union (routinely called "Russia") as it was with Japan. A defeated Japan would be required to limit the size of its army and navy in the future, but some Japanese commercial and financial interests in Manchuria would be preserved. Pink administration of certain railroads in Manchuria with free use by other nations was proposed, but Orange troops were to be removed from mainland Asia and Pink troops from Yellow territory. Finally, there was a proposal that the Japanese mandated islands be jointly administered by Red and Blue with a proviso that Blue would leave the mandated islands to Red if Red compensated Blue with the British West Indies.[12] This is an interesting foreshadowing of a later exchange of bases for destroyers.

The analysis was sound, and the selection of objectives was wise. The speculations in 1934 about the creation of power vacuums came close to the mark as events unfolded in the decades that followed. The connection between foreign and domestic policy was also appreciated, and the psychological predisposition of the American people was understood by the authors of the minority report:

> The disturbed economic situation of the US would probably be relieved by the conduct of a war which should reduce unemployment,

increase business and wages and realize the accomplishment of economic recovery that the government is now trying to perform. American public opinion and sentiments are, in general, opposed to the conduct of war, and it would require flagrant enemy acts and properly handled propaganda to arouse the nation to the point of prosecuting a war effectively.[13]

Other concerns and some penetrating glimpses into the future emerged as the officers thought through the problems of coalition warfare. They expressed reservations about the capacity of the Soviet Union to hold up in "a long drawn out major war," and expressed concern for the 121,000 Japanese residents of Hawaii. It was noted that "Australia looked to the United States Fleet rather than to the British Fleet for her security."[14] (The speaker was not identified, but this comment may have come from Halsey.) The officers had confidence in the potential of the United States to overwhelm any foe, or almost any combination of foes, but they regretted the nation's short-term lack of preparedness. By 240M (240 days after mobilization) the Blue coalition would be superior to Orange, but until then the situation would be dangerous.[15] The United States had to depend upon others and good luck while it built its armed forces for war. The committee speculated about what the Japanese would do, concluding that they would go on the strategic defensive: "Orange will consider, but not adopt, a surprise submarine attack against the Blue Fleet, assembling in Hawaiian waters. . . . Orange will consider, but not adopt, a plan to attack either the Blue or Red Fleet before a junction is effected. . . . Orange Fleet will assume the strategic defensive and conduct a war of attrition with submarines."[16]

The committee finished its presentation by saying that the degree of cooperation achieved by the Allies in the Great War was about as much as one could expect. And then they added a comment that brings Roosevelt and Churchill to mind: "The most important factors in determining the degree of cooperation and unity of effort that an alliance can obtain are the personalities of its civil and military leaders." They also unknowingly described Dwight D. Eisenhower in noting, "Tact and diplomatic skill are essential qualifications for an allied Commander-in-Chief."[17]

Some of the committee's observations reached beyond the 1930s and beyond World War II. In the question-and-answer session someone asked how it would be possible to defeat Japan and still give that nation a chance to do well economically. It was not easy in 1934 to anticipate a post–World War II Japan, Inc., but an unidentified committee member replied that Holland, once a great naval power but now without a great fighting navy, had "retained her advantage of commercial position and . . . profited greatly."[18] This hint at a rosy future for a demilitarized Japan—and much more in the work of the class of 1934—draws a smile of recognition from those familiar with the events of the ensuing decades.

AWC Commandant Gen. George S. Simonds—former chief of the army's War Plans Division and future assistant chief of staff under MacArthur—praised the committee for its work, describing the lot of an army planner: "He has no real work to keep him from going mad, except housemaid's work; all the rest is forced exercise in the form of endless rehearsals for a destructive and terrifying performance which never comes off and which, if it does come off, isn't like the rehearsals." But Simonds asserted that the committee had made a real contribution in a region of "inevitable conflict" and probable armed conflict. Orange and Pink would be first on the stage. In his final remark, Simonds expressed his opinion that the study raised basic issues that "you will have to think about if you are on the WDGS, or the staff out in the Philippines, or in command of the Philippines, or other responsible positions."[19] Considering the parts they would play later, one pauses to wonder what Halsey, Wainwright, and others were thinking as they listened to their commandant in 1934.

# 5

# 1935
## *The Nazi Confederation*

The United States is committed to the war in Europe but
sooner or later will have to deal with Japan.
**—STUDENT COMMITTEE,**
"PARTICIPATION WITH ALLIES," 1935

The "Participation with Allies" portion of the 1935 War Plans course demonstrated just how in touch the Army War College faculty was with contemporary international affairs. It also showed the students' high level of sophisticated analysis and their application of all instruments of state power to
address the complex political-military issues handed them by their faculty.
The scenario presented a problem in Europe, but Japan's readiness to
exploit the European situation to its advantage in the Far East raised the
prospect of American involvement in a two-ocean war. From at least 1934
onward the committees assigned to "Participation with Allies" kept two and
sometimes three theaters of war in mind. The AWC class of 1935 committee's response to the problem came very close to foreseeing the actual
events of 1938–41. The student briefer of the committee report was not
engaging in hyperbole or buttering up the faculty on 17 April 1935 when he
said,

> This situation was conceived by the Faculty some months ago, and
> events of today outside the walls of this institution are in a fair way to
> substantiate the Faculty's flight of fancy to a degree most flattering
> to the perspicacity of that august body. Indeed the members of War
> Plans Group #4 have experienced some difficulty in keeping sepa-
> rate the developments of the problem from the news in the daily
> press.[1]

Scholars of the period will also struggle to distinguish actual events from the college-invented scenarios.

The task of the committee was to digest the situation presented before writing instructions to guide key U.S. officials.[2] As the situation developed, an alliance of the United States, Britain, France, and Italy faced an enemy coalition called the "Nazi Confederation," consisting of Germany, Austria, Hungary, and Yugoslavia. The United States, Britain, and France, all with Asian/Pacific interests, also kept a wary watch on Japan. The record of the committee's work lays out in detail the problem, the students' solutions, and the rationale for their decisions in writing instructions.

In the summer of 1934, the faculty-designed scenario began, war in Europe seemed inevitable. A January 1935 coup d'état put the Nazis in power in Austria. An Austrian political and economic pact with Germany followed. Italy, with the approval of Britain and France, reacted by seizing the Brenner and Reschen passes and occupying two Austrian towns. A revolt in the Italian Tyrol followed. War was declared on 10 January, with Italy facing Germany and Austria. France occupied the Saar and sent troops to the Rhine. In order to control the Adriatic, Italy deployed troops to Albania on 20 January; Yugoslavia mobilized and returned certain territories to Hungary in consideration for a guarantee of Yugoslavia's northern frontier. Hungary cast its lot with Germany and Austria, and demanded territory from Czechoslovakia. In the middle of February, a German-financed revolt broke out in the Ukraine. At the end of February, the scenario continued, a Nazi Confederation was created, consisting of Germany, Austria, Hungary, and Yugoslavia. Yugoslavia was promised Albania and Fiume. France joined Italy. Czechoslovakia was overrun and occupied "largely by Hungarian troops." France held the west bank of the Rhine from the vicinity of Cologne to Mainz, with bridgeheads in Koblenz and Mainz. French public opinion, while insisting on defense, was opposed at the outset of war to undertaking more than was essential for security, and the advance to the Rhine satisfied that.

Russia closed its western frontier, suppressed the revolt in the Ukraine, and reinforced its Far East army.

Japan, bound by a secret understanding with Germany, mobilized in early March and concentrated a large force in northwestern Manchukuo. The Japanese demanded a free hand in China and cessation of further fortification of Singapore and Hong Kong. Japan notified the United States that any movement of the U.S. fleet west of the 180th meridian—roughly Midway Island, halfway between Hawaii and Wake Island—would be considered a hostile act. The Japanese also asserted sovereignty over mandated islands that they were fortifying. Great Britain, urged on by Australia and New Zealand, sought the cooperation of the United States in enforcement of a mutual policy in the Pacific and Far East.

In the fighting on the western front during February and March, German operations were characterized by unrestricted aerial warfare, including the use of chemicals, against Italian and French industrial and population centers and against shipping in the Mediterranean.

Popular American attitudes were anything but bellicose. The American people loudly demanded that the United States not enter the conflict no matter what the cost. Laws were passed withdrawing protection to U.S. nationals or property in the war zone, and legislators, mindful of Great War debts, forbade loans to belligerents. But then came the Japanese ultimatum denying the U.S. fleet free movement west of the 180th meridian, which hurt the pride of Americans and opened their eyes to the real threat to their commercial future. On 22 March, Japan closed the Sea of Japan and the China Sea to all foreign ships not licensed by the Japanese government. On 30 March, the United States and Britain declared a state of armed neutrality in the Pacific, a reaction warmly received by the U.S. public.

Shortly thereafter, several American and British ships were destroyed in the ports of Le Havre and Cherbourg by Nazi aircraft. On 10 April the United States and Britain declared war on the Nazi Confederation.

Proceeding from this scenario, the committee, assuming the roles of political authority, president of the Joint (Army and Navy) Board, and army chief of staff, prepared memoranda of instructions for the army and navy commanders in the field and for the representative appointed by the president of the United States to the Inter-Allied Council.[3] The main decisions of the planning group were succinct:

> (1) The United States is committed to the war in Europe, but sooner or later will have to deal with Japan.
>
> (2) Our war aims are to prevent the Nazis or any other Confederation becoming supreme in Europe, and Japan becoming all powerful in the Far East. It will not suffice that our assistance be limited to money and supplies, and it has been decided to send an expeditionary force to Europe. All we need to send to France is a respectable force . . . and we can save our main effort for Japan. . . .
>
> (3) It is essential that a strong naval force be stationed in the Pacific.[4]

The main objective of the Nazi Confederation, the committee determined, was to regain all territory lost by the member nations in the Great

War and to extend their territory in Europe to the southeast: "This strategic time will probably be coincident with the entry of Japan into the war with the objective of neutralizing American and British effort in Europe." Germany, Austria, and Hungary, the revisionist powers, were the foe. The sense in those countries that they had been cheated in the postwar treaties was widely known. As the committee put it, "Since [Hitler's 1933] advent it has been increasingly apparent that Germany will no longer abide by the provisions of the [Versailles] treaty."[5]

But linking Germany and Japan in a military axis in 1935 put a two-front war on the American plate, thus anticipating the real world of November 1936. AWC planners expected integration of German and Japanese plans; that would have complicated British and American counterplanning. But there is little evidence of close cooperation in the real world as Germany and Japan went their willful and independent ways before and during World War II, to their mutual disadvantage.

Japan's aim was hegemony in East Asia. Whether it was to be called a "co-prosperity sphere," an empire, or a kind of Japanese Monroe Doctrine, the end sought was the same: Japanese domination in the Far East and a much smaller role in the region for non-Asians. The timing of the Japanese bid for hegemony in the AWC scenario of 1935 was tied to the development of scenario events in Europe. It was important to Japanese planning that the United States and Britain commit to Europe so that Japan would have a free hand in the Pacific, as it did during World War I, particularly in the initial phase of military operations. The German-Japanese connection in the scenario presented the problem of the two-ocean war to Britain and the United States. There would be differences between the scenario of 1935 and the actual events of 1939–41, but it is noteworthy that the committee decided to defeat the Germans before turning to the defeat of Japan. While the committee was correct in anticipating that the American public would be more readily prepared to fight the Japanese than to fight in Europe, the bombing of American ships by Nazi aircraft in the scenario decided the issue: Germany would be defeated first.

The students did their homework. Some members of the committee were tasked as a subcommittee to summarize the texts of the treaties binding on the United States and to write fact sheets on several controversies in which the United States had interests. They were scrupulous in attempting to determine both the legal requirements of the treaties to which the United States was signatory and the policy of the U.S. government. Soldiers of that era were particularly—perhaps exceedingly—sensitive to the principle of civilian ascendancy. They knew that it was not for soldiers of the United States to make national policy, but they were often unsure just what U.S.

policy was. In the absence of clear political guidance, the soldiers studied the texts in order to divine what their civilian masters expected of the army and the navy. Thorough summaries of treaties, declarations, and contemporary issues were provided by a subcommittee to guide the deliberations of the whole committee regarding U.S. obligations and constraints.

The following treaties, conferences, declarations, and issues were summarized: Versailles, 29 June 1919; Trianon, 4 June 1920; St.-Germain, July 1920; Neuilly, 9 August 1920; Sèvres, 10 August 1920; the separate U.S. treaties with Germany, Austria, and Hungary, 18 October 1921; the Washington Conference (Nine-Power Treaty), 6 February 1922; the Shantung controversy; the termination of the Anglo-Japanese alliance (at the expressed wish of the United States, Canada, and Australia); the Siberian question; the mandated islands; Lausanne, 24 July 1923; Locarno, October 1925; the Pact of Paris (Kellogg-Briand), 1928; the London Naval Treaty, 1930; the Four-Power Treaty, 15 July 1933 (Germany, France, Britain, and Italy); the German-Polish Declaration, 26 January 1934; and the scheduled Naval Conference of 1935.[6]

Accordingly, the committee was keenly aware of contemporary issues and the backgrounds of those issues. Analysis came out of solid research beyond mastery of contemporary international issues. It included an examination of cultural dictates and domestic constraints to policy in the United States and among possible belligerents on both sides.[7]

Sensitive to antiwar sentiment among the American people, the planners were nevertheless convinced that sufficient cause could arouse the American public. A subcommittee examined and reported on American psychology, on the ability of the administration to get the support of the American people, and on the reaction of the people to developing international relations. The purpose of these efforts was to find propaganda themes that would win public support.[8] A theme to emerge from an annex to the main report was suspicion of the Japanese among the American people and how this attitude might be used: "For many years the western states have been alarmed at Japanese immigration. To them 'yellow peril' is very real. Unquestionably these states would use all their influence to have the United States declare war against Japan on slight provocation and would give whole-hearted assistance to the prosecution of the war."[9]

This analysis explained remarks in the final student presentation to the effect that motivating Americans for a war in the Pacific was much easier than motivating Americans for another war in Europe. Racism was alive and all too well in the America of the mid-1930s, as would be demonstrated by the incarceration of Japanese-Americans in the name of national security after the bombing of Pearl Harbor. Although no one put it so crudely, racism could be exploited easily by the use of anti-Japanese propaganda. But more than racism is involved. Suspicion of Japan and sympathy for China were consistent in American attitudes, at least until 1949. In the late 1930s the preference is clear. In October 1937 Gallup asked where American sympathy was. The response: Japan, 1 percent; China, 59 percent; neither, 40 percent. In May 1939 the same question elicited this response: Japan, 2 percent; China, 74 percent; neither, 24 percent.[10]

The committee was confident that the administration would be able to manage the support of the public, pointing out that "since the Civil War, the trend has been to increase the power of the Executive." Since 1932 "this trend has been intensified and will enhance the power of the administration to control events and to influence the public to support its policies." The committee noted that the congressional elections of 1934 "continued the Democratic majority at an unprecedented strength," and it speculated that the Democrats would have their way. After describing the president and his advisers as more "press conscious" than any previous administration and capable of securing a "favorable presentation of the Administration's case on any subject," the students looked to the other side of the Atlantic to assess the potential of propaganda there.

They believed that "the Nazi government of Germany has used all means of propaganda and advertising with telling effect." Similar means could be quite as effective in influencing American public opinion, "especially in the emotional stress of impending or actual international conflict." The report concluded that not only could the administration manipulate public opinion into accepting a war policy, but the Roosevelt administration could be expected to stimulate "a wave of popular enthusiasm as soon as the issues become clearly defined and threaten our national interest."[11]

The scenario and student reactions to it were enlightened. The prospect of a two-ocean war with the United States fighting simultaneously as a coalition member against a German-led coalition and with Japan foresaw the actual situation of 1941–45. (See map 1, appendix I.) The sensitive and accurate assessment of public opinion in 1935 and recognition of the importance of propaganda are equally striking.

As the scenario unfolded, the American people were determined not to be tricked into another war in Europe. The general attitude was that neither loans to belligerents nor the promise of protection to Americans foolish enough to put themselves in a war zone should drag the republic into another war. Nevertheless, when American merchant ships were sunk in French ports by German aviation, America responded with a declaration of war. The students correctly concluded that peacetime pronouncements would count for little once the lives of innocent countrymen were taken arbitrarily by an aggressor.

In another flash of insight, the students anticipated a propaganda ploy by the Soviet Union. When the Japanese concentrated troops in Manchuria at one point in the scenario, the Soviets reinforced their troops on the border. Since it looked like war between Japan and the Soviet Union, "Communist agitation in the US was greatly reduced at once.... Several of the strongest peace organizations changed their peace-at-any-price attitude."[12] This fairly describes the new line of Communist propaganda taken when the Germans turned on the Soviet Union in 1941.

The committee's description of French public opinion in 1935 was equally accurate. The students believed that there was a willingness on the part of France to take some symbolic action when the Nazi coalition invaded Czechoslovakia, but there was no desire to engage in decisive combat with Germany. France convinced itself that it would be enough to put French troops on the Rhine. This action by the French in the make-believe world of 1935 is strikingly like the course actually taken in 1936 during the Rhineland crisis and in 1939 after the German invasion of Poland, in the so-called Sitzkrieg that lasted until the spring of 1940. In the March 1936 remilitarization of the Rhineland, Hitler gambled that the French would not contest by arms the movement of his troops into the demilitarized zone, and he was right. The AWC students accurately anticipated in 1935 the French behavior demonstrated both in March 1936 and in the Sitzkrieg. The reason for German delay on the French front in the 1935 scenario was a decision to defeat Italy in an estimated 180 days before turning to the defeat of France.[13] The French were reluctant about going on the offensive, just the reverse of French doctrine in 1914, and reluctant about doing anything bold without a British presence or British guarantees. So it was also when war games became actual events.

The committee also got right not only the close cooperation between the Americans and the British but also some of the nuances of the relationship before and after the United States' entry into World War II. The administration sensed that the United States would not be able to avoid war and hesitated to get too far ahead of the American people. Movement toward intimate cooperation with Britain had to be paced with a growing conviction by the American public that there was a threat to the United States. The development of cooperation with Britain in the 1935 scenario mirrors Roosevelt's policy from 1939 until the American declaration of war in December 1941. The scenario read, "Near the end of the second month of the war in

Europe the administration felt justified in announcing its purpose of 'cooperating with Great Britain in determining a policy to be followed in the Far East.' This announcement met with the approval of the public."

The incremental steps toward war overcame the "still considerable distrust of France and Italy because of their failure to repay war loans of the First World War." In the end, the American public, as it would in 1940–41, set aside reservations to endorse warmly the intimate relationship with Great Britain: "The growing union with Great Britain, emphasized by the joint action in the Pacific, has been popular," the scenario emphasized. "The necessity of acting in concert with Great Britain in both the European and possible Pacific theaters," it concluded, "grew to be generally appreciated."[14]

Committee assessment regarding the British dominions correctly asserted that the Pacific dominions were not enthusiastic about a British war in Europe. Australia and New Zealand expected a fight much closer to home. It was clear to all that if Britain engaged in a European war while also fighting a war in the Pacific, priority would go to the European theater. Therefore, Australia and New Zealand recognized their reliance upon the United States for their security and pressed the British to cooperate with the Americans. This estimate by the planners of 1935 proved sound, as the United States dominated the Pacific in World War II and by degrees later accepted former British responsibilities around the world.

After a thorough analysis the committee decided to transport U.S. troops and supplies to Europe in order to assist in the defeat of the Nazi forces and to concentrate the U.S. fleet in Hawaii in order to prepare for war with Japan. It was assumed that Britain, France, and Italy would be capable of defeating—or at least containing—the Nazi Confederation. This assumption permitted the United States to withhold forces for possible use against Japan. The United States was determined to play a relatively modest role in the European war, but it wanted a voice in peacemaking. The aim was to establish a durable future peace. Vindictive peace had proved to be a mistake.

Nothing like the Blitzkrieg of 1940 was even suggested. The United States promised to send at least 250,000 troops to Europe but not more than 500,000. U.S. troops would be started to France by 30M (thirty days after U.S. mobilization) and were to complete training and be ready to take over a section of the front by about 270M. Memory of the slow-moving Great War is evident here in the expectation that there would be time for a deliberate U.S. buildup. And why not? The French Army was expected to number some 4.5 million men at 180M, and France was allied to Britain and Italy (in the scenario). The German Army only recently had been increased from

**TABLE 1** ★ Comparative Strengths in Theater of Operations at 90M and 180M

**ALLIES AT 90M**

| Country | Airplanes | Land Forces | Sea Forces (Tons) |
| --- | --- | --- | --- |
| Britain | 1,464 | 100,000 | — |
| Italy | 2,452 | 1,750,000 | — |
| France | 8,500 | 3,381,000 | — |
| Total | 12,416 | 5,231,000 | 2,644,000 |

**NAZI CONFEDERATION AT 90M**

| Country | Airplanes | Land Forces | Sea Forces (Tons) |
| --- | --- | --- | --- |
| Austria and Hungary | 100 | Austria 150,000 | |
| Hungary 250,000 | — | | |
| Czechoslovakia (seized) | 500 | — | — |
| Yugoslavia | 800 | 1,000,000 | — |
| Germany | 4,700 | 2,000,000 | — |
| Total | 6,100 | 3,400,000 | 173,000* |

**ALLIES, NAZI FORCES, AND JAPAN AT 180M**

| Group | Airplanes | Land Forces | Sea Forces (Tons) |
| --- | --- | --- | --- |
| Allies | 19,251 | 6,650,000 | 3,296,000 |
| Nazi Confederation | 9,400 | 5,350,000 | 181,000 |
| Japan | — | — | 759,000 |

*Source:* Prepared by War Plans Group 4, 17 April 1935.

*At 90M Japan had sea forces totalling 748,000 tons.

the treaty army of one hundred thousand. Professional soldiers knew that the German Army was not fully trained for protracted war against a first-class foe. Surely the European allies were sufficiently superior to the enemy coalition that there was no urgent need for American soldiers. (See table 1.) In about nine months some 250,000 American soldiers would be in Europe. Then the United States would share in the defeat of the German-led coalition before turning to the problem in the Far East.

Strong U.S. naval forces stationed in Hawaii would cooperate with the great British Navy operating out of their "impregnable" base in Singapore. Again, as in the estimate of the situation in Europe, there was no sense of great urgency: "[The Japanese] generally begin their wars by surprise attacks before there is any declaration of war," said the committee. "This must be guarded against, but with the strong forces allied against them it does not seem probable that they will detach any important force for distant operations away from their homeland."[15] After all, it was reasoned, the U.S. Navy was superior to the Japanese fleet in battleships by a ratio of 15:9. The

Japanese advantage was in other types: cruisers, destroyers, and submarines, and in land-based aviation in the mandated islands. But the U.S. fleet, the British Mediterranean Fleet (the Italians and French took up the slack in the Mediterranean), and the British ships already in the Pacific combined to enjoy a 2:1 advantage over the Japanese. Therefore, while a bold tactical blow by the Japanese was possible, the committee believed that the Japanese would assume a defensive strategy. They would use their light forces in an outer line to harass and cause attrition among the enemy, while forming an inner line close to the home islands consisting of battleships with supporting land-based aviation. The planners concluded that the Japanese would be tough, but sheer allied weight would defeat them.

The naval responsibilities of the allies were carefully spelled out in the committee report. In the Atlantic, the U.S. Navy assumed responsibility for sea control west of longitude 50 degrees west. The British accepted responsibility for the Atlantic east of that line. An American liaison officer was sent to London to work with the Admiralty. The French would control the western Mediterranean, and the Italians were responsible for the eastern Mediterranean. The committee was overly optimistic regarding the Atlantic, failing to foresee the effectiveness of German submarines from 1939 to 1943: "As it is believed that Nazi submarines cannot be effective for some time, probably a year, vessels sailing for English ports will be unescorted until intelligence reports indicate that protection is necessary."[16]

The 1935 iteration of "Participation with Allies" was a creative and comprehensive reach into the future. It showed an impressive appreciation for the foreign forces around the world and a grasp of how they affected U.S. security interests. The participants were particularly astute in assessing attitudes in the United States and in France. Their work would also be useful to planners in the War Department's General Staff facing a blank sheet of paper and contemplating U.S. courses of action in a two-front war after 1938.

# 6

★ ★ ★

# 1936

## *The Central Coalition*

Our aim was to insure that the Allies would have
at least a 3:2 preponderance on the Western Front,
which we considered the decisive front.
**—STUDENT WAR PLANS REPORT,** 1936

On 2 October 1935 Malin Craig was relieved as commandant of the U.S. Army War College and became chief of staff of the army. George Simonds, the previous commandant, was Craig's deputy chief of staff until May 1936. On 5 November 1935 Craig tasked the college to study the organization of the U.S. Army division and higher units. The college was in the mainstream of the army. Both Craig and Simonds were thoroughly familiar with both the Army General Staff and AWC. Simonds had served as chief of WPD from October 1927 to September 1931 and as deputy chief of staff under MacArthur, so he was aware of war planning and everything else that happened on the army staff. Craig had been chief of cavalry from 1924 to 1926 and the army assistant chief of staff, G-3 (training and operations), from 1926 to 1927, so he was no stranger to the general staff.

The major innovation for the class of 1936 bearing on war planning was the addition to the curriculum of a feature called Foreign News. It came under the aegis of the G-2 faculty. "The purpose of this new feature was to encourage habits of careful but rapid newspaper reading and the prompt evaluation of the information in its relation to international affairs in general and the manner in which it might or might not affect the present and future of this country."[1] The world was divided into five regions, plus the United States. Students tracked events in one region and reported significant events to the class in short presentations. In the course of the year, each student would track two regions. The college maintained a real-world focus, and it was well connected to the very top of the military hierarchy.

During the War Plans Period in 1936, students were organized into committees to address four war situations: three Color Plans of the kind that students had been working on almost from the founding of the college, and the third version of "Participation with Allies," the problem introduced in 1934. The Color Plans were Green (Mexico), a minor effort in which the army was paramount; Orange (Japan), an overseas effort in which the navy was paramount; and Red (Britain), a major effort requiring equally great contributions and cooperation by the army and the navy. The stated purposes of "Participation with Allies" in a war in Europe were to bring home lessons learned in the Great War and to prepare for possible alliances in the future. As fate would have it, when the German government denounced the Locarno Pacts of 1925 and reoccupied the Rhineland on 7 March 1936, War College students were wrestling with a similar situation.

The 1936 alignment of contesting coalitions was like that of 1935, with one significant difference: Italy, an ally of the United States in the 1935 scheme, was a member of the German-led Central Coalition in 1936. Italian aggression in Abyssinia and Benito Mussolini's bombast had removed Italy from the side of the angels, a clear indication that the planners at the college were in touch with contemporary international developments.[2] The scenario moved quickly, presenting students with a United States at war. America had attempted to maintain its neutrality, but a series of attacks on American shipping on the high seas and in allied ports and other provocative incidents resulted in a declaration of war against Germany and Italy on 5 March 1936.

Germany, Italy, Austria, and Hungary comprised the Central Coalition at war with France, Britain, Greece, Turkey, and now the United States. Neither side had had success as of 5 March. The French Army and the British expeditionary force were on the Rhine, and the Germans were massed for an attack on Czechoslovakia. Italian troops were mobilized along their frontiers from the Alps to the Mediterranean and the Adriatic. Austria and Hungary had mobilized on their frontiers with Yugoslavia and Rumania. The British Commonwealth supported Britain, but only Canada was prepared to send an expeditionary force to Europe. Australia and New Zealand feared that the Japanese would take advantage of events in Europe and attempt to dominate the Far East while Britain was focused on events closer to home. It was believed that Germany and Japan had an agreement to cooperate militarily. The Soviet Union had mobilized in anticipation of a German, Polish, or Hungarian expansion in the Ukraine and to defend Siberia against Japan. Poland and Bulgaria were neutral, but they were tilting toward the Central Coalition just as Czechoslovakia, Yugoslavia, Rumania, the Soviet Union, and Belgium were leaning toward the allies. Central Coalition submarines were operating in the Mediterranean, in the Bay of Biscay, off the British coast, and in the Atlantic.

The student committee was to prepare memoranda that (1) stated the United States' war aims (the ends); (2) specified the extent of U.S. military and economic participation in cooperation with allies (the means); (3) instructed the Honorable A (the president's representative in Europe, based on President Wilson's Colonel House); and (4) laid out the Joint Army and Navy Basic Plan for war (the ways). The tasks assigned required the students to think through the implications of war from national strategy to military strategy to theater operations. The nature of the problem presented to the students made it clear to them that they were not being trained as mere technicians of violence. That part of their professional development was behind them. The War College educated the students by forcing them to think as philosophers of war, but not as fuzzy-headed philosophers. The formulation of strategy required clear-sighted analysis of ends, ways, and means at the national level and their synchronization.

The students' statement of war aims contained no surprises, but it is interesting to note the emphasis on a durable peace, the contributions of allies, and public support. This was obviously a reaction to what the student officers had experienced in their own lives as the high expectations of the peace following the Great War had been dashed, and as the likelihood of another round of wars loomed on the horizon. Certainly the aims were to defeat the Central Coalition and to restore peace on terms favorable to the United States and "conducive to international political and economic stability." But the committee went a step further in resolving that the allies would be made to understand that the United States would not tolerate an imposed peace treaty that planted the seeds of revenge in the hearts of the vanquished. Their sensitivity to the consequences of the economic terms of the Versailles treaty is apparent: "Those nations should be made to realize that the United States will not be a party to, but will actively oppose, any after-war scheme designed to continue economic dominance over [enemy] Coalition countries after the termination of hostilities."

The failure of Allies to pay their war debts was also evident in the efforts of the planning group to fix in advance the contributions of the alliance members. It was difficult to be explicit in forecasting the military and economic contribution of each ally, since war is filled with surprises. One of the allies might provide credits and materiel, another might have its cities and ports destroyed, and yet another might pay with a disproportionate number of battlefield deaths. Indeed, a member state might *be* the battlefield. Nevertheless, as in the previous two years, the student committee tried to fix responsibilities while still in the planning stage. Perhaps it is quintessentially American to believe that war can be conducted in a businesslike manner. In any event, the committee members made some interesting distinctions. Credits in funds, they said, would go only to Britain and France. Raw materials would be shipped to allies generously, but manufactured goods would be limited. The group's solution to this problem was expressed in the form of instructions to the president's representative to the Inter-Allied Council. The officers were well aware that sooner or later the administration would have to explain its actions to the Congress and to the American people.

In the question-and-answer session attended by the entire college community after the student report on 15 April 1936, a member of the audience asked how "the Honorable A was to insure himself before he turned loose the money. . . . What tangible things would you consider security?" The response was that the British and the French might either transfer some of their possessions in the Western Hemisphere to the United States or grant them independence. In either event, that would mean "getting rid of a foreign power in the American half of the world."

The committee's Joint Army and Navy Basic Plan for war in 1936 reacted to a scenario that painted a much more serious situation in Europe than had been presented in 1935. Again, a wary eye was kept on Japan, but no one really expected the Japanese to cross the vast Pacific and menace the American West Coast. Study of the 1935 student work or consultation with naval colleagues would have revealed to the 1936 planners that the Japanese fleet had short legs. That is, while it was an excellent fleet, it was designed for strategic defense, lacking the capacity to sustain distant operations far from port. Nevertheless, the Japanese contributed to the enemy coalition in drawing the attention of Russia and the United States to Japan.

The land force contribution of the United States to the European theater was much greater in 1936 than it had been in the 1935 student solution. That was due both to the estimate of a lesser threat posed by the Japanese in 1936 and to the fact that from the beginning of the situation given to the committee, the United States was at war in Europe. In 1935 the plan had called for a probable deployment of 250,000 men to Europe and a maximum of 500,000. In 1936 a field army of 750,000 would be dispatched to Europe within 180 days, and three field armies with more than 2 million soldiers were expected to be in the theater within 360 days. Some 870 American aircraft were to be on the Continent within 170 days of the declaration of war. Echoes of 1917 can be heard in the insistence that the Americans would be a separate and distinct force.

The U.S. Navy expected to play a limited role in European waters, "as it finds it necessary to keep the bulk of the fleet in the Pacific." Cruisers and destroyers would be assigned to convoy duty in the Atlantic, but the main American naval effort would be concentrated in the Pacific to maintain lines of communication there. Some of the destroyers and auxiliaries were destined for Europe "as they are recommissioned, to supplement the Allied naval forces operating in the Mediterranean and North Sea." That is, some old ships would be taken out of mothballs and returned to the fleet. Such retreads were considered adequate for chasing submarines in the Atlantic, but the navy always reserved its Sunday punch for war with Orange. Student analysis of friendly and enemy strengths and weaknesses clearly assessed the allied fleets to be superior to the enemy fleets. Therefore, some marginal U.S. augmentation of the British and French fleets in European waters was probably all that was needed, according to that assessment. A desperate Battle of the Atlantic was not expected by the AWC planners of 1936.

In addition to the assumption of allied naval superiority, the students made several other basic assumptions: that the Central Coalition would defend in the west and attack in the direction of the Black Sea; that the allies, including the United States, would make their main effort in the west in an invasion against the main enemy, Germany; and "that victory cannot be obtained in less than two years. Accordingly, the Allied and Associated powers must be prepared for a long war." The experience of the 1914–18 war had taught military planners that a contest of long duration involving the most advanced industrial nations in the world would probably be a war of materiel. Thus, the group's strategic assessment concluded, "From an economic standpoint, the Central Coalition should immediately invade Czechoslovakia to secure its industries and resources and push its advance into Rumania to secure its oil fields. . . . Japan should be secured as an ally for the aid it could give in interrupting the trade of the allies to the Far East."[3]

The missions of the armed forces and the government were expressed in clear and simple terms: the army would conduct an offensive in Europe with the United States' allies to defeat Germany and Italy; the navy would convoy merchant ships in the Atlantic and maintain sea lanes in the Pacific; the civil authorities would organize maximum support of the military efforts of the United States and allied forces. Prudence demanded that the army retain some of its forces for the possible war with Japan. Therefore, one field army was kept in a "position of readiness" in the United States. Because the United States "may become involved" in Alaska, the Aleutian Islands, Hawaii, or the Philippines or along the U.S.-Mexican border, reinforcement on a very selective basis was necessary. Accordingly, eighty-one thousand troops were sent to reinforce Hawaii, Panama, and Alaska. "The Philippines," the work group concluded, "will have to struggle along with what they have."

The students drafted emergency legislation designed to be available to the political authority for implementation as the nation entered into war or faced a national emergency. Draft bills covered a multitude of topics and circumstances, most of them concerned with mobilizing people and material resources. Among them were bills dealing with manpower, industrial mobilization, materiel procurement, private property, marine insurance, war trade, and war financing. Presidential proclamations were drafted when legislative action was not required. Various agencies and boards enumerated in the Industrial War Plan of 1933, such as the War Resources Administration and the War Trade Administration, were established by the committee. The students also wrote plans for imposing censorship, managing propaganda, controlling aliens, and influencing neutrals. They believed that no governmental agency other than the War and Navy Departments thought seriously about war preparation. The prevailing attitude was that the military alone must anticipate all the details and loose ends that were sure to require action in modern war.[4]

The officers at the Army War College in the mid-1930s invested much thought in the meaning of war away from the battlefield. Since the premise of a long war lay behind planning for the 1936 "Participation with Allies" problem, the consequences of modern war were sure to be far-reaching. War would affect and be affected by economics, politics, and psychology. Student officers grasped the increasing importance of public information and morale and were strikingly sensitive to popular opinion for many reasons. The men attending the college recalled the roller coaster of American public opinion from antiwar sentiment in the early days of the Great War, to enthusiasm for war and the utopian peace that would follow, to disappointment that became disillusionment and isolationism in the years after the war. The volatility of American opinion struck close to home. The officers planning for war in the mid-1930s had served in a frontier army, in an army of millions, and in the tiny army between the world wars. The instability of international relations and the fickleness of public opinion—and its importance in a democratic state—had been palpably demonstrated to these soldiers. They wondered how publics, American and other, would respond to the new devilish weapons that reduced the distinction between soldier and civilian. Aviation would be important, but there was no broad consensus among professionals as to how catastrophic the bombing of population centers would be. It would be terrible, but no one knew how terrible. It was generally assumed that poison gas would be used in bombs. The consequences of gas, incendiary bombs, and high explosives falling on cities and factories, in accordance with Italian strategist Giulio Douhet's writings, were unknown. One could only surmise the physical and psychic effects of such measures as these, intended to break the will of the enemy. It was not at all clear how populations and governments would react to weapons of mass destruction and loss of civilian life on an unprecedented scale. Civilian morale might collapse, or it might stiffen.

There were other unknowns. Submarines, tanks, motorized and mechanized forces, and aircraft carriers had been studied extensively, but there were vast differences of opinion as soldiers speculated about the significance of the new and improved weapons. Only actual war would show who was right. Still, the biggest question mark attached itself to popular opinion and what would happen if weapons of mass destruction were used against civilians.

Consideration of manpower priorities demonstrated how one issue influenced others, and how in the final analysis decisions relied as much on professional predispositions as on science. The army officers were notably self-effacing in allocating human resources: "As the Navy is the traditional first line of defense and must be brought to full battle efficiency without delay, it is accorded the first priority in personnel. Second priority is given to the GHQ Air Force, due to the desirability of having trained personnel ready to fly new planes as they are produced and the difficulty of the training requirements."[5] The predominantly army audience for the student presentation did not universally acknowledge the wisdom of these personnel priorities. Indeed, during the question-and-answer period after the oral report, the entire strategic direction was challenged. A member of the audience wondered if the committee had made a mistake in dedicating so much to a war in Europe when "possibly our national future interests may be protection from what may happen in the Far East." "Further, the British Commonwealth of Nations would probably look to the United States to pull its chestnuts out of the Far East if we could be persuaded to do so. What was the reason of *[sic]* committing that large a force to such interests as we may have in Europe, in contrast with what our future interests may be in the Far East?"[6]

The phrasing (or transcription?) is rough, but the thrust of the question is clear enough: Are American interests to be found in the Far East rather than in Europe? The remark about British chestnuts was prophetic. Under great pressures everywhere after the German successes in 1939–41, the British were eager to have the Americans take up the slack in the Pacific. Singapore was one chestnut under discussion in the American-British Staff Conversations (ABC) of 29 January–27 March 1941. The British, fighting for survival in their home islands, were unable to provide security for Australia and New Zealand in an ocean dominated by Japan. Only the Americans could confront the Japanese with a prospect of victory if the British were deeply involved in a European war. But the Americans were torn between the Atlantic and the Pacific.

The response to this question of where primary U.S. interests lay in 1936 anticipated the "Germany-first" strategy to which the Allies would later adhere despite pressures in the United States to make the main effort against the infamous foe that had attacked Pearl Harbor without warning. The committee assumptions about the general nature of the anticipated war were that it would be total; economic capacity would be decisive; it would be long; and after initial setbacks, the allies would win, if they would stick together. And Germany would be defeated first. The group spokesman in 1936 put it this way: "It was a rather complicated proposition. Our aim was to insure that the Allies would have at least a 3:2 preponderance on *the Western Front, which we considered the decisive front.* Hence, the three field armies to Europe."[7] The committee's appreciation of the general strategic situation of the United States is the backdrop of the Germany-first decision: "We felt that with the fleet in the Pacific, one field army in the United States would provide very comforting security. We did not feel that there need be any great apprehension as to the security of our West Coast, the Hawaiian Islands, or the Panama Canal. The Philippines, of course, we expected would be overrun by Japan very shortly."[8]

The work done by the group of fifteen officers assigned in 1936 to "Participation with Allies" in coalition warfare looked in retrospect very much like a dress rehearsal for World War II. It could have been a study done at the War Plans Division of the General Staff in 1939, 1940, or 1941. One could quibble over their miscalculation regarding Poland's possible alliance with Germany, but that would overlook the conclusion of the German-Polish nonaggression treaty of 1934, still fresh in the minds of those in the class of 1936. Similarly, they failed to predict the fall of France, but so did everyone else.

They came stunningly close to predicting how World War II would break out, how the contending coalitions would evolve, what the strategic objectives of all parties would be, and the outcome.

American war planners in 1938–42 undoubtedly profited from knowledge of the work of the 1936 student committee. A German-led coalition confronting the United States and its friends on one side of the world, and a menacing Japan on the other side, was precisely the equation that had to be solved by army and navy war planners in the real world of 1938–42. It was nearly a replay of the student exercise.

Nine members of the class of 1936 served in the War Plans Division of the War Department General Staff between 1936 and 1944. One of them, Carl A. Russell, rose from the grade of major to brigadier general in continuous service in WPD from 1 July 1939 to 28 November 1944. Another, Robert W. Crawford, advanced from lieutenant colonel to brigadier general by serving in WPD from 14 March 1939 to 22 June 1942.[9]

# 7

★ ★ ★

# 1937

## Europe and the Pacific

It is a war in which the economic and material factors
may play the major part, rather than a war which may
be quickly ended by military operations.
**—COMMITTEE 6,** WAR PLANS PERIOD,
"PARTICIPATION WITH ALLIES"

Academic year 1936–37 saw continued tasking of the Army War College by its former commandant, Chief of Staff of the Army Malin Craig. The college was asked to study the organization of corps and armies "composed of divisions of the type recommended by the War Department," a reference to the so-called triangular division consisting of three rather than four regiments, the division type that would fight in World War II. The college summary of the course refers to the response of AWC to War Department needs: "The course reflected the trend in the reorganization of the army, and the War College was called upon to make several studies in connection with similar studies being made by the War Department."[1]

In the War Plans course, six planning groups were formed. Three of them formulated "coalition plans exemplifying our major efforts on the North American continent, varying in magnitude and strategical concept, in which both the Army and Navy had important roles to play."[2] These were purely academic exercises, for they necessarily cast Britain in the role of the enemy. There were, however, no other candidates for the job. If one wanted a bogeyman on our East Coast whose defeat would require serious planning for an extensive effort by the U.S. Army and Navy, one came up with Red. No other nation was capable of projecting land and sea forces onto America's Atlantic coast. An unintended but fortuitous product of planning for this unlikely showdown was the amassing of mountains of data that would be useful when the United States turned in earnest to planning for hemispheric defense as a part of the Rainbow planning process. The data on Newfoundland, Iceland, Greenland, and the Caribbean would find its way into later plans, and the appreciation of British strengths and weaknesses would prove as useful in giving the British a real hand in 1940 as it was in giving them the make-believe boot in 1937.

Consistent with the practice of providing AWC students with a wide range of contingency planning requiring varying degrees of effort by the army and navy in various theaters, the other three student groups turned to wars outside North America. The college summary of the academic year put it this way:

> Of the remaining three war planning groups, one represented a major joint overseas operation in the nature of a strategic offensive in which the Navy interests were paramount initially; the second involved a minor effort in which the Army played the predominant role; and the third involved participation with allies on another continent in which the Army and Navy played equally important parts.[3]

Reference to the "paramount" interests of the navy as usual meant Orange, the navy's favorite war, the one with Japan. The army's "predominant role" usually meant someplace in the Western Hemisphere, a place where the army could from a standing start prevail, allowing the navy to drop off the army and to be prepared for further missions in the Atlantic or Pacific. The reference to "equally important parts" being played by the services meant the big war. For the third consecutive year the student committee assigned to "Participation with Allies" planned for war in Europe, the one that would become the World War II European theater of operations: "This is a war in which all major powers of the world are involved. . . . Involving practically the entire world, it very probably will be a war of long duration. . . . It is a war in which the economic and material factors may play the major part, rather than a war which may be quickly ended by military operations."[4]

Scenario events and real-world events require the reader to be very attentive to which world one is in. Presumably the students working on the "Participation with Allies" problem, war in Europe, were similarly muddled as they read the morning newspaper before engaging in very similar events in the college scenario. In the scenario, the enemy coalition consisted of Germany, Poland, Italy, Austria, Hungary, Albania, Greece, Turkey, and Japan. The United States and the British Commonwealth remained neutral for the first year of the war, joining France, Russia, Czechoslovakia, and Rumania only when German and Italian submarines and aircraft sank U.S. and British ships. On 10 May 1938 the United States declared war on Germany and Italy only. By the time the United States entered the war, the German-led coalition had already overrun Czechoslovakia, Rumania, and the northern half of Yugoslavia. German and Italian troops faced French troops, but there was not yet an offensive by either side in Western Europe. In the Far East, however, the Russians and Japanese were fighting north of Lake Baikal.

The degree to which the 1937 scenario mirrors the real-world events of 1939–40 is eerie. (See map 2, appendix I.) In the real world, German and French troops watched one another from September 1939 until the spring of 1940 in the so-called Sitzkrieg. Soviet and Japanese forces had already engaged in serious combat from June through August 1939 along the Outer Mongolian–Manchurian border, as Gen. Georgi K. Zhukov skillfully used over one thousand tanks against the Japanese.[5]

The situation posited to the AWC student committee described what had happened in Europe and Asia in the year before the American declaration of war.[6] Germany, Italy, and Japan comprised the Anti-Communist Coalition States. In the spring of 1937, Germany, Italy, Austria, and Hungary invaded and overran Czechoslovakia without a declaration of war. Germany and Italy conducted a passive defense along their French borders, and "France concentrated along her threatened borders but did not advance." Russian and Rumanian troops invaded Hungary, the Germans drove east, and Yugoslavia joined the allies. Italy secured the central Mediterranean and interfered with French and British shipping. The Spanish Civil War ended in 1938, according to the scenario. Japan moved into Siberia in the winter of 1937–38 in the vicinity of Lake Baikal, then turned to the south and began active operations in China. Britain reinforced its forces in the Pacific to restrain Japan.

In the spring of 1938 the Japanese threatened South China ports and the Dutch East Indies. In May the United States and Britain met and agreed "that the two nations should join in efforts with the Allies to bring about a peace settlement by the application of force." On 10 May the president asked for a declaration of war, and the Congress obliged. By 31 May the Congress had passed all enabling legislation.

The president declared the United States an active participant in the war. Then he directed the navy to establish and protect sea lines of communication to Europe for a U.S. expeditionary force. He further directed U.S. forces to be employed in Europe. The Joint Board was to make recommendations for his approval. As much of the air forces "as can be spared for the expeditionary force" was to prepare without delay for participation. The president concluded by saying that support and assistance to allies should not risk vital U.S. interests. The professional soldiers continued to be confident that American industrial capacity was enormous and that it would be the margin of difference in a long war of materiel. They also knew that simultaneous and early demands would be made of it to supply, arm, and equip American combat forces and the training base while at the same time supporting Russia, China, and perhaps others.

Before coming to decisions, or even recommendations, the committee proceeded in the best General Staff tradition to make an estimate of the situation. The student officer who made the oral presentation to the entire college community formulated the task by saying there were three questions to be answered at the outset: What can we do? What do we think we should do? What will our allies demand of us or permit us to do?

The first question required an estimate of enemy and friendly capabilities. The committee's work in determining the total war-making potential of all belligerents—and identifying likely future belligerents—was comprehensive. It combined encyclopedic breadth and thoughtful analysis of relevant economic, political, psychological, and military elements of power. In responding to the second question the committee outlined in exhaustive detail the possible courses of action available to friend and foe. It then estimated the enemy's probable course of action. Only then did the committee decide on the friendly course of action. To answer the third question, the committee began by considering capabilities of the allies, already determined in response to the first question, then estimated the war aims of the allies and what they would need to attain those aims. From that point it was a matter of deducing what the allies might want from the United States.

The committee drew these conclusions about the general nature of the war they would fight. The war would be total, and it would be long. The allies, if they cooperated, would win after initial setbacks. Economic capacity would be decisive. The implication was that modern war would be decided by the intelligent establishment of priorities and allocation of resources, principally American resources. Public support, it was assumed, would lag behind events, but it would be there when needed.[7]

A few new wrinkles in planning for coalition war in 1937 were driven by the scenario. The immediate cause of the U.S. declaration of war against Germany and Italy was the familiar violation of freedom of the seas. The last straw was the sinking of U.S. ships by Italian submarines and aircraft in the Mediterranean. The United States was certainly concerned with Japanese conduct in the Far East, but America was not at war with Japan; the British were. As a consequence, one of the early decisions was for the United States to assume allied responsibility for sea control in the Mediterranean while the British countered Japanese military strength in the Pacific. Another factor arguing for these arrangements was the immediate readiness of the U.S. Navy, the first line of defense, as compared with the lack of readiness in the U.S. Army. The army was unprepared. Mobilization, training, concentration, and deployment take time. If the Americans were to make a military contribution early on in the war, that contribution would be naval. There was great uneasiness about a Europe-first strategy, particularly in a navy that had trained for more than thirty years for a great Trafalgar-like battle in the Pacific. Despite the navy's uneasiness, the army planners scrupulously adhered to the president's clear guidance to fight the war in Europe. His admonition "not to risk vital United States interests" was interpreted to mean that the continental United States could not be left unguarded and that Japan bore watching. Response to the scenario dictated that elements of the fleet deploy to the Mediterranean. That short-term decision out of the way, student planners turned to their estimate of the situation for the longer term.

The economic estimate was short and to the point: "The Allies control the great bulk of the economic resources of the world in all categories from raw materials to finished products, as well as the financial resources."[8] The longer the war lasted, the more allied manpower and sheer economic weight would assure allied victory.[9] There was only one proviso: "that trade routes connecting the far-flung British Empire, the United States, South America, and Europe be maintained so as to function efficiently." In that connection the estimate noted that Britain imported 45 percent of its food supply: "Enemy air and submarine blockage could seriously disrupt imports and could cause the economic collapse of Great Britain while endangering an American expeditionary force in Europe."[10] Heavy losses were anticipated, but the combination of the two greatest fleets in the world would almost certainly ensure that the sea lines of communication would remain open to allied shipping.

Similar assessments were made of the capacities of allies regarding finance and munitions.[11] In the long haul the allies would prevail, but it would be a while before U.S. industry could begin cranking out war materials:

> The United States has the greatest potential munitioning capacity in the world. It will require at least a year, however, before the major portion of that potential capacity can be made actual capacity. . . . Once in production the United States can not only supply her own needs but will have the capacity in many lines to provide a surplus for the Allies if required.[12]

The committee was professionally objective about the reason for the American lack of preparedness for war. The United States had tried to stay out of the war by avoiding any provocation of belligerents: "Because of national policies of limited preparedness and strict neutrality, no expansion had been effected in the munitions industries of the United States, and no Allied war orders had previously been placed in this country."[13] The military officers of the 1930s would have preferred a higher state of national readiness for war, but they had no doubts regarding the ascendancy of political over military considerations. They saluted and obeyed civil authority. Military strategy would follow national policy.

In their political estimate, the students asserted that the American people could be motivated to fight Japan more easily than they could be brought to fight a European power. This assertion had also been found in the student assessments of 1934, 1935, and 1936. There was a certain amount of concern for the great numbers of resident aliens in the United States, in American overseas possessions, and in Latin America, but preoccupation with Japanese in California, Hawaii, and the Philippines far exceeded concerns about, for example, German and Italian residents in the United States. "Even in the Hawaiian group, 40 percent of the inhabitants were either Orange nationals or descendants of Orange nationals," the students reported.[14] Perhaps attitudes regarding the loyalty of Japanese-Americans can be ascribed to some other cause, but racism pure and simple is the most likely candidate: "The dependencies of the United States with a population composed largely of a colored, oriental, and mixed races cannot be depended upon to render a great deal of assistance in the event of war against a foreign power."[15] Europeans, including the large concentrations of Germans and Italians in North and South America, were simply less ominous than the Japanese to army planners in 1937. We shall see that in succeeding years the focus on hemispheric defense and the evolution of long-range bomber aircraft, like the B-17 Flying Fortress, intensified planners' attention to the numbers of Germans and Italians in South America.

The propaganda line (that was what they called it) recommended by the planners to win public support was to emphasize the need to bring the war in Europe to an end by defeating the enemy coalition before Japan moved against the United States. The committee was confident that both the political system and the government of the United States would earn "the great popular backing" of the American people. It noted the popularity of the president and his party's successes in the elections of 1934 and 1936 in coming to the conclusion that the president could effectively carry the American people into a war in Europe.[16]

The members of Committee 6 did not accept the conventional wisdom about the disadvantage of democratic nations in facing dictatorial states in war. They believed that democracies elicited the willing cooperation of their citizens. The dictatorship's advantages of centralized control and enforced stability were recognized, but the committee added an interesting qualification: "However, in the long run, especially should military reverses occur to any of the dictatorships, this advantage to the Coalition would eventually disappear."[17] The key to success would be the allied capacity to cooperate and direct the efforts of the alliance toward common objectives. Allied advantages in materiel and population would tell if only the allies pulled together and their populations supported the war.

In the question-and-answer session following the committee presentation, the issue of Russian reliability arose. This was a reaction to the assertion in the report that with its dictatorial government, "Russia can be counted on for a prolonged war calling for self-denial and hardship."[18] Some believed that Russia was a weak link requiring "bolstering up during the entire war effort and that there was serious danger of her complete collapse."[19] Still another assessment was that "although the Russians can be counted upon to fight vigorously in defense of their homeland . . . their effective utilization elsewhere is questionable."[20] Of course, evaluating combat performance in advance was more art—or a good guess—than science, but it was obvious in these remarks and in all planning that the officers fully considered the combat effectiveness of friend and foe. They also recalled the separate peace made by Russia with Germany in 1917.

Col. Don F. Pratt said the Russians were even less trustworthy than "the others." Col. Charles E. Thomas pronounced the view of the classic Realpolitiker: "My reading of history indicates that you can trust any country so long as its interests make it worthwhile for it to keep the promise. I think this group has set up a situation where it is to Russia's interest to play the game." And then Thomas began to sound more like a child of the 1960s than a vintage 1937 army colonel: "My history also leads me to believe the United States is not at all an exception to the rule; if you don't believe me, read a few of the solemn treaties we have entered into with the Indian tribes."[21]

In its evaluation of the military forces of the major powers, the committee showed soundness, if not brilliance.[22] The Russians were tough troops, especially in defense, but not well trained, well led, or well equipped. It was interesting that Joseph Stalin and Marshal Mikhail Tukhachevski were singled out in the committee for praise in April 1937. In June, Tukhachevski and seven other generals would be executed for allegedly conspiring with the Germans and the Japanese. Many other executions would follow in the great purge that debilitated the Red Army and contributed to the German successes in Russia in 1941 and 1942.

The wide-ranging discussion during the question-and-answer session moved to the problem of allies in general. Observations were not kind. They show both hard-headed analysis and a general skepticism about foreigners.

The sharing of naval bases in the Mediterranean elicited a particularly interesting monologue by the always-salty Capt. Edward J. Foy, USN, a faculty member at the college. He castigated the British, pontificated on both morals and morale, and suggested that Europeans were no more honest now than they had been in Machiavelli's time. Unhappy that the U.S. Navy was stuck in the restrictive waters of the Mediterranean while the British fleet was roaming "his" ocean, a real ocean, Foy said, "The British, as usual, in this game have cleared out to do something which was comparatively easy." Based upon his recent command of a cruiser in the Mediterranean, he reported that "Toulon is infested with Communists and is a very dangerous place to send American ships. I refer to the morale of the crew, as well as the morals." He then returned to the question of reliability with a sea story. He said that since the Spanish Civil War,

> the nations of Europe have found that they could not rely on anybody's promises; the Italians would look you square in the eye and say they would quit sending people to Spain, and the next day send them. After the embargo was put on Spain . . . we were tied up to the dock in Naples and next to us were two large transports being loaded with soldiers, so-called volunteers, and with war materials, ostensibly for Ethiopia. But any Italian naval officer would tell you they were actually headed for Spain, in spite of the most solemn promises. In the same way the French kept feeding soldiers and supplies across the French border, even after the 6th of March when they were supposed to have stopped that sort of thing. So, when it comes down to whom you can trust and whom you cannot, I think the answer is that you cannot trust any of them, and it is well for us to realize that.[23]

Committee evaluations of foreign militaries were part of the process. The Germans and British received high marks. The Japanese were loyal, clean, self-sacrificing, tough, and prepared to fight to the last man. Their navy was just slightly inferior to the British and U.S. navies, and their aerial support (interestingly) was assessed as being weak. The overall evaluation was that the Japanese had an efficient fleet. It would be dangerous for any other fleet to take them on in their home waters. Fascism was believed to have unified the Italians and given them a sense of purpose. They were not, however, expected, to measure up to the Germans. The Italians had a large air force, but their planes lacked reliability and their pilots lacked training.

Their fleet, like the German fleet, was small and efficient. The Czechs were rated fair, but they had been almost entirely overrun. The Yugoslavs were considered very good despite tension between the Serbs and Croats. The Rumanians lacked offensive capability. And so forth. But observations about the French show excellent insight into that critical point where politics and the military come together, where statesmen and generals meet.

The French Army was highly regarded for its morale, training, combat efficiency, supply, command, and staff, but there were doubts regarding the will of the French people and the stability of their government. The committee expressed these doubts in several places in the report. Owing to the composition of the French government, French tenacity and will were suspect. The committee warned of the presence of both Communists and Fascists in France.[24] "As of May 31, 1938, the stability of the French government may be taken as temporarily assured, but its future stability may falter in the face of a military defeat." The committee concluded, "Should her boundaries become overrun and the Coalition armies advance over French territory, her position in the Allied group may become perilously weak; on the other hand, the landing of a strong Allied force in France and the use of French territory as the base of advance would impart a feeling of security to the French people."[25] Much of the report of Committee 6 was characterized by sound analysis and sensitivity to nuance, perhaps nowhere more clearly than in the prediction of what later would be called a "Sitzkrieg" followed by French collapse. In its assessment the French Army was overrated. The will of the government and the people was accurately described.

The committee saw two courses of action available to the enemy (German-led) coalition. The first was to go on the defensive in the west, to contain the French, crushing Czechoslovakia, Yugoslavia, and Rumania and continuing east against Russia. Japan would strike Russia from the east. The rationale for this course was the early possession of the natural resources of the Soviet Union, Czech industry, and Rumanian oil. The coalition would then be self-sustaining and operate on interior lines: "The possibility of a coalition success against Russia seems favorable, considering that pressure can be exerted against both of her flanks, and also that there was a chance that under pressure her government might collapse."[26] Success depended upon the containment of the allies in the west.

The second course was the one that the committee expected the enemy to select: defeat of France in the early days of war. The second phase was stated succinctly: "After subduing France, operate against Great Britain by air attacks and blockades." Then, in the third phase, "in conjunction with Japan, conduct a combined offensive against Russia."[27]

The students selected for the Germans what appeared to be the high-payoff, high-risk option: the defeat of the nation regarded as the most powerful land power, France. Rolling up the relatively weak nations of Eastern Europe posed no problem to the German-led coalition. Russian offensive capability was not highly rated. It would not be difficult to contain the Russians, particularly with the Japanese on their back. The Germans were credited with being "aggressive and apparently determined that by rapid maneuver and open warfare the stalemate of trench warfare of the World War will be prevented."[28] The Germans would make their main effort in France.[29]

It remained for the committee to decide a course of action that took into account the interests of America and its allies as well as the capabilities of all concerned. Two friendly courses of action were considered. The first was to conduct offensive operations against Japan while on the strategic defensive in Europe. The object was to knock Japan out of the war while keeping Russia in. A variation of this plan called for an offensive via Italy to the Balkans, the Mediterranean offensive to be simultaneous with the Pacific offensive. The object was to isolate Turkey, menace the coalition from the south, and ensure free passage of allied shipping in the Mediterranean. The alternative, course two, called for containing the Japanese by reinforcing the British fleet in the Pacific and conducting offensive operations against Germany from France. This was the course chosen.[30]

The rationale was instructive. Recall that the United States was not at war with Japan, but a threat from that quarter was appreciated. The prestige and power of the British fleet provided a happy solution:

> A Japanese threat against the United States is brought to a minimum by the presence of the British Fleet based in Singapore. Japan, to all intents and purposes, is effectively contained in her islands and cannot operate at great distances away from her homeland. She may therefore be ignored in attacking the Coalition, especially as her interests have now become diverted from Russia to China.[31]

When actual hostilities began and actual courses of action were considered in the real world, the British allies would concur in the American conclusion expressed in just a few words: "The heart of the Coalition is Germany." However, the British were less enthusiastic about engaging in decisive combat with Germany soon after American entry into the war as a belligerent. The students would send the American expeditionary force "with the armies of France and Britain directly against the heart of the Coalition."[32] The Americans were consistently ready to go for the jugular;

the British were inclined to be more circumspect. They preferred a strategy of nibbling at the edges to weaken Germany before risking the decisive battle. But that was in the future.

The committee recommended and the president approved sending a seven-division field army and supporting troops to France, a total of four hundred thousand men. It was estimated that the American force would be in France within six months. In this plan, as had been the case for each of the AWC plans since 1934, there were the usual admonitions about the U.S. force not being sent piecemeal to be used as fillers by some allied general. The U.S. force would be an independent command under U.S. officers in a U.S. sector of the front. The land force contribution of the United States was consciously modest, for it was sent primarily as a sign of solidarity. There was no sense of urgency. It was assumed that the allies would have no problem containing the Germans until the Americans arrived to join in the offensive into Germany.

Of interest, given later actual events, was the consideration and rejection of proposals to conduct landings in Africa, the Baltic, the North Sea, and Italy. The plans were discarded because the landings would be too expensive in terms of men and materiel. It was also thought that once ashore in Italy, allied forces would face mountain barriers favorable to the defender.[33] Concentration of allied military force against the enemy center of gravity, Germany, was the best means of attaining victory in a world war. This was the professional opinion of the American soldiers in 1937. It would not change.

This 1937 version of "Participation with Allies" was the fourth consecutive consideration of the problems of coalition warfare undertaken at the Army War College. It addressed American concern with a two-ocean war in the context of a friendly alliance. The basic considerations of 1937 were the same ones that would perplex the Americans and the British in their deliberations before the U.S. entry into World War II and after. They had to decide where to put their main effort, against Germany or against Japan. Once they decided to defeat Germany first, they had to agree on whether the offensive would be direct or indirect. That was what the fifteen student officers of Committee 6 did in 1937, and that was what they presented in their oral report to the college community on 10 April 1937.

Some 367 AWC graduates in the classes from 1934 to 1937 heard the rationale and decision regarding priorities of the friendly coalition in war against a German-led coalition and Japan. Some seventy officers had actually done the detailed planning for a two-front war. Between 1939 and 1943, three members of the class of 1937 served in the War Plans Division of the War Department General Staff. Matthew B. Ridgway joined as a major on 30 September 1939 and departed a brigadier general on 24 January 1942, a critical period for war planning in the transition from peace to war. Charles S. Kilburn and Henry A. Barber were the others, both of whom retired as generals.[34]

Planning at AWC from 1938 to 1940 would take a different direction.

The Army War College building, under construction in 1906. The statue of Hohenzollern King Frederick II of Prussia *(right center, in fenced area)* was a gift of Kaiser Wilhelm II. After World War II the National War College occupied this building. AWC and Frederick were moved to Carlisle Barracks, Pennsylvania. **U.S. Army Military History Institute**

Aerial photograph of Washington Barracks, later Fort Lesley J. McNair, with the Army War College in the lower right, circa 1919. From 1907 until 1940, AWC met in the building shown here. **U.S. Naval Historical Center**

Rear Adm. Harry E. Yarnell *(left)* welcomes Rear Adm. William A. Moffett *(third from left)* to NAS San Diego in September 1932. Moffett, as chief of the Bureau of Aeronautics, won acceptance for aviation in the fleet without the acrimony that characterized the army's introduction of aviation. Capt. John H. Hoover, USN *(right)*, AWC 1937, would earn four stars. **U.S. Naval Historical Center**

Maj. Gen. George S. Simonds (AWC 1920), commandant, AWC, May 1932–January 1935, shown here in Washington, D.C., 4 June 1934. Before becoming commandant he had been deputy commandant; chief of cavalry; chief of the War Department General Staff, War Plans Division; and military adviser to the U.S. delegation, 1932 Geneva Disarmament Conference. He established a War Plans Division at AWC and instituted "Participation with Allies," requiring students to plan for coalition-versus-coalition warfare from 1934 onward.

**U.S. Army Military History Institute**

Gen. Malin Craig, chief of staff, U.S. Army, at his desk in the State, War, and Navy Building, Washington, D.C., 7 October 1935. Craig followed Simonds as AWC commandant, serving from February to October 1935 before moving up. He continued coalition war planning and added a reading, briefing, and lecture program that under his successor became "Current News of International Affairs."

**U.S. Army Military History Institute**

Col. D. D. Eisenhower, cigarette in hand, briefs Lt. Gen. Lesley J. McNair on 14 September 1941 regarding the Third Army Louisiana Maneuvers, Lake Charles Junior College, Louisiana. McNair would die by friendly fire in France in 1944 as strategic air was used in a tactical role, and Eisenhower would advance quickly to five stars.
**U.S. Army Military History Institute**

War Plans Division, Washington, D.C., 23 January 1942. *Left to right:* Col. W. K. Harrison; Col. Lee S. Gerow; Brig. Gen. Robert W. Crawford; Brig. Gen. Dwight D. Eisenhower; Brig. Gen. Leonard T. Gerow, chief, WPD; Col. Thomas T. Handy; Col. Stephen H. Sherrill; Col. John L. McKee; and Col. Jay W. MacKelvie. Eisenhower followed Gerow as chief, and Handy succeeded Eisenhower. **U.S. Army Military History Institute**

Maj. Gen. Thomas T. Handy *(fourth from right, sitting)* at a promotion ceremony in 1943. WPD became OPD on 9 March 1942. Handy (AWC 1935 and Naval War College 1936) served in WPD/OPD from August 1936 to October 1944, except for one year spent with troops (June 1940–June 1941). During the interwar period WPD routinely had 11 officers. That changed: on 6 December 1941 there were 66 officers; on 8 March 1942, 93; on 31 December 1942, 204; and on 21 October 1944, 319. **U.S. Army Military History Institute**

*Left to right, sitting:* Winston Churchill, Capt. Roderick McKenzie, Lt. Gen. Mark W. Clark (AWC 1937), Maj. Gen. Lyman Lemnitzer (AWC 1940), and *(standing closest to Churchill)* Maj. Gen. Alfred M. Gruenther (AWC 1939) on a subchaser during the prime minister's visit to Clark's Fifth Army, 19 August 1944. The recent AWC students wear stars.

**U.S. Army Military History Institute**

Presenting French colors to the mayor of liberated Cherbourg. The mayor holds the flag, and next to him is Maj. Gen. J. Lawton Collins (AWC 1938). Also present: Maj. Gen. Raymond O. Barton, 4th Infantry Division *(face closest to mayor's head);* and *(left to right)* Maj. Gen. Matthew B. Ridgway (AWC 1937), 82d Airborne Division; Maj. Gen. Manton S. Eddy, 9th Infantry Division; and Maj. Gen. Maxwell D. Taylor (AWC 1940), 101st Airborne Division. **U.S. Army Military History Institute**

General of the Army Douglas MacArthur signing the Instrument of Surrender on the USS *Missouri,* Tokyo Bay, 2 September 1945. Behind MacArthur are Lt. Gen. Jonathan M. Wainwright and Lt. Gen. Sir Arthur E. Percival, both of whom had just been released from Japanese prison camps. Facing the camera above MacArthur's cap is Wainwright's 1934 AWC classmate, Adm. William F. Halsey. **U.S. Naval Historical Center**

Gen. Omar N. Bradley, chief of staff, U.S. Army, confers with senior generals at the Pentagon, 31 March 1948. *Seated, left to right:* Gen. Jacob L. Devers, Army Field Forces; Bradley; Gen. Mark W. Clark, Sixth Army; and Gen. J. Lawton Collins, deputy chief of staff. *Standing, left to right:* Maj. Gen. H. R. Gay, Military District of Washington; Gen. Thomas T. Handy, Fourth Army; Gen. Courtney H. Hodges, First Army; Lt. Gen. Walton H. Walker, Fifth Army; Lt. Gen. Leonard T. Gerow, Second Army; Lt. Gen. Alvan C. Gillem, Jr., Third Army; and Maj. Gen. S. J. R. Irwin, V Corps. **U.S. Army Military History Institute**

War correspondents gathered in New York City on 25 January 1950 to honor prominent military leaders, among them marine, army, and navy AWC alumni. *Left to right:* Gen. Clifton B. Cates, USMC (AWC 1940); Adm. Forrest Sherman; Gen. R. L. Eichelberger (AWC 1930); Fleet Admiral William F. Halsey (AWC 1934); Fleet Admiral Chester W. Nimitz; Adm. Thomas C. Kinkaid; and Vice Adm. Merlin O'Neil, commandant, USCG.

**U.S. Naval Historical Center**

Three of the senior officers in the front row saluting as Adm. Forrest Sherman's body arrives in Washington from Naples on 25 July 1951 were AWC graduates. *Left to right:* General of the Army Omar N. Bradley (AWC 1934); Gen. Hoyt S. Vandenberg; Gen. J. Lawton Collins (AWC 1938); Adm. Lynde D. McCormick; Fleet Adm. Chester W. Nimitz; Gen. Clifton B. Cates, USMC (AWC 1940); Adm. Thomas C. Kinkaid; and Adm. William M. Fechteler.
**U.S. Naval Historical Center**

Gen. Clifton B. Cates, commandant, USMC *(left)*, and his successor, Lt. Gen. Lemuel C. Shepherd, meet in the commandant's office on 6 November 1952. Cates (AWC 1940) and Adm. John H. Hoover (AWC 1937) reached four-star rank. Fleet Adm. William F. Halsey (AWC 1934) and his AWC classmate, General of the Army Omar N. Bradley, achieved five-star rank. **U.S. Army Military History Institute**

# Part III

# DEFENDING THE WESTERN HEMISPHERE AND ORANGE REVISITED

# 8

# 1938

## *Orange and Purple*

The United States can look with perfect serenity upon the
developments in the Pacific situation in the decades to come.
**—DOUGLAS MACARTHUR,** 25 JULY 1936

After reaching out boldly to participate with allies in Pacific and European wars for four consecutive years, Army War College students in the War Plans Period of 1938 were assigned modest tasks. The class of 1938 did not work out a plan for American participation in a world war. Instead, a work group was directed by the faculty to plan an army-navy expedition to South America under the rubric "Participation with Allies." Correspondence between the War Plans Division of the War Department General Staff and the Army War College turned the "Participation with Allies" work group to hemispheric defense.[1] Orange was reconsidered, and the traditional Color Plans, Red and Green, were retained in the curriculum. The objective of the War Plans course, as usual, was to give the students planning experience in the full range of possible wars. Even as war clouds were forming, training General Staff officers for the most probable war competed with a need to train them for all eventualities. The plan prepared for an overseas effort was Purple for South America. In this case, Purple was Brazil.[2]

Red was actually a coalition of Britain, France, and Canada, an unlikely prospect in 1937–38, but one that required students to put on their thinking caps as they addressed a major threat to the Atlantic Coast and the northern frontier. The annual course summary indicates that it was a pure training exercise with little likelihood of implementation: "A war between Great Britain and the United States may well be thought of as suicide for both. It is difficult to imagine any set of circumstances developing in the relations of these two great democracies and World War allies that might lead to the final point of war. There is every possible reason to the contrary."[3]

Planning Green postulated a revolution in Mexico. In this scenario, the Mexican government is overthrown and "a Blue military government is established pending the establishment of a stable government in that country capable of fulfilling its international obligations." Mobilization is unnecessary, and there is no need to enact conscription. The U.S. military proceeds from its peacetime state of preparedness to intervention. The premise is that European powers might intervene in Mexico to collect payment on debts if the United States does not regulate affairs there.[4]

As the prospect of war in the near future moved from the realm of the possible to that of the probable, the students were directed to reflect on American capabilities and vulnerabilities. Defense of overseas possessions and reaction to violation of the Monroe Doctrine became the focal points of war planning from 1938 until the War College closed in 1940, at which time students became de facto General Staff officers. Something far more complicated than Green was to be considered: "A special study was made on the subject of 'Overseas Possessions and Their Influence on the Strategic Position of Mother Countries in War.' To the strategical studies of the overseas possessions of the United States was added a study of Brazil and Argentina, having in mind possible violations of the Monroe Doctrine."[5] The phrasing of this "special study" returned planners to the 1904 ruminations of Bliss: defense in the hemisphere, and American vulnerability in the Pacific because of the Philippines.

In the American military, a sure sign that a situation is getting serious is a sudden interest in intelligence by planning and operations officers. Changes in the G-2 course of 1938 reflect the rediscovery of the importance of intelligence, a usually neglected and underfunded activity, as events heated up and pointed to war. One committee studied the attaché and translation systems and recommended improvements in them. Another committee reported on the causes of the "Spanish Revolution" (the 1936–39 Spanish Civil War) and the participation of other nations in it. The aim was to deduce military lessons. The official summary of academic year 1937–38 at AWC concluded, "Events in progress in the wars in Spain and China were reflected in the studies of various committees during the school year. Interest was also displayed in conditions in the Western Hemisphere."[6]

There was a sense that the outside world was closing in. Introspection and review of national preparedness by the army highlighted American vulnerabilities and shortages, almost all of which could be made up in time.

The more modest scope of the problems worked out by the class of 1938 suggests a phased approach to readiness for war. The first task was to protect American overseas possessions menaced by Orange and those parts of the Western Hemisphere where there were large German and Italian populations. Consideration of offensive operations in the Pacific and in Europe would come later. Now was the time to circle the wagons for defense of home and hearth.[7]

The possibility of an Axis attack via South America to Mexico and the southern frontier of the United States has been treated seriously by some historians and scornfully by others. According to one of the official histories, "the threat to the countries of the Western Hemisphere took on terrifying proportions" after the debacle in Europe from April to June 1940, and "the military staffs prepared an emergency plan for a large-scale descent on the coast of Brazil to counter any major Axis move in that direction." This is a reference to Purple. We shall see that the college planned for such a contingency from 1938 onward, a consequence of presidential concern following the concessions made by Britain and France to Germany at Munich regarding Germans residing in the Sudetenland region of Czechoslovakia. The completed plans of 1938 and 1939 at the War College became the Rainbow 4 plan approved by the Joint Board on 7 June 1940 and by the president on 14 August 1940.[8]

Later historians have called these schemes the "geopolitical fantasies" of Franklin D. Roosevelt. Among the fantasies was the fear that Germany would invade Brazil via French West Africa and "purchase" revolutions in Central America at one million to four million dollars per country.[9] The effects of bombing in Spain, China, and Ethiopia and the American development of the long-range B-17 bomber in 1935 did nothing to allay fear of attack from the air. The bulge of Brazil was now within range of bombers flying out of Dakar, Senegal. The possibility of intercontinental flight and destruction from afar was new, real, and frightening as violence erupted in Europe, Asia, and Africa in the 1930s. Characterizing security concerns in terms of "terrifying proportions" was not entirely an exercise in hyperbole.

Mobilization planning was one of the main thrusts of academic year 1938. As the faculty made clear to the class when the students began their war plans work, there was hardly a serious contingency that the Regular Army could handle without augmentation from the reserve components and civilian society: "All our War Plans requiring an effort greater than that which the Regular Army can meet alone are at present based upon and are dependent upon the Protective Mobilization Plan and the Industrial Mobilization Plan."[10] Whatever schemes might be devised to ensure the security of the nation against military aggression, in the United States they all began with mobilization. The deliberate policy of limited preparedness provided for a ready navy, but the army and industry needed time to translate potential power into available power.[11]

George C. Marshall understood that great wealth could be translated into great power, but the United States would be vulnerable in the early days of war as the small peacetime army expanded to war strength. "Overindulgence in 'lessons learned' between July and November of 1918 was hazardous for an army that needed to be thinking about 'the first 6 months of the next war,'" Marshall insisted.[12] He identified the error in training officers for directing an army that simply would not exist in the United States when war came. In 1937 he warned that

> to base most of the instruction on well-trained units of full strength and complete as to corps troops, materiel, etc., is to qualify officers for something they will never find during the first years of an American war. . . . We must be experts in the technique—and the special tactics of handling hastily raised, partially trained troops, seriously deficient in corps and army establishments and heavy materiel; . . . we must be experts in meeting the confusion and chaotic conditions of the first months of a war when discipline is poor, officers green and information of the enemy invariably lacking.[13]

In a letter to Brig. Gen. Lesley J. McNair dated 4 March 1939, Marshall expressed continuing concern for the Leavenworth faculty's lack of appreciation of the degree to which the United States depended upon the reserve components:

> Too many of them are only theoretically familiar with the air component and the National Guard. . . . We must be prepared the next time we are involved in war, to fight immediately, that is within a few weeks, somewhere and somehow. Now that means we will have to employ the National Guard for that purpose, because it will constitute the large majority of the war army of the first six months.[14]

When the class turned to the mobilization exercise at the end of February 1938, it had already done the "G courses" (the G-1, G-2, G-3, G-4, and War Plans Division courses designed to prepare students for the General Staff) and Analytical Studies to provide a knowledge base for further work. The mobilization exercise was a part of the "Information Period." Later the students capped the academic year by using all previous learning in the formulation of four war plans.

For the mobilization exercise, the ninety-four-man class was divided into ten groups of seven men each, one group for each of Corps Areas I to IX, and one to play the War Department. Their tasks were to study mobilization plans and regulations, learn the detailed procedure for mobilization under the Protective Mobilization Plan (PMP), and prepare data on troop availability for use in subsequent war plans. The intent was clear. Plans were to be based upon an understanding of reality. No deus ex machina, no magic wand, no amount of wishing would provide a mobilized U.S. Army overnight.

The remaining twenty-four students were organized into twelve-man groups to conduct two special studies. One group was to study coastal "Frontier Defense and Joint Overseas Expeditions." The second would study "Overseas Possessions and Their Influence on the Strategic Position of Mother Countries in War."[15]

A consensus concept was emerging. A mobilized America could handle almost any war, but to mobilize people and things for a big war would take a year or two.[16] During the period of preparation for a great effort, it would be prudent to concentrate on protecting the American base. The base would be defined as the line Alaska-Hawaii-Panama and the Western Hemisphere. That was the thinking that shaped the backdrop for the 1938 versions of Orange and the new Purple Plan. With Orange, the AWC planners of 1938 produced a bold plan that, for reasons that will become clear, was drastically modified by the AWC group tasked to do the Orange Plan in 1939.

## Orange Revisited, 1938

The Joint Estimate for War Plan Orange considered the courses of action available to Japan and ruled out an offensive in the South Pacific. Even after a successful encounter with the U.S. fleet, it would be very difficult for the Japanese to establish a base in Hawaii and maintain it. The study group concluded that the Japanese would seize Guam and the Philippines and then go on the strategic defensive, forcing a war of attrition. This meant that the United States would be forced to fight a long and expensive war. Heavy losses on both sides were anticipated.[17]

The estimate included these assumptions and conclusions: The Japanese military was first rate; the U.S. Army was good but deficient in tanks, antitank weapons, antiaircraft artillery, and some types of ammunition; the U.S. Navy was excellent, "but it is doubtful if it is adequate to maintain itself in the sphere of an enemy in the Western Pacific." The economic advantages were on the side of the United States and would increase with the passage of time; the Japanese would have the upper hand for about a year in virtually all ways, then the United States would dominate. Germany and Italy would maintain a benevolent neutrality toward Japan rather than declare war on the United States, unless England, France, or Russia were to enter the war on the side of the United States. The suspicion of Japanese residents, even U.S. citizens, was unambiguous: "Orange nationals in large numbers and Blue citizens of Orange extraction [live] in the Philippine Islands, Hawaii, Panama, and on the Pacific Coast. There is little doubt as to their loyalty to Orange, as a large number of them are even suspected of being in the military service of Orange."[18]

Considering the recognized need for mobilization time, the War Plans Group 3 solution for Plan Orange was bold, optimistic, and mistaken. It consisted of four phases:

1. The line Alaska-Hawaii-Samoa-Panama is secured by 70M (70 days after mobilization).
2. The joint expedition departs San Diego 85M and arrives at Torres Strait 111M.
3. The Philippines are secured. U.S. forces are built up. Offensive operations are conducted against the Japanese.
4. Japanese ports are blockaded, and Japan's lines of communication are cut.

The earliest expected date for ending the war is 1,080M. (The Navy Basic Plan said that "a favorable conclusion of the war cannot be expected by Blue prior to 1440M.")[19] Translation: the army's best estimate was that it would take a minimum of three years to defeat Japan (and the navy's estimate was no less than four years).[20] The aims were to maintain the status quo in the Far East and to prevent the Japanese from doing what was inimical to American interests.

Japanese aims were more specific: to dominate East Asia; to lead an Asia for Asians; to expand Japanese economic and military influence; and to obtain racial equality and prestige for the Japanese. The Orange Plan written and presented by Group 3 was familiar to all the students in the class of 1938, because it was repeated as a map problem for the entire class.

The study group made several assumptions. One was the broadly accepted assertion, which prevailed almost until the bombs fell on Pearl Harbor, that "war with Japan is not probable in the immediate future, [but] war with Japan is ultimately inevitable."[21] When they struck, the Japanese would take advantage of both strategic and tactical surprise and use their initial advantages to grab Guam and the Philippines.[22] Then Japan would go on the strategic defensive, assuming the tactical offensive only when very favorable opportunities presented themselves. The Japanese would enjoy superiority in the Far East in the early days of war. Then American superiority in materiel would inexorably overwhelm the Japanese.

A key consideration in developing a strategy for a Pacific war was the ability of the U.S. garrison to resist Japanese offensive operations in the Philippines. The question was how long the Americans could hold out.

If it were assumed that the garrison would be quickly overrun by the Japanese, then a bold thrust into Asian waters dominated by Japan would be a risky, if not irresponsible, undertaking. Denied forward bases, damaged U.S. ships would have to return to Pearl Harbor, under escort, to be repaired. Despite an absolute advantage enjoyed by the United States when comparing the two fleets, the Japanese might gain local advantage as light Japanese forces inflicted damage and casualties on the U.S. fleet making the long crossing from Hawaii to the Philippines.

If the garrison held, the study group assumed that victory would be relatively cheap. The alternative to a bold stroke was a conservative strategy entailing a deliberate campaign in which bases would be secured as the fleet advanced. The availability of a base in the Philippines was critical to the strategy to be chosen.

The AWC work group of 1938 chose the bold stroke. It assumed that the garrison would hold; on 111M a naval battle would begin; on about 120M American troops would land in the Philippines to ensure that the fleet had an advanced base. From that base unrelenting pressure would be put on Japan until the Japanese had had enough of blockades and came to terms. The reason for the optimism was revealed in a key assumption in the student presentation: "It must be noted that these operations are based on the assumption that the Philippine garrison, *recently augmented by a well trained and well equipped Native Force,* will be able to maintain a stiff resistance to Japanese aggression, especially on the Island of Luzon."[23] The "Native Force" was neither well trained nor well equipped in 1938, nor would it be in 1941. The capability of the U.S. garrison was also overrated, and the efficiency of the Japanese invaders was underrated.

Gen. Douglas MacArthur bears responsibility for the inflated expectations of the Philippine garrison by some planners. In a letter of 25 July 1936 to Gen. Hugh A. Drum, then commander of the Hawaiian Department, MacArthur wrote, "The United States can look with perfect serenity upon developments in the Pacific situation in the decades to come." The confidence of the man at the top almost certainly influenced officers lower in the chain of command, but not all of them. Jonathan M. Wainwright wrote in a letter to his daughter-in-law on 17 August 1941, "The P. A. [Philippine Army] troops are not well trained so I will have a job getting them ready to fight." Bradford Grethen Chynoweth is scathing in his criticism of MacArthur, his staff, and what he found upon assuming command of a Philippine division just before the war with Japan began. He says that "MacArthur's Army was mostly a political myth" and calls MacArthur "lazy, shiftless, frivolous, uncommunicative, and uncooperative . . . and a SUPREME EMOTIONAL ACTOR." He describes the situation as being hopeless.[24]

In the discussion period after the student presentation, the reporting group was taken to task for risking all on a roll of the dice. After praising the committee for a thorough job and fine technique and method, an officer in the audience—it may have been Captain Foy, but the transcript does not identify the speaker—accused the group of recklessly risking too much on pure hope:

> In war you cannot assume that you are going to win every fight. Here you have stuck your neck out . . . 9000 miles . . . and are supposing by a long stretch of the imagination that your expedition will not suffer a major, serious defeat. What happens to the expedition, what happens to the war in the Pacific, and what is the attitude of the American public, and where are you [if defeated]?

This critic thought it "too precarious a plan to undertake." The committee chairman could not defend the position taken by his work group. He apparently had not thought through the meaning of defeat and lamely repeated that the navy "believes it can defeat Japan." He concluded by saying, "I admit, if the Japs beat our Fleet, the war is over."[25]

Captain Foy, the naval member of the faculty, is again worth citing and paraphrasing at some length because of his strategic insights and his always amusing way of making serious points. Foy exercised his acerbic tongue and salty wit before underlining a primary teaching point. He said that the "committee certainly cannot be accused of pessimism; every break is assumed to go their way . . . everything 'clicks' . . . and [they] win the war." Foy then gives the landlubbers a sense of what the navy had learned in over thirty years of playing Orange on a floor of the Naval War College in Newport:

> I won't say that this highly imaginative plan is an unheard of thing in the Navy. It isn't at all. It is played year after year at the Naval War College. There is always somebody who thinks he can win the war that way, and it is fortunate that there are people who think that way.

Otherwise we would get into a groove of thinking and become stale. However, the game is played over and over again at Newport and this particular solution invariably loses. . . . The fact that it has been brought up I think is very good . . . and I'm glad it was used by the committee because I think it is the last time you will ever come in contact with it unless you go to the Naval War College where it is licked over and over again on the game board.[26]

One justification for the risky bold stroke proposed by the study group was the presumed insistence by the American people on a quick victory in the Pacific. Captain Foy found it difficult to understand that rationale: "The idea of assuming that the American public is so impatient as to force us to gamble our national defense on one throw of the dice, I think, is absolutely beyond comprehension."[27] He described the dangers in putting all of one's eggs in one basket and thereby risking the very survival of the fleet. He also was incisive in his remarks about timing:

I have heard lots of people discuss a quick advance of the Fleet to Dumanquilas [Philippines], an immediate advance to arrive there some 30 to 40 days after the declaration of war, and I think it can be defended in certain circumstances. But this scheme which is designed to put on speed in answer to the impatience of the American people, which doesn't get started for Hawaii until three months after the war has been declared, is certainly, to my mind, without any virtue whatsoever.[28]

The remarks of students and faculty in this discussion period provide a sense of what was learned by being required to do the detailed work inherent to war planning. The following comment has the ring of the newly converted (or the sound of a student who has just learned something): "If war with Japan is inevitable, we should follow the only possible course there is, and that is, either build up the defenses of the Philippines and build a navy twice as strong as Japan's, and if that can't be done, then look around for allies, and if England cannot be spared from the Mediterranean, then get Russia or someone else; I think we have to look for other allies." Another student wanted to be sure that he had heard correctly that the United States forces would probably be overrun quickly: "I want to ask a very ignorant question. Why is it assumed that the Philippines will be lost immediately? Is it entirely out of the possibility the Fleet could support the Philippines and successfully resist the Japanese taking that?" The committee response was not encouraging. Apparently research led them to what insiders had been saying for some time: "We hope that the Philippine defenders will be able to hold Luzon until the Fleet arrives in four months, but we are not sure of it, and we expect that they [the Japanese] will have over-run Luzon. We do want to get a base in Mindanao. Of course when we arrive there if the Philippine defenders are doing more than we expect, we will push on to Manila."[29]

A student, one Maj. J. Lawton Collins, later Gen. "Lightning Joe" Collins, raised three contentious issues in his remarks: the location of the major base, the status of bases when the Philippines are granted independence, and the degree to which the United States had a "fortified" base in the region. He concluded by observing that there was "very little coordination between the Army and Navy on this question."[30]

It happened that Captain Foy had written his Individual Staff Memorandum, the major student paper, as a student in the AWC class of 1932 on the question of the status of bases in the Philippines after independence. He summarized his paper and said that his conclusions were to get out and stay out. Should the United States retain interests in the Far East, we should "get a Guantánamo at Dumanquilas Bay and make it an American Hong Kong." What he meant by that was to establish "a naval base as well as a commercial base but to do it on the basis of building a commercial base." He came to this conclusion because he did not believe that the U.S. Congress would foot the bill for a purely military base. He did believe, however, that the development of a commercial base "would be available to the Navy in time of war." Foy concluded his remarks with a most damning observation. Even if Manila is not denied to us, "when you get over there you find that it is a virgin bay with no installations to be of any use to you."[31] After forty years there and a great deal of talk, the U.S. naval base in the Philippines was neither fortified nor capable of supporting the U.S. fleet in war.

This discussion of the college's 1938 version of Orange demonstrates that insiders had known for some time that the Philippines could not be held long enough to be reinforced from the outside. Others in the class were indignant as they discovered that the army and the navy had failed to establish the fortified base assumed to be in the islands and essential to a short-war strategy.

Further, what was later called by the public an "island-hopping" strategy appeared as the naval strategy preferred in Newport in 1933 and, as we shall see, in the Army War College in 1939. It was based upon a simple recognition that lacking a fortified naval base in the Far East, bases needed to be established for logistics and aviation as the fleet sailed toward Japan. However bold American soldiers and sailors considered themselves to be, hard-headed pragmatism dictated a slow and relatively cautious strategic offensive in the Pacific. The decision in 1940 to defeat Germany first, already recommended at the college by the classes since 1935, provided further rationale for a deliberate and conservative strategy in the Pacific. The strategic thinking at AWC, as illustrated in the plans worked out by students in 1938 and 1939, shows how bad ideas were discarded and better ideas adopted through the process of war planning at the college.

## Plan Purple, 1938

The college required a group of students to plan Purple in response to a request from the War Plans Division of the War Department General Staff for a study of hemispheric strategy and recommended troop deployments.[32] The premises for Purple were infiltration into the Western Hemisphere by Germany and Italy, and a concern for the Japanese migration to Latin America. Civil war in Brazil finds Germany and Italy furnishing arms and men to rebels, according to the scenario. The number of Italian and German immigrants and their descendants, it is feared, could extend European influence in the hemisphere. In its estimate of the situation, the committee noted that there were 1,353,700 Italians, 155,000 Germans, and about 180,000 Japanese in Brazil. The actual influence of Germany and Italy was significant. The German language was taught in schools and used "even in the municipal councils" in some regions. It was further noted that "strong friendship [among] Germany, Italy, and Japan was strengthened by the pact signed by these three nations November 25, 1936." The United States was worried about the economic, political, and military penetration of South America by powers from outside the hemisphere, a violation of the Monroe Doctrine. It was assumed that Spanish and Portuguese possessions in Africa and in the eastern Atlantic would be made available to Germany and Italy because of the support rendered by those two countries to Gen. Francisco Franco during the Spanish Civil War. The Canary Islands, the Cape Verde Islands, Guinea, and West Africa were mentioned in that connection.[33] The United States, along with Argentina, supported the legal government of Brazil. The committee decided to send a corps of four divisions to Brazil.[34]

Despite words of encouragement from Captain Foy, the committee's conclusions were challenged by classmates during the discussion that followed the presentation.[35] There was an unwillingness to commit an army corps from the still small U.S. Army to Brazil when the deteriorating world situation in 1938 could involve the United States in a major war in the Pacific or in Europe.[36] One member of the audience said that deploying a corps to

Brazil was a roundabout way to whip Germany and Italy. The committee responded by pointing to its task: fix a problem in the hemisphere. This led to a discussion of the navy's ability to accomplish the mission by means of a blockade, particularly the ability to sustain a blockade off the coast of South America if Italy or Germany declared war on the United States. Similarly, there was speculation about how events in the Far East might affect the activities in the Western Hemisphere.

The post–World War II American practice of providing military assistance and advisory groups to friendly countries in need of help was anticipated in the observations of one officer. He saw it as an economy-of-force measure and cited as examples contemporary German actions in Austria, Franco's making use of German and Italian advisers, and British experience over the centuries in providing leadership for "native troops." Foy concluded his critique: "When you try to find shipping to haul American complete units enormous distances and try to support the units over there in adverse climatic conditions, it seems to me the expense would be decreased and probably we would succeed if we did use some of the cadre idea in the conduct of those operations."[37]

Clearly, it was necessary to be prudent about committing U.S. forces to one theater when circumstances might require those forces in some other part of the world. This was the primary lesson of the exercise. The army could scrape up a corps-sized expeditionary force for use in Brazil, but that "corps" lacked headquarters and support troops. And deployment of the corps overseas left the strategic reserve shelf bare. Planners wondered if it made sense to deploy such a force to South America when the center of gravity might soon be in Europe or in the Pacific. But the principle of first things first focused attention on defense of vulnerable possessions in the Pacific and preservation of the Monroe Doctrine. The faculty assigned AWC students their academic tasks after consultation with the War Department General Staff. As war drew closer, planners began to think of minimum requirements to be accomplished until the nation was ready for great offensives. The college mirrored the concerns of the General Staff in preparing Purple in 1938, and the close relationship between the college and the General Staff continued into 1939, 1940, and the war years.

The War Plans Division alone had seven members of the class of 1938 assigned to it between 1 March 1939 and the end of the war. John E. Hull joined WPD/OPD as a lieutenant colonel on 2 December 1941 and departed a lieutenant general on 2 September 1945. He succeeded Thomas

T. Handy (AWC 1935) as assistant chief of staff, WPD, on 21 October 1944. Handy, in turn, moved up to become deputy chief of staff under George C. Marshall on 21 October, after having served in WPD/OPD from 1936 to 1940 and from 1941 to 1944. Hull and Handy worked closely with Eisenhower, Marshall, and the civilian leadership and were, like other members of the AWC class of 1938, to be found at the center of most of the policy and strategic decisions of World War II.[38]

The War Plans Division also requested in 1937 and 1938 that the college study the "Strategy of a Blue–South American combine against a German-Italian challenge to the Monroe Doctrine" and the "Relative value of defensive war along the line Alaska-Hawaii-Panama, or along the line Aleutians-Guam-Samoa, versus offensive war in the Western Pacific."[39] These studies were among the more significant individual written projects done by students in the class of 1938.[40] The correspondence between the college and WPD clearly demonstrates that the college responded to the needs of War Department planners with both individual studies and committee work.

# 9

# 1939

## *Orange and Purple Again*

When we consider the actual situation in the Philippines today,
it seems to me nothing short of a crime that the Army and Navy
let themselves get into the hole we are in in the Philippines.
**—MAJ. J. LAWTON COLLINS**, 1939

The mission of the Army War College in 1938–39 was unchanged, but there
were changes in the course suggesting that war was just around the corner.
The curriculum was reduced by sixteen calendar days in compliance with
War Department instructions to relieve "the shortage of officers on duty
with troops during the intensive summer training period."[1] And a complete
mobilization course was added, an obvious attempt by the General Staff to
get some help from officers at the college in reviewing and improving a system that would soon move from planning to execution. In the G-2 course a
special study was added on the collection of foreign military intelligence by
nonmilitary personnel, another action suggesting serious interest in heightened readiness for war. The official 1939 course summary added, "Throughout the course increasing interest was manifested in the Western Hemisphere." Again recognizing that the United States was most vulnerable in the
first months of a major war, the prudent first step was to secure the country's
base before projecting power to distant theaters of operations.[2] The continental United States, the hemisphere, and some American overseas possessions constituted the base that was to be secured before any more ambitious
overseas schemes might be undertaken. Committees were organized to plan
the defense of Hawaii, Alaska, the Panama Canal Zone, and the Philippines.[3]
There was a sense of clearing the decks for imminent battle as noted deficiencies were corrected and the army and navy prepared for war.

The Color Plans prepared by the students in 1939 were the same ones prepared by the class of 1938: Red, Green, Orange, and Purple. Including Red in 1939 defies explanation, considering the actual international situation. The rationale offered by the chief of the War Plans Division in his annual orientation for the new students at the Army War College rings hollow: "It is unsafe to assign probability to these different assumed emergencies. Some, at the moment, appear reasonable; others appear to be so utterly at variance with the indications of the day as to be farcical." But he went on to say that planners cannot afford to be bound exclusively by the mood, currents, and trends of the day: "Now a war plan cannot be formulated to meet a condition which exists today. . . . A war plan must be formulated to meet some future condition . . . [so] accept the assumptions furnished you by your faculty adviser, and build a plan based upon those assumptions."[4]

Green was repeated every year to exercise an army operation from a standing start. The scenario was unchanged. The Mexican government is overthrown; the United States establishes a military government to ensure that no other power intervenes on our frontier to exploit the Mexican instability; the standing army performs the assigned mission without mobilization.

## Orange, 1939: Step by Step

The planning for Orange profited from the work of groups assigned to study Alaska, Hawaii, and the Philippines in 1938–39, and from more than thirty years of thinking about war with Japan. The previous year's Orange Plan was useful as a foil, and the presence of U.S. Navy officers in the class and on the faculty was helpful. As already noted, the navy took a proprietary interest in the Pacific, and naval officers brought to the Army War College their practical seagoing experience and Orange war-gaming experience at the Naval War College.

A fresh look at Hawaii to review the missions there raised familiar concerns, chiefly the ethnic composition of the island population and unity of command. The non-Japanese in Hawaii worried about the 152,000 Japanese who made up 38 percent of the total population there and over half the population of Oahu. The committee reported that 24 percent of the Japanese were aliens and 76 percent were U.S. citizens, remarking, "A fear psychosis exists among the non-Japanese of the Hawaii population to exaggerate . . . the real menace presented by these Japanese residents."[5]

There was a general unease regarding command arrangements in some specific functional areas: "The Hawaiian area, as a whole, can be most effectively defended if all the forces available for the defense are placed under one commander. I see no reason for dividing responsibility . . . between two co-equal and independent commanders."[6]

The study group singled out air defense for special mention: "The senior air officer present—Army or Navy—should command all the defense aviation."[7] The need for unity of command was understood by all military professionals and surfaced regularly in plans and exercises, but it was put in the "too-tough-to-fix" category. The services resorted to incantations about cooperation, since neither the army nor the navy was prepared to accept command by a member of the other service.

The group studying the Philippines confirmed that the islands would probably be lost early in the war.[8] In response to a discussion of the future of the Philippines, the commandant, Maj. Gen. John L. DeWitt, made some splenetic remarks about the government and leadership in those islands:

> I don't think that after 1946 [the target date for independence] the Philippines will be either a commonwealth, colony, or republic with reference to the United States, but of Japan. I believe the government there today is as near a dictatorship as it can be. . . . The recent victory of Franco in Spain will lead to a development of fascism in the Philippines through Spanish influence [and] activity of the German colony in Manila. . . . If [Manuel Quezon] is alive at the end of that time [1946] we are liable to see a prompt joining of the so-called Rome-Berlin-Japanese axis by the Philippine Government under the influence of Japan. . . . I don't think we, as a nation, can depend on them after 1946.[9]

A group of three students—one of them Capt. Leslie R. Groves, later General Groves of Manhattan Project fame—wrote a minority report saying that the United States should get out of the Philippines. Their reasoning was that having a base in the Philippines increased the possibility of the United States stumbling into war and encouraged Philippine irresponsibility and high-handed conduct toward other nations. The American people, they said, would not go to war to protect American business interests in the Orient.[10]

While these views may not have been in the mainstream of the army officer corps, it is clear that at least some of the officers considered a U.S. presence in the Philippines provocative, and some saw the garrison there as a liability rather than an asset. Others were just plain angry about how inadequate American defenses remained after forty years there. Faculty member Maj. J. Lawton Collins was scathingly critical:

> If we need any further justification for long range war planning, we have it in the consideration of this Orange Plan. . . . I would like to raise the question if it would not have been possible to have a base there today if 25 or 30 years ago we had made a genuine estimate of the Philippines. When we consider the actual situation in the Philippines today, it seems to me nothing short of a crime that the Army and Navy let themselves get into the hole we are in in the Philippines. Manila and Olangapo are not defensible by any force we have had in the Philippines since the early days; the repair ships and everything are separated widely from one another. Manila Bay is too big to defend from the land point of view; there are too many beaches and too many ways it can be attacked. Yet we have poured hundreds of millions of dollars into the organization of the defense of Corregidor, and we all agree that we cannot hold it. To me, that is a tremendous indictment against the Army and the Navy.[11]

The future World War II leader and chief of staff went on to say that the army and the navy should have done long before what the students at the college were doing in 1939: scrap the defense of Manila and defend Dumanquilas Bay. The latter could be defended "from the land point of view." Collins concluded his denunciation of American military ineptitude by saying that his observations during service in the Philippines confirmed the correctness of the students' conclusion.

General DeWitt joined in the strong condemnation of U.S. national policy and military strategy regarding the Philippines, stating that U.S. policy, from the acquisition of the islands in 1898 to 1939, had been muddled and that the United States was about to pay for those errors:

> We cannot, even as conditions are today, reinforce the Philippines. We are going to lose them right away. We are 9,000 miles away; the Japanese [are] next door. . . . There is one thing that I can never get out of my mind . . . the moment strained relations start between the United States and Japan, the same tenseness will exist throughout the entire world. The minute we begin . . . to use diplomatic pressure and tell the Netherlands East Indies we are going to take all their oil, rubber, etc., that they are now giving to Japan in order to bring economic pressure on Japan, it is going to bring on a World War right away.[12]

DeWitt concluded his remarks by saying that it was time for the United States to begin maximum mobilization. Collins and DeWitt had presented lucid appreciations of national policy and an accurate assessment of American vulnerability in the Far East. DeWitt described quite accurately how two years later economic pressures from the United States would force Japan's military hand and bring on war between the two countries.

Not all officers brought such passion to the issue, but the one-hundred-page student estimate of 18 May 1939 reflected a thorough and realistic appreciation of the factors that would shape the expected war between the United States and Japan.[13] It reads like a history of events rather than a projection into the future: the Japanese possess a warrior spirit ready for self-sacrifice; some ten million men could be mobilized; expect a long and tough fight.[14] Because war in Europe is likely, it seems improbable that either Japan or the United States will get much help from European friends; since Japan is a "have-not" nation, in the long run the U.S. economic advantage will wear down Japan.[15] The United States can expect Canada, Australia, New Zealand, China, and Russia to be on the American side: "French Indo-China, [the] Netherlands [East Indies], India, Malay, etc., being exposed to Orange aggression, their home countries may be expected to sympathize with Blue, but to act against Orange only in defense of their own territories."[16]

Both the United States and Japan need strong air and naval bases to drive home an attack on the other.[17] The initial advantage belongs to Japan: "Blue is superior to Orange in ships and men and can maintain this superiority east of the 180th Meridian. Not until adequate bases have been seized and developed can Blue expect to maintain superiority west of that Meridian." Japan will capture the Philippines and Guam and may "attempt to capture Alaska, Samoa, or even the Hawaiian Islands, not with the idea of a diversion, but for the purpose of inflicting serious damage on Blue. Her possession of any or all of these might materially delay or prevent a Blue advance to gain control of the West Pacific."[18]

The Japanese plan is summarized as follows:

1. Seize the Philippines and Guam.
2. Establish bases in the Carolines and Marshalls.
3. Seize bases in the Aleutians.
4. Organize an outer defense on the Aleutians-Carolines-Marshalls line.
5. Employ naval attrition tactics from advanced bases.
6. Conduct all-out naval engagement when Blue has been reduced by attrition and becomes vulnerable to Orange.[19]

The students could not have been more on target had they had the Japanese war plans in hand. Orange would position itself for the strategic defensive early in the war and to wear Blue down. Blue would counter with a step-by-step advance across the Pacific securing bases as it advanced; the Japanese fleet would be defeated and Orange commerce would be destroyed.

This is not the 1938 solution of making a bold thrust to the Philippines that would force the Japanese fleet to engage the U.S. fleet in decisive battle early in the war to prevent American interdiction of Japan's sea lines of communication to the resource-rich south. The 1939 planners knew that a long war would try the patience of the American people, but they were determined to take no unnecessary chances. Their plan "secures the Blue communications and does not expose the fleet to the risk of a major disaster."[20] It built on previous plans and became the Pacific portion of the strategy that would guide the United States and its allies during World War II.[21]

Because it was important that army planners appreciate the naval point of view and some of its methods, each year a high-ranking naval officer presented that view and some operating principles to the class. In a lecture, Adm. Robert L. Ghormley, assistant chief of naval operations, reiterated the distinction between the readiness of the army and that of the navy. The navy "must at all times be practically mobilized and ready to move on short notice [and] to commence operations upon the declaration of war." On the other hand, "the economic conditions of our country and the geographical position of the United States will not permit the partial mobilization of the whole army in time of peace." He then came to his point: "These conditions do, however, permit the partial mobilization of Army defenses in Hawaii and the Canal Zone, two key defensive position's *[sic]* in the Navy's strategical plans." The army was expected to "defend the continental United States and the vital positions in our outlying possessions," so that the navy would have available the forward operating bases that would allow that service to take the initiative against the enemy.[22]

Ghormley did not expect a declaration of war: "It seems to be the present fashion for an enemy to strike a telling blow at a time when, on the surface, the situation is serene and trouble is least expected, or when the attention of the world is focused on areas far from the scene of the intended blow. This is followed by offensive action without the formality of a declaration of war." He specifically expected violation of the Monroe Doctrine, damage to the Panama Canal, submarine attack or mining operations against our fleet while at anchor in operating areas, and "a seizure of the Philippines or Guam."[23] By this time it was generally believed that the garrison could not hold until reinforcements arrived, and that was Ghormley's view as well.

The fate of the garrison was not explicitly addressed, but that must have been on the minds of the professional soldiers, many of whom had served there and had friends serving there.

Ghormley speculated on air power: "The world has not yet seen a main fleet action in which aircraft may be considered as a real component of the engaged forces. In my opinion the battle of the air will take place soon after the initial contact, each force attempting to gain control of the air before the main gun action takes place."[24] He was right as far as he went. Little could he know that in the next war sea battles would be decided with great destruction, often without any main gun action.

Maj. (later Gen.) Charles L. Bolte (AWC 1937) opened an interesting line of questions about a two-ocean war and the effectiveness of naval aviation. He asked if the navy would have two fleets in a two-ocean war "or if the principle of concentration means you would always provide for substantial forces in one ocean . . . with smaller forces in the other ocean." Ghormley thought it would be a "wonderful thing" to have two great fleets, but that was simply not possible: "I think the concentration would be in the ocean which looked the more dangerous. In the Atlantic, we have England and France that are a kind of bulwark at the present time. . . . So it seems to me the natural concentration, in view of the Japanese, German, Italian tie-up, is for the biggest concentration to be in the Pacific as it is at present."[25] The admiral's qualification, "at present," allowed for the unforeseen, as must be done. Just about one year after his lecture, France was overrun by Germany, the French fleet's future was unknown, and Britain was fighting for its survival. The "bulwark" was gone.

The following exchange after the admiral's presentation regarding naval countermeasures to enemy air power comes close to anticipating the events of 7 December 1941.

Bolte asked, "Do you consider the hostile air threat so dangerous that it might drive the fleet out of a very large harbor or away from a very large anchorage?"

Ghormley wanted specifics: "Hawaii, a base at Truk, or San Francisco?"

Bolte: "Let's take Pearl Harbor. Would the presence of hostile air, to the extent of not over three carriers, drive you away from Pearl Harbor, or to sea?"

Ghormley: "Ships depend upon maneuverability." He went on to say that to enjoy that maneuverability, one would prefer to be at sea. On 7 December the aircraft carriers were at sea; the battleships were not.[26]

Respect for Japanese military and naval competence collided with racial stereotypes, often leading to humorous assessments. For example, Japanese pilots were assumed to have poor eyesight, as evidenced by their squinting. In the first post–World War I assessment of Japanese competence in the air, the Royal Air Force informed the Committee of Imperial Defense in March 1920 that the Japanese are not apt pilots, probably for the same reason that they are indifferent horsemen. A British wag noted, "Japanese incompetency in the air is very significant and on the whole satisfactory."[27]

Heightened tensions in the world in the spring of 1939 were reflected in these plans and even more clearly in the tone of the discussions among students and faculty that followed the student presentations. The officers found themselves constantly looking over their shoulders. As they addressed a plan in one region, they wondered just how to allocate meager resources to near-simultaneous crises breaking out in distant corners of the world. The Far East and Europe, for example, intruded as they worked out a plan in the Western Hemisphere.

## Purple Revisited, 1939

The 1939 version of Plan Purple was much like that of the previous year. The situation presented to the work group finds Brazil in a civil war. Germany and Italy support the rebels, hoping to gain influence in the region, and the United States supports the government of Brazil. The United States enforces the Monroe Doctrine by sending a corps-sized expeditionary force to Brazil as the navy positions itself to interdict support of the rebels by sea. Not surprisingly, available forces cannot meet the operational requirements of an overseas expedition, even the relatively modest requirements so close to home. The problem is that the American force to be deployed is not balanced, lacking hospitals, engineers, logistics, military police, and air defense.

In addressing the problems of assembling the expeditionary force, the students discovered that they were robbing Peter to pay Paul. Their recommendation was to establish a balanced expeditionary force consisting of not less than a reinforced corps of three war-strength divisions and supporting troops. As was so often the case, the most stimulating part of the exercise was the discussion of the student work. When a question arose, for example, as to the positioning of the U.S. fleet to support the army in Brazil, concern for regions outside the Western Hemisphere was evident in Captain Foy's response: "[The fleet] will be in [the Panama Bay area], cruising around, so that it can be brought into the Atlantic when wanted. It is placed so that it is a staying hand on any aggressive action by Japan; merely an indication to Japan that we are not abandoning the Pacific because we have a little trouble down in South America."[28]

Those who were struggling to ensure hemispheric defense might have been a bit disconcerted by the cavalier approach of the navy to "a little trouble down in South America," but the navy was consistent. It focused on war with Japan—always—as Foy made clear: "[The corps in Brazil] will certainly be deserted by the Navy because we will have a much more important job to keep the Japs out of one side and the Germans and Italians out of the other."[29]

The net effect of aviation and air defense capabilities was unclear to professional military men, and it was much on their minds. Despite the German and Italian combat experiences in Spain, it was not settled whether military aviation would be decisive or simply a nuisance to land and maritime combat. "Air is perfectly untried," Captain Foy pointed out in this regard; "it is all theoretical and you can make any assumption you want." This was an honest assessment, not a denigrating throwaway line from an old salt. Wild claims abounded, but only the bloody lessons of the next war would validate some claims and refute others.[30]

Awareness of the many hot spots around the world was evident again in the answer to a question about air defense. One member of the audience asked the study group why it lined both littorals of the United States with considerable coast artillery defense and antiaircraft units for a relatively minor effort in South America. The response was, "The Rome-Berlin-Tokyo axis creates diversions all over the face of the earth." It was difficult to know the direction from which the main threat was to come. The committee decided to be safe rather than sorry.[31]

In his annual lecture to the college on 31 March 1939, as the students began the war-planning portion of the course, the chief of the War Plans Division, Brig. Gen. George V. Strong, mentioned "a so-called Rainbow Plan, which is now being drafted."[32] This was the first mention of the Rainbow Plans in the college curricular materials, but Strong knew that what the college had been doing in the War Plans Period since 1934 was Rainbow-like. He was in close touch with the college via correspondence; six of his officers were from the classes of 1935, 1936, and 1938; and it was a short distance from the War Department to the college.[33] Students had been required either to plan for a two-front war or to be keenly aware of the possibility that while they were planning for war in Europe, war in the Pacific was inevitable. Even while the students focused on Brazil, a wary eye was kept on German, Italian, and Japanese activities around the world.

Rainbow was on Strong's mind as he told the class that he, as chief of WPD, and the students shared a problem: matching real on-hand assets to the requirements necessary to execute the various plans in their earliest phases. His remarks about his responsibilities in the real world dovetailed nicely with the hypothetical problem the students were grappling with in Brazil. The distance between academic scenarios and existential war fever was narrowing. The fog lifted to reveal Germany, Italy, and Japan as aggressive states dangerous to America. This made planning easier as the problems took on distinguishable form, but planners were bedeviled by the prospect of providing the resources required in the short term. It was generally recognized in all planning that the United States could defeat any likely enemy coalition in the expected long war of materiel that would be decided by national economies. The problem for General Strong and for the students was how to address the here-and-now problem of resources available in 1939. Even as he addressed the War College students, Strong was deeply engaged in the Protective Mobilization Act of 1939. Purple and the deployment of a corps overseas were feasibility testing of real-world plans.[34]

The study groups from 1934 to the outbreak of the shooting war in Europe in 1939 had been working on problems of high interest to the war planners on the General Staff all along. Ghormley's concern for the security of overseas bases and Strong's desire to shake out the mobilization plans and to round out a corps-sized expeditionary force show the extent to which students were involved with the War Plans Division of the War Department General Staff. The class of 1940, the last AWC class until 1950, would go to work under the direct supervision of the War Plans Division.

# 10

★ ★ ★

# 1940

## *School's Out*

Close cooperation with the War Department was continued by the
study of subjects of special interest to the War Department.
**SUMMARY OF THE COURSES AT AWC
SINCE THE WORLD WAR,**
1939–40 COURSE

The process of clearing the decks for action continued into academic year
1939–40, accelerated by a rapid deterioration in international relations. As
conflicts multiplied, professional soldiers had good cause to believe that the
next war would be even worse than the last. Aerial bombardment and the
use of poison gas might not be limited mainly to military targets, and the
effects of the mobility provided by motorized and armored forces had yet to
be demonstrated in combat involving first-rate armies on both sides. As the
Army War College class of 1940 assembled in September 1939, the Wehrmacht was concluding its swift victory in Poland. Before the class completed
its scheduled program at the college in the late spring of 1940, Hitler's armed
forces had overrun Denmark, Norway, the Netherlands, and Belgium, and
the Germans were in Paris. British troops were evacuated from Dunkirk,
and the British found themselves fighting alone for their survival. The pace
of events was shocking.

As in 1938 and 1939, mobilization was a featured subject in 1940. In several other small ways the probability of war was manifested at the college at
the beginning of the academic year. Reflecting an awareness of the American aversion to involvement in war, even as it seemed that war was
inevitable, the "Influence of Public Opinion on the Conduct of War" was
studied.[1] Puerto Rico was added to the list of overseas departments to be

studied, further evidence of concern for hemispheric defense. The State Department detailed four Foreign Service officers to take the G-2 portion of the course. The army was pleased at this response to a longstanding invitation to civilian agencies to become more involved in the preparation of contingency plans and emergency measures in the event of war.

The college summary of the course in 1940 says, "Close cooperation with the War Department was continued by the study of subjects of special interest to the War Department."[2] The historical ride that had been scheduled was dropped. A third of the class was ordered to special duty in the War Department beginning 8 June, and the remainder of the college engaged in a special course consisting of studies of special interest to the War Department General Staff.[3] The identity of interest toward which we have seen the college and the staff moving since 1934 was now complete. The college closed its doors. Potential students, the front-runners of the officer corps, had a war to fight. The next students to gather at the college would be the class of 1951 at Forth Leavenworth.

## The Last Orange, 1940

The last Color Plan of the last prewar AWC class was Orange. The plan was very much like the Orange of 1939, except that it was worked out while a real war was taking place in Europe. Since 1934, no plan for war in the Pacific had been considered by student study groups without due regard for the situation in Europe, so it was unnecessary to tell the Orange planners of 1939–40 to keep Europe in mind. Newspaper headlines suggested as much.

As in 1939, the deliberate step-by-step advance in the Pacific was the solution preferred by the AWC planners of 1940. Bases would be established as the U.S. fleet advanced so that it could be logistically supported from proximate bases, but also because of increasing respect for air power. Bases would be established in the immediate rear of the fleet. These bases would serve also to permit land-based aircraft to support the fleet, for navies were now fast becoming conscious of the necessity for greater air support than the fleet itself could furnish.

American planners believed that the Japanese had prepared airfields to support the Imperial Navy, some of them illegally on the mandated islands. The U.S. Navy needed land-based as well as carrier-based aircraft: "Admittedly this method of advance is a slow process, but surer than any other.

Further, it is the easiest from which to withdraw."[4] In the event of an early drubbing—not out of the question, as the U.S. fleet was being concentrated in the Pacific or occupied with another antagonist in the Atlantic—it would be possible for the fleet to regroup and refit to fight another day. Always in the background was the important assumption that time favored the United States. As the war dragged on, the United States would grow stronger as the resource-poor Japanese grew weaker. There was no need for risk taking early in the war.

In estimating strengths and weaknesses of the United States and Japan, the 1940 plan was consistent with those of the recent past and foresaw the events of 1941–45. Despite some absolute American advantages, the Japanese enjoyed local advantages that would be magnified when they attacked the Philippines and Guam, probably without warning. American strength would ultimately tell as the United States advanced via the Marshall, Caroline, and Mariana Islands and recaptured Guam and the Philippines by phases after concentrating in the Hawaiian Islands. In due course the Japanese lines of communication would be cut and Japan would be defeated. The committee hoped that invasion of the Japanese home islands would not be necessary, but that and ground combat on the Asian mainland remained possibilities. However, the students expected that the enemy would be broken by means "primarily naval in character."[5]

In the discussion period, someone asked about Russian assistance and "What about Joe Stalin?" The study group spokesman replied, "We would like to have Russia put pressure on the Japanese on their frontiers, but this isn't a Rainbow plan; it is just between the United States and Japan, and so in that instance the best we can hope for is sympathetic relations between Russia and the United States in their venture. We would like to bring them into it; the more the better."[6]

Realizing that "American land operations cannot begin for a long time," members of the group came up with some schemes that anticipated methods of the Cold War. Among the creative short-term substitutes for American land power in the early phases of the war were a trading company and tourist bureau in Rangoon to handle supplies; American advisers to the Chinese Army; financing and organizing Chinese and Korean "sabotage, revolution, and anti-Japanese acts"; and various ways to enhance Chinese military effectiveness.[7] A special Annex Y was designed to hurt Japan by building up the military and economic effectiveness of China.[8] One of the schemes was to organize a scientific expedition that would really be a U.S. military mission.[9] The need to do something to hurt the enemy before the

U.S. Army could be mobilized and deployed produced some creative thinking in the realm of what later came to be called dirty tricks.

## Rainbow X

One group from the class of 1940 was assigned to develop a plan called Rainbow X. It began working on its task in the winter and spring of 1940, before the quick German successes in France, but after Denmark and Norway had been defeated. The premise for this plan was German domination of the Continent and German air and submarine operations against Britain before American assistance was available. During World War I a great French Army supplemented by a British expeditionary force had managed to keep the Germans out of Paris for over three years before American soldiers arrived in France. Although it was considered improbable that Germany could overrun the West, the prospect was obviously of great interest to the General Staff.[10] A German-dominated Europe would require a complete reconsideration of pace and priorities.

George C. Marshall became the army's chief of staff on 1 September 1939, the day the Germans invaded Poland and just a few days before classes began at the college. It was a busy day for the new chief. He was made a permanent major general (two stars), he was promoted to temporary general (four stars), and he met with President Franklin D. Roosevelt. Marshall's initial challenge was to build and equip the U.S. Army while at the same time the United States acted as "the arsenal of democracy." He had to make decisions regarding the distribution of weapons and equipment to Britain, a de facto ally in 1940, possibly to the Soviet Union and China later, and to U.S. forces. Moreover, among the U.S. forces choices had to be made regarding the allocation of resources to the training base and to the fighting force to be deployed. It would make little sense to send to Britain those critical items required by the U.S. forces if it became probable that Britain would be defeated by Hitler. Reflection on this issue forced one of the first strategic principles of the United States to emerge, and a clear preference of the president: to keep Britain in the war. It would be a mistake to deny Britain the means of its survival, survival vital to America's security. Defeat of Britain would leave the United States alone in a hostile world. Therefore, estimates of the British capacity to go it alone against Germany were critical to decisions about allocating war materials. Britain became the central focus in 1940 for the U.S. Army war planners.

The undermanned and overworked General Staff, and most particularly the War Plans Division, quickly—and reasonably—involved the college in Rainbow planning. Students had been working on problems of coalition warfare and thinking through the implications of a two-ocean war since 1934. Conditions in the spring of 1940 approximated scenarios exercised over the past seven years.

In their Joint Estimate of Rainbow X, wars in Europe and the Far East were explicitly connected by the West European colonies in the Far East and the Berlin-Rome-Tokyo axis:

> The Dutch East Indies, with their immense resources, are a tempting prey under present conditions. This would particularly be the case should Germany overrun Holland. Japan in that case might take them under "protective custody." To prevent such action would require large British and American forces in the Western Pacific, and it is highly questionable whether they would care to become seriously engaged with the Japanese near Japanese home bases.[11]

American and British planners would sort out just how to go about fighting a truly world war not only involving nations from around the world but also requiring fighting by the allies in theaters in remote corners of the world. To avoid dissipating their efforts, priorities had to be established.

Assuming German dominance of Europe, the college study group outlined the concept of the war as follows:

1. Put pressure on Germany by "creating additional theaters on the German flanks, so as to disperse German effort and force the expenditure of resources and reserve supplies."
2. Engage in the "economic strangulation" of Germany at the same time that pressure was being applied to its flanks.
3. "The Allies will avoid decisive military operations until Germany becomes over-extended or weakened, at which time they will strike a coordinated blow in a decisive direction."
4. "It is intended that all Allied measures will be continued until the German Army is defeated, the country occupied, and the people subjugated."

The group estimated that the war would require a maximum effort by all allies for at least two years, and the priority of effort was clear: "The Allied attitude in the Pacific will be purely defensive, based on a strategy of first concentrating every effort toward the defeat of Germany."[12]

Rainbow X in 1940 marked the seventh year of planning for coalition warfare at the college. The concept was reported to the college community on 21 May 1940 as Wehrmacht divisions raced down the Somme valley to the English Channel. Within a month Germany dominated Europe. From 1934 to 1937 a two-ocean war had been contemplated. From 1938 to 1940 the focus was on mobilization and hemispheric defense in the transition to war. In 1940 a dramatic new situation arose as France was defeated and Britain fought for its very survival.

From time to time students wondered aloud just what all the turmoil in distant corners of the world really meant to the national security of the United States, thus reflecting the isolationist predisposition of many Americans. One officer pontificated, "We are fat, we are rich, we are desirable, and as long as we are that, we are prey."[13] The fall of France, an undeclared war in the Atlantic, and tensions between the United States and Japan provided some concrete steps to a declared war.

# Part IV

# SUMMING UP

# 11

★ ★ ★

# War College Plans and "Official" Plans

The main thing that saved the Army was the school system.
**—GEN. THOMAS T. HANDY,** AWC, 1934

The war plans developed at the Army War College between the world wars would be little more than historical curiosities had they remained within the walls of the college, unknown to the war planners on the General Staff. Such, however, was not the case. The army's leadership knew about the planning and just about everything else that happened at the college, frequently requesting that the college prepare plans for a General Staff that was always short of officers. The War Plans Division of the War Department General Staff had eleven officers assigned, including the boss, the assistant chief of staff, a brigadier general. They were spread very thin as they addressed the extraordinary range of complex and important tasks for which they were responsible. (See appendix F.) In the entire period from 21 September 1921 to 31 December 1940 only ninety-two officers served in WPD.[1] The evolution of AWC war planning, particularly from 1934 to 1940, the transition of the members of the class of 1940 from student to staff officers, and the actual war plans developed and approved by the army and navy staffs indicate that college war planning was known to the men officially responsible for planning and ultimately responsible for the Rainbow Plans.

## War College Preparation and
## Great Decisions of World War II

The principal elements of the actual conduct of World War II can be seen in
the 1940 Rainbow X prepared at the college. It was given to the entire college community as an oral presentation on 21 May 1940, eight months
before the Anglo-American staff talks of January–March 1941 were conducted and six months before Adm. Harold R. Stark, chief of naval operations, wrote his famous Plan Dog memo, the formal title of which is "Memorandum on National Security Policy." He said in November 1940 that the
United States was likely to gain most advantage by stressing "Germany
first." This became official policy through ABC-1, the final conference document of the American-British Staff Conversations in March 1941, and the
U.S. Joint Army and Navy War Plan, Rainbow 5, developed in May and June
1941. Stark's conclusion, a strong offensive in the Atlantic and a "strict
defensive" in the Pacific, carried great weight because it came from a senior
navy source. The navy's fixation on Orange was well known. Stark's recognition of the need to send large air and land forces to Europe or Africa,
or both, in order to keep Britain in the war reversed the Atlantic and Pacific
priorities of the navy. German domination of Europe made it essential that
the United States and Britain work hand in hand, lest the United States find
itself alone in a hostile world.[2] The options available in 1939 and 1940 are the
same ones the students considered from 1934 to 1940, and their "Germany-
first" decision was the same as Stark's.

In *American Strategy in World War II: A Reconsideration,* published in
1963, Kent Roberts Greenfield, the army's chief historian from 1946 to 1958
and a distinguished scholar of World War II, reflected on the great decisions
of the war. Greenfield listed eight Allied decisions and one American "foundation": the survival of Great Britain and its postwar freedom of action as a
Great Power.[3] A comparison of his analysis to the student Rainbow X of 1940
shows that the students were either very good or very lucky.

First on Greenfield's list was the complete defeat of the enemies. The
Allies "would not stop fighting until they had these enemies at their mercy."
This is similar to the students' expression of the same principle in their
point number 4: defeat the German Army, occupy the country, subjugate
the people.

Second, Greenfield listed "the decision of the United States that Germany was the Number One enemy." The students asserted that the allies
would defeat Germany before turning to the offensive against Japan.

Third was the decision to invade North Africa, an operation subsumed under the student plan to create additional theaters on the German flanks in an attempt to "disperse" the German effort.

Fourth was the decision to give the bombing offensive a weighty claim on American resources, one aspect of the "economic strangulation" of Germany and Japan recommended by the study group. The wisdom of assigning such high priority and resources to strategic bombing was later questioned. Resources might have been better invested in army divisions. But the point here is that the college planners in 1940 and the wartime planners concluded that blockade and bombing would be emphasized before bloody invasions were conducted.

Greenfield's fifth great decision deals with a specific event, the U.S. Navy's victory at Midway in June 1942, about which commentary in 1940 is not to be expected. However, that event cried out at the time to use resources to exploit the victory. It caused the Americans to go over to the offensive in the Pacific in violation of both the student concept of the war and the Anglo-American strategic understanding reached at the ARCADIA Conference. This is an excellent illustration of the influence of battlefield success or failure on strategy.

Sixth, Greenfield cited the decision to conduct a two-pronged offensive in the Pacific. This decision was not explicitly mentioned by the 1940 group, but it certainly vindicated the student plan to seize bases as the fleet advanced, what was popularly called island-hopping, rather than risk all on a single bold stroke at the source of Japanese power.

Seventh was the cross-Channel attack by the Allies to regain entry onto the Continent. The exact circumstances and required military operations were not identified in the student plan of 1940, but it said that after wearing down the Germans "the Allies . . . will strike a coordinated blow in a decisive direction."

Greenfield's final point was that the Allies had built into their strategy the possible need to invade Japan if blockade and bombing failed to bring Japan to its knees. So had the planners at the college. It was unclear whether terror bombing or targeting the enemy's industrial base was the more promising course of action, or if either would obviate the need to invade the foe's homeland. The students of 1940 inclined to bombing such targets as munitions plants, because "it is difficult to break the will to war of a nation by terrorizing the civil population by air bombing."[4] This conclusion was validated by the British popular reaction to the Battle of Britain and to the rocket attacks later, and by German popular reaction as industrial production rates rose late in the war after Germany had taken a terrific pounding from the air.

Although the force of events and various turning points during the war exerted influences that could not be foreseen—for example, the initial German successes, the Battle of Midway, Soviet resiliency, and the atomic bomb—the study group that worked out Rainbow X in 1940 produced principles or guidelines that look very much like those ultimately accepted by the Anglo-American alliance. This was an outcome of the process set in train during the War Plans Period at the college in the 1930s, particularly "Participation with Allies," that forced coalition-versus-coalition warfare in the thinking of the officers who would be the brain of the army in the war now visible on the horizon.

In the planners' oral presentation of Rainbow X to their classmates, several concerns emerged that are interesting to readers who know what actually happened in the war years. Hardly new, but very much on their minds, was the unavoidable and time-consuming need to mobilize the U.S. Army. The plan was to have 1.2 million men in France 360 days after mobilization. The planners assumed a reinforcement of France and Britain more or less like that in 1917, with some training time for the American troops "under the protection of the French and British armies." Military professionals believed that the rapid buildup of the Wehrmacht from an army of one hundred thousand would require some time before it was ready for serious combat. College planners further assumed that the pure weight of the allies would wear down the Germans ultimately. But because they held German war-fighting ability in high regard, and because they estimated that it would take over a year to bring effective U.S. land forces to bear on the Germans, they recommended a strategy of economic attrition and peripheral operations to get the Germans fighting in several directions at the same time.[5] Initial caution was particularly recommended regarding the so-called West Wall: "Major offensive action should not be undertaken here until Germany has been considerably weakened by military action on other fronts or by economic or political action."[6]

The students of 1940 knew that the class of 1939 had confirmed what was generally believed by most officers: the U.S. Army could not field a balanced expeditionary force for about a year, and the fielded force would not be effective for about eighteen months. Moreover, a mass of divisions was not sufficient without the corps, army, and General Headquarters troops that would make an American expeditionary force self-sufficient and sustainable. Respect for the German Army and the need to mobilize the U.S. Army resulted in a recommendation for a deliberate approach in Europe, starting with some nibbling at the edges of German strength.

Some political leadership—a former naval person of great imagination comes to mind—might see southern Europe as a "soft underbelly," but experienced soldiers recognized that the mountainous terrain of the Balkans or Italy favored the defender with decided tactical advantages. "If Italy comes in on the side of the Allies, an attack can be made against Germany along the Italian frontier," said the committee. But, they reminded their listeners, "this is very difficult terrain and little progress was made here during the last war." In fact, it proved next time to be the assaulting infantryman's nightmare.[7]

The student solution in Rainbow X was to defeat Germany first and then to turn to Japan. And in the European theater the allies initially would defend on land while conducting air and sea offensives. The students anticipated a German air offensive against Britain, but they assumed that the allies would ultimately turn it back and enjoy air superiority as they began their land offensive. "If we would build a sufficient number of those bombers with long range to go over in big quantities, that is from 800 to 1000, I believe we could make the German Blitzkrieg look like child's play," said one officer during the discussion.[8] All of this would take time, as the United States transformed potential strength into actual power and allocated it to allies, the training base, and the fighting force. As one member of the group discussing the student presentation put it, "The only definite element in our set-up which is available to fight today [is the Navy]."[9]

## Rainbow Plans and AWC Planning

On 12 November 1938 the Joint Board sent a problem to the Joint Planning Committee for study. The JPC was asked what military courses of action were available to the United States in the event of violation of the Monroe Doctrine by one or more of the Fascist powers and a simultaneous extension of Japanese influence in the Philippines.[10] The formulation of the problem was strikingly similar to what Tasker Bliss had proposed more than thirty years earlier when he was asked to pose the first problem for the newly established U.S. Army War College and General Staff. Over the winter of 1938–39 the problem of providing courses of action was studied as the Germans annexed the remainder of Czechoslovakia. In April 1939 the JPC report to the Joint Board listed the dangers in German and Italian penetration of the Western Hemisphere, among them a threat to the Panama Canal and pressure that could be applied to U.S. foreign policy. Nevertheless, the report concluded that German offensive action in the Western Hemisphere was unlikely, since Germany could expect British or French intervention. A Japanese attack on the Philippines or Guam was considered unlikely in the near future. However, the JPC believed that concerted aggression by Germany, Italy, and Japan should be considered in future planning.[11] The projected series of new plans was called Rainbow.

At the behest of the War Department General Staff, the AWC class of 1938, in addition to the bold-thrust version of Orange, worked out Purple, the army-navy expedition to Brazil designed to thwart German and Italian penetration into the hemisphere. The AWC class of 1939, in addition to the deliberate step-by-step version of Orange, was doing the second iteration of Purple even as the JPC was grappling with its similar task. Defense of the Western Hemisphere south to the bulge of Brazil, 10 degrees south latitude, would become Rainbow 1. All of the Rainbow Plans would include defense of the hemisphere as the sine qua non. Rainbow 2, 3, and 5 were, among other things, to prevent violation of the Monroe Doctrine to 10 degrees south latitude. The Purple Plan exercised at AWC in 1938 and 1939 was just what the army and navy planners needed. It finds its way into all the Rainbow Plans.

Rainbow 4 was both more ambitious and more traditional. It was to protect all the territory and the governments of the Western Hemisphere against external aggression. Neither the Color Plans nor plans worked out at the Army War College under the "Participation with Allies" rubric had been expressed quite that way previously. Rainbow 4 in fact restated the Monroe Doctrine. However, Plan Purple was useful to those who would take the entire hemisphere into account, as were the old Green, Red, and Crimson Plans. They provided a mass of current geographic, political, social, and economic data on the Western Hemisphere essential to sound war planning. And Purple, Green, and Red were being reworked at the college even while the JPC was responding to the Joint Board's tasking of November 1938. The data compiled by War College planners on the hemisphere from Newfoundland to and including Brazil was comprehensive, current, and available to Rainbow planners.

Rainbow 2 assumed the United States to be in concert with Britain and France. It stated that the United States would not provide maximum participation in Europe, but instead would sustain the interests of the "Democratic Powers" in the Pacific and defeat enemy forces there. Rainbow 3 called for protection of U.S. possessions in the western Pacific as rapidly as possible, consistent with Rainbow 1.

The differences between Rainbows 2 and 3 recalled considerations that had been turned over frequently in both the "Participation with Allies" plans of 1934–37 and the Orange Plans, especially those of 1938 and 1939.

As early as 1934 AWC had tasked a committee to plan for a U.S.-Russian-British-Chinese coalition confronting Japan and Manchukuo. The committee was required to list objectives, outline the conduct of the war, determine the extent of American naval and military participation, and estimate the extent of participation of each of the allies. Incorporating the actual events of 1931–32 in China into the curriculum for the class of 1934 was quick work, but the scenario was ready when the class of 1934 reported for the course in the summer of 1933.[12]

In fighting Japan as a part of an allied coalition or alone, two familiar courses of action were invariably considered at the Army War College from 1934 onward. One was the bold stroke required to get at Japan quickly. That was essentially Rainbow 3, getting to the U.S. possessions in the western Pacific "as rapidly as possible," as in the AWC 1938 version of Orange.[13] The 1939 version chose a deliberate campaign in the Pacific, essentially Rainbow 2. Thus planning at the Army War College from 1934 onward (and planning at the Naval War College going back to 1906) shows an appreciation of the implications of bold and cautious plans for victory in the Pacific. The nuances and details were known to the naval and military professionals who attended the senior service schools of the army and navy whenever war with Japan was considered.

But the most significant difference regarding Orange was the navy's view of the struggle in the Pacific as a mano-a-mano epic context, a battle on the order of Trafalgar, Tsushima, or Jutland, a shootout at the OK Corral in which war with Japan was "the American mission." This view contrasted sharply with the prosaic army view—most clearly since 1934 and the introduction of "Participation with Allies"—which incorporated some very serious thinking about a two-ocean war with the United States being a member of an alliance in which Orange was but a part of a larger strategy. The degree to which the navy's view was a product of its own self-image—a sense of uniqueness incomprehensible to landlubbers; the implications of being the first line of defense; and the cultivation of its function as protector of the (imagined) China trade—is worthy of speculation. So is the significance of the location of the Naval War College in Newport, Rhode Island, far from the political center. The facts are these: the navy saw victory in a war with Japan as its reason for being; the army saw war with Japan as a part of a two-ocean war, perhaps the lesser theater of that war.

Rainbow 2 was also interesting for what it said about the two-ocean war. Assuming an alliance of the United States with Britain and France and given the memories of how the United States had entered the Great War, some-

thing less than maximum participation by the United States seemed necessary in Europe. The French and British would hold the line there. The
United States would look out for its interests and those of Britain and France
in the Pacific while participating to some lesser degree in Europe. No one
foresaw that Germany would crush France and drive Britain from the Continent mere weeks after the JPC delivered the Rainbow Plan courses of action
to the Joint Board in April 1940. Something like the American troop buildup
in Europe during World War I was expected. As the United States mobilized,
trained, and shipped troops to Europe, the British and French would contain
Germany. When the U.S. troops were ready, the allies would conduct an
offensive to defeat Germany. Meanwhile, the U.S. fleet, a force already prepared to fight, would take up its tasks in the Pacific.

The less-than-maximum U.S. effort in Europe called for in Rainbow 2
looked much like the AWC "Participation with Allies" of 1935. The assumption in both cases was that the allies were superior to the "Nazi Confederation." All the United States needed to send was, in the words of the 1935
AWC planners, a "respectable force—and we can save our main effort for
Japan."[14] A force of 250,000 to 500,000 U.S. troops in Europe in nine to twelve
months was thought to be sufficient. German successes in the spring of 1940
changed all that.

Rainbow 5 was much like the "Participation with Allies" plan of the AWC
students in 1936. Rainbow 5 saw a need to project American forces "to the
Eastern Atlantic and to either or both the African and European Continents
as rapidly as possible" in order to defeat decisively Germany or Italy or
both, in concert with France and Britain.[15] The AWC plan of 1936 reacted to
a scenario that portrayed a much more serious situation in Europe than that
of 1935. It required 750,000 American troops in six months, over 2 million
within a year, and almost 900 American aircraft in Europe in less than six
months.[16] On the naval side, escort ships were assigned convoy duty, but
the bulk of the U.S. fleet was kept in the Pacific. In the 1936 AWC plan it was
still assumed that the presence of the British and French fleets in European
waters would permit the U.S. fleet to keep its major combatants in the
Pacific. The Rainbow 5 of 30 June 1939 made no specific reference to the
Pacific.

Rainbow 5 also resembled the AWC work of 1937.[17] The scenario that
year portrayed the United States at war with Germany and Italy, but not
with Japan. One of the early decisions was that the U.S. fleet would assume
responsibilities in the Mediterranean, thus releasing British ships to
counter Japanese strength in the Pacific. This was a variation on the familiar
naval theme. Since the army needed time to mobilize and the navy was

ready to go at all times, the swiftest response to the president's decision assigning priority to war in Europe was a naval response. The students of 1937 anticipated both the Sitzkrieg of 1939–40—a state of war with little combat—and the decisive German victory over the weak nations of Eastern Europe. They also decided for offensive operations against Germany from France, going for the jugular in the exercise as the U.S. Army would do in the course of World War II. The decision was to place four hundred thousand U.S. troops in France in six months. Landings in Africa and Italy were also considered.

Considering the evolution of World War II strategy, the distinction between Army War College plans and "official" plans is a distinction without a difference. Bold concepts, thorough research, and detailed planning for the coming war characterized the work done at the college. The AWC planning from 1934 to 1940, strategic decisions by key war planners from 1938 to 1941, and the actual events that unfolded between 1941 and 1945 are remarkably similar. Part of the reason for the similarity is that the circle of army insiders between the world wars was a small, cohesive, and homogeneous group.

# 12

★ ★ ★

# Professionals in a Small Army

By 1940 the military establishment had grown into a loose confederation of agencies. . . . Nowhere in this federation was there a center of energy and directing authority. Things were held together by custom, habit, standard operating procedure, regulations, and a kind of genial conspiracy among the responsible officers. In the stillness of peace the system worked.

—JAMES E. HEWES, JR., *FROM ROOT TO MCNAMARA: ARMY ORGANIZATION AND ADMINISTRATION, 1900–1963*

That the concepts and language of Army War College and General Staff planning documents are so similar is not surprising. The officer corps of the 1930s was a homogeneous group of mostly Anglo-Saxons in a subculture sharing a common professional education and common values, a "genial conspiracy." Officers replaced one another in the United States and in a limited number of overseas assignments in a friendly game of musical chairs.

The officers at the college and on the General Staff enjoyed close personal and professional relationships begun at West Point and reinforced at the Infantry School at Fort Benning, at the Command and General Staff courses at Fort Leavenworth, and at the Army War College in Washington. The army was small. In each of the years from 1923 to 1939 there were about fourteen thousand officers. Men like George S. Patton, Jr., Omar N. Bradley, and Dwight D. Eisenhower had known one another for decades before serving together in World War II, and George C. Marshall knew the officer corps sufficiently well to keep track of those he would put in positions of great responsibility when the army expanded. The officers who rose to the top as commanders and staff officers were constantly evaluating one another, most readily in a school environment.

The links between the college and WPD are found in the plans and in the planning process, but personalities also tied college and staff together. Who the planners were, where they were assigned in the transition from

peace to World War II, and what they thought of one another constituted an
important part of the human dimension of war planning. Many of the student planners at the college during the years of peace found themselves in
positions of influence from World War II to the Cold War, and they worked
with men they had known for years. Among the insiders of a small army it
would have been difficult to maintain secrecy about the planning at the college, even if that had been attempted.

There were many formal and informal ties between the War Department
General Staff, particularly the War Plans Division, and the Army War College. On 1 March 1938, in the annual presentation of the assistant chief of
staff, War Plans Division, that kicked off student war planning, Brig. Gen.
Walter Krueger said that because WPD was small, "additional officers that
may be needed will be drawn from the student body of the Army War College." He had made a similar statement in his 26 February 1937 lecture to
the college, so it is not surprising that in 1940 some members of the class
were put to work on plans before the course ended. Later the entire class of
1940 terminated academic exercises to work under WPD, as directed by
Chief of Staff General Marshall.[1]

Proximity of the college at Washington Barracks (now Fort Lesley J.
McNair), a short trolley ride from the War Department, made it convenient
for General Staff officers and other officials of the War, Navy, and State
Departments to lecture at the college and for students to consult with officials and conduct research in the War Department. Washington in the
1930s was not, in the words of John F. Kennedy a generation later, a town of
northern charm and southern efficiency. It was a small southern city, more
provincial capital than world center. Built between 1871 and 1888, the Executive Office Building was "Old State" and housed the Departments of State,
War, and Navy. (The War Department began its move to the new Pentagon
on 29 April 1942. State moved to its present site in 1946. It was two miles
from the college to State-War-Navy during the period 1934–40.)[2]

Both formal relations and friendships among the officers assigned to
the college and the General Staff meant that all but the most closely held
secrets were generally known at both places. In the U.S. Army of the 1920s
and 1930s, an officer could know all of the officers of his branch and year
group, most of his contemporaries, all of the senior officers, and many others. It is almost certain that he would have known the best and the worst.

When the United States entered World War II, 260 of 305 general officers were graduates of the Army War College.[3] Two-thirds of all graduates

**TABLE 2** ★ AWC Graduates Who Attained the Rank of General

| Year | Graduates | Generals |
|------|-----------|----------|
| 1934 | 84 | 49 |
| 1935 | 92 | 60 |
| 1936 | 95 | 61 |
| 1937 | 96 | 61 |
| 1938 | 96 | 64 |
| 1939 | 92 | 69 |
| 1940 | 102 | 72 |
| Total | 657 | 436 |

of the college from 1934 to 1940 would serve during World War II as generals, a total of 436.[4] (See table 2.) Names from this group appear and reappear in the memoirs of the generation of U.S. Army officers that came to its maturity just as World War II broke out. By the time they attended the Army War College, they knew many of their classmates and had already evaluated them.

Maxwell D. Taylor believed that his classmates in the second year of the Leavenworth course were the most able group of officers of that size with whom he was ever associated: "Almost all had distinguished careers in World War II, including such men as Mark W. Clark, Matthew B. Ridgway, Walter Bedell Smith, and George E. Stratemeyer."[5] Clark's biographer mentions that Ridgway and Smith also made an impression on Clark and adds, "The Leavenworth system, imposing conformity and standardization, shaped several generations of graduates into a homogeneous pattern. The result enabled the Army to use officers as interchangeable parts. Anyone educated at Leavenworth was at home in any headquarters."[6] Clark attended the Infantry School's advanced officers course at Fort Benning in 1924, and Ridgway was a classmate there, too: "Clark found it stimulating to be a part of an alert young group of officers." It was there that Clark "began seriously to read military history and started his own collection of professional books."[7]

During his tenure as assistant commandant at the Infantry School from June 1927 to November 1932, George C. Marshall directly influenced some three hundred to five hundred students and sixty to eighty instructors.[8] Of Marshall's Fort Benning, Edwin Forrest Harding said his comrades there were "the most brilliant, interesting, and thoroughly competent . . . men I have ever been associated with." He mentioned J. Lawton Collins, Charles L. Bolte, Omar Bradley, William M. Hoge, Harold R. Bull, and Truman Smith.[9] Many of the same names would be found on a list of senior commanders of World War II. Among the army's division and corps commanders were, to name a few, Leonard T. Gerow, Jonathan M. Wainwright, Collins, Ernest N. Harmon, Manton S. Eddy, Clark, Ridgway, Taylor, and Lucian K. Truscott, Jr. Ten corps commanders came from the AWC classes of 1934–38. Twenty-nine of thirty-four World War II corps commanders came from the 1926–38 classes.[10]

Collins's personal experience illustrates how he regularly served with men who would distinguish themselves in a great crusade. Collins worked with William H. Simpson, later an army commander in World War II, and his old friend Charles Bolte while he was on the AWC faculty. Among the students who passed through the college while he was there (1936–40) were Lyman L. Lemnitzer, Anthony C. McAuliffe, Taylor, Leslie R. Groves, Alfred M. Gruenther, Stratemeyer, Hoyt S. Vandenberg, and John E. Hull. When the college closed in June 1940, Collins served on the Secretariat of the General Staff in General Marshall's office along with Bradley, Stanley R. Mickelson, Bedell Smith, and Taylor. Earlier, at Fort Benning, Collins had been closely associated with Joseph Stilwell, Bradley, Clarence R. Huebner, and Bolte, when Marshall ran the Infantry School. Similarly, his peers at Fort Leavenworth would go on to distinguish themselves in World War II. He was conscious of being a part of a core of well-trained and reflective professionals in a small army.[11]

Taylor said that Leavenworth turned out well-trained future commanders and General Staff officers, "all speaking the same professional language, following the same staff procedures, schooled in the same military doctrine, and thus ready to work together smoothly in any theater of war."[12] He might have added that they were also ready to work together at the college.

The Army War College allowed for introspection and removed the sense of competition that existed at Leavenworth, but the need to work smoothly with one's comrades was evident in all staff efforts. War planning by committee or work group was easier because of the general socialization of professional soldiers, the Leavenworth experience, the Fort Benning experience, and personal knowledge of one another. For example, Bolte, Clark, Ridgway, and Walter Bedell Smith were together in the class of 1937. Almond, Bradley, Halsey, Harding, Hershey, Hodges, Maxwell, and Wainwright were in the class of 1934.[13]

Assignment from the General Staff to the college faculty was commonplace. Men routinely moved from college to staff and back again. The annual assignment of several graduates of the college to the War Plans Division of the General Staff was also routine.[14] For the AWC classes from 1934 to 1939 the following numbers of graduates, by AWC year group, were assigned to WPD: 1934, four; 1935, five; 1936, nine; 1937, three; 1938, seven;

1939, eight; and 1940, four. Other General Staff sections also received recent graduates regularly. In March 1940 there were 127 graduates of AWC classes 1934 through 1939 in high-level staff positions in Washington, more than half of them in key General Staff jobs.[15] In 1941 there were 215 AWC graduates from the classes 1934 through 1940 serving in the War Department, more than 70 percent in key General Staff positions.[16] On 3 April 1942, five of six brigadier generals and thirteen of nineteen colonels serving in Eisenhower's Operations Division were officers who had passed through the college between 1935 and 1940.[17]

Student work, including the topics of the Individual Staff Memoranda (ISM), the major student project, written by all members of the class, was often assigned after AWC consultation—and sometimes an exchange of correspondence—with the various staff sections of the War Department General Staff.[18] The ISM done by students were "exactly like the form used in the War Department in preparing a Memorandum for the Chief of Staff."[19] The college forwarded individual student projects requested by the General Staff and those the faculty believed to be of special interest to the staff. For example, in 1932 thirty-eight of the eighty-four ISM were sent to the War Department, including one by George S. Patton and another by Captain Foy.[20] (Patton's subject was "The Organization, Tactics and Equipment Suitable for Meeting the Probable Characteristics of the Next War," and Foy considered whether a U.S. naval base should be retained if the Philippines were granted independence.) These ISM were among those responding to the General Staff requests of the class of 1932 and are representative of the kinds of studies done by the college and passed on to the General Staff. Students had the opportunity to deal with issues of current concern to those at the top of the military hierarchy. They also had an opportunity to be "discovered" as bright fellows with a future.[21] The small sections of the General Staff had the benefit of the thinking of those bright fellows—if the powerful AWC commandant approved the project—and could take what was useful and toss out what was not.

And interesting notions were not the exclusive preserve of students. In 1931, while still assistant chief of staff, War Plans Division, Brig. Gen. George S. Simonds wrote a note proposing that one of the students examine a notion that would reappear almost a decade later in quite different circumstances: "An interesting study for Ind. Memo. next year.—'Would it be worthwhile for England to cede her possessions in the Western Hemisphere to the US in consideration of the cancellation of all debts?'" Someone added in pencil, "If so, what disposition should we make of them?" The question was answered on 3 September 1940 with the trade of old U.S. destroyers for ninety-nine-year leases on British bases in the Western Hemisphere.[22]

There was nothing automatic in the give and take between the General Staff and the college regarding student work on useful projects. The faculty made judgments about the suitability of the topics requested by the staff, recommendations were made to the commandant, and he decided if the studies would be done.[23] Serious thought went into how best to use student time. Staff and college interests overlapped, but they were not congruent. The staff was pleased to use the free skilled labor, but the commandant decided where student effort would be spent. The 30 January 1934 offer by the commandant to the War Department's G-3 stipulated that students would work only on subjects "that either now or may in the future be up for consideration by the War Department General Staff." On 8 February 1934 the chief of infantry provided a list of subjects to the commandant, making it clear that the subjects "have been suggested by specific questions that have arisen in this office during the past year." "Busy work" was clearly not the intent.[24]

Responses to the studies done by students and forwarded to the staff varied from simple acknowledgment of receipt to rather expansive commentary. One of the students failed to cover himself with glory in his ISM without apparent damage to a promising career. In 1934 future fleet admiral William Halsey was assigned the topic "Japan's Attitude at the Forthcoming Naval Conference." The comment on his paper was, "The study is not sufficiently extensive nor exhaustive to be of great value." His grade: Satisfactory.[25]

The security issues important to the General Staff at the time can be found in the list of topics staff sections asked the classes to study. In 1932, for example, WPD listed, among others: Was there a conflict between political and military strategy among the Allied governments in the Great War? Is the policy of "Paramount Interest" the best that can be used to ensure coordination and cooperation between the army and the navy in joint operations? The G-3 Division was interested in motorization, mechanization, whether the tank was an infantry or cavalry weapon, and mobilization. The G-2 Division wanted the students to study the international objectives of the "Russian" government, whether Alaska was an asset or a liability to national defense, and subversion in the military and how to combat it.

Three papers touched on the Philippines in 1932, suggesting that the navy was not alone in identifying Japan as the most likely threat to the United States in the years before attention turned to Europe. The army staff was shaping its position for disarmament discussions. In any event, the staff's proposed list of topics to be studied by War College students was a kind of barometer of security concerns by year throughout the 1930s.[26]

Not all student work was brilliant. Only twenty of the eighty-two Individual Staff Memoranda done by students were sent to the General Staff from the class of 1935.[27] In that year Malin Craig, AWC commandant (and soon to be army chief of staff), asked the War Department's G-2 for a "list of subjects on intelligence matters which, in your opinion, would make worthwhile topics for a two weeks' individual study by students of this college." The request was made on 5 March 1935. Within two days he had a promise to provide the list requested.[28] This and many similar examples of quick responses suggest that cooperation was excellent and that there was probably a daily courier service linking the college and the War Department. Person-to-person correspondence frequently resulted in a response within forty-eight hours. There were advantages to locating the army's senior service school in the nation's capital. There were also advantages in having a commandant whose star was rising.

The topics sent from the War Plans Division to the Army War College in 1938 reflected an increasing sense of urgency, and they were more specific than those proposed earlier in the decade:

> —Specify by name and location the minimum number of critical points, not extensive areas, which if occupied by US naval or land forces would tend most efficiently to delay the advance of enemy forces toward each of the critical areas of the US and its possessions.
>
> —Are the economic and political advantages of sufficient importance for the US Government to subsidize 30 percent of the US Merchant Marine?
>
> —Relative value of defensive war along the line Alaska-Hawaii-Panama, or along the line Aleutians-Guam-Samoa, versus offensive war in the Western Pacific.
>
> —Strategy of a Blue–South American combine against a German-Italian challenge to the Monroe Doctrine.[29]

All of these WPD requests were honored. The last one mentioned was done at the college in 1938 and again in 1939 as Plan Purple, the defense of the government of Brazil from a German-Italian-sponsored insurrection. Planning focus shifted from Europe to the Western Hemisphere in 1938. The reason for the shift in War College planning is these requests to the college from the General Staff's War Plans Division.

But even the best questions to the army's best thinkers did not necessarily evoke imaginative responses. Col. Ned B. Rehkopf, assistant commandant, said of the student efforts in 1938 that only one was radical. He added, "Perhaps I've come to the wrong place for revolutionary ideas." The college forwarded only ten of that year's Individual Staff Memoranda to the War Department.[30] Perhaps Rehkopf was showing the pique and frustration well known to the teacher who has extended himself for his students only to be disappointed by the ingrates. Rehkopf had asked Robert L. Eichelberger, then a lieutenant colonel and secretary to the army's chief of staff, for some facts regarding the use of actual staff memoranda from the sections of the General Staff by the office of the chief. Rehkopf wanted to assure himself that his students were getting realistic preparation for General Staff work, and he probably wanted to motivate them by telling them that what they were doing at the college was important to the General Staff. Eichelberger's four-page response was polite, thorough, to the point, and prompt. Between 18 and 23 April 1938, Rehkopf wrote two letters to the Office of the Chief of Staff, and Eichelberger answered both in a most considerate manner, suggesting a collegial rather than hierarchical relationship between staff and college. The fact that the current chief of staff of the army was former commandant at the college partially explains the relationship.

Rehkopf referred to these letters when he announced to the class their next duty assignments: "Each officer who graduates from the War College may reasonably expect to serve a tour on the General Staff of the War Department or General Staff with troops at some time."[31]

In addition to the regular exchange of correspondence and student work in support of the staff, an officer working on a special project could call for help from the Army War College and find a sympathetic officer in a key position there. John D. Reardon, Air Corps, a member of a board at the War Department studying a number of air force issues, asked that the college assist by assigning students to study the issues. Commandant George Simonds, aware of current issues being studied by the General Staff because he had run the War Plans Division as assistant chief of staff from October 1927 to September 1931, assigned students to the air force issues.[32]

It is not surprising that the commandant was responsive to the needs of the staff. Simonds was a strong link between the college and the War Plans Division for much of the interwar period. He was a member of the first postwar class in 1920, and upon graduation he was assigned to the faculty. From 1922 to 1924 he was assistant commandant, and from 1932 to 1935 he was commandant.[33] While assistant commandant, Simonds served on the Fiske Board, established to define the division of duties between the Command

and General Staff School at Fort Leavenworth and the Army War College in Washington. Essentially the board recommended and Pershing approved that the college's mission was to train officers for:

1. high command and staff above the corps level,
2. duty with the General Staff and in the Office of the Assistant Secretary of War (whose principal concern was industrial mobilization), and
3. Corps Area Command and General Staff duty.[34]

Examining the army's school system and putting professional education into perspective requires a broad appreciation of the military profession. The experience was useful to Simonds in his later positions of leadership as assistant chief of staff, War Plans Division, and as commandant of the Army War College. Historian Harry Ball noted that "Simonds was not averse to having his students take on studies that the War Department General Staff needed."[35] Simonds kept the college in the mainstream of national security thinking. During his tenure there he continued the division of the year into "Preparation for War" and "Conduct of War," but as former director of WPD and military adviser to the American delegation at the arms limitation conference in Geneva, Commandant Simonds emphasized "Preparation for War."

Chief of Staff Douglas MacArthur, from the earliest days of his appointment, took a personal interest in rapid mobilization for war.[36] Simonds had served as assistant chief of staff for almost a year under MacArthur, so he understood the thinking and desires of the new chief. As one of MacArthur's principal staff officers, Simonds produced plans to comply with MacArthur's insistence that mobilization plans be geared to war plans and that mobilization plans be flexible enough to support the Color Plans. Simonds continued as commandant to support the chief of staff just as he had as assistant chief of staff, on the General Staff, and as an expert in disarmament negotiations. Whether because he was directed to do so or because he recognized the need, Simonds added two weeks to address mobilization as a part of the War Plans course in his first year as commandant (1932–33).

In his second year Simonds reestablished the college War Plans Division and ensured that the navy and Air Corps faculty members were part of it. This action reflected his recognition of the absolute need for close cooperation among air, sea, and land forces, a need most evident from the perspective of a war planner. Just as joint operations meant coordination of the U.S. services, alliances meant that there was a need for a better understanding of the dynamics of coalition warfare. Therefore, it was on his watch as commandant that "Participation with Allies" was added to the usual Color Plans worked out by students each year. Simonds left the Army War College in January 1935 to become deputy chief of staff to MacArthur. His professional activities toward the end of his career were in direct support of MacArthur, who had appointed him commandant and then brought him back to the General Staff as his closest assistant. Under Simonds the college was certainly not an academic backwater out of touch with army concerns.

Simonds's successor as commandant was no less influential. Malin Craig would serve as commandant for less than a year, from February to October 1935, before he succeeded MacArthur as chief of staff. Duty as commandant of the Army War College in the decade before World War II was obviously one of the most prestigious assignments in the army and a steppingstone to higher perches in the military hierarchy. One can be sure that officers noticed patterns of advancement and paid attention to men of achievement like Simonds and Craig. Later, as chief of staff, Craig turned to the bright men he had left at the college to do special projects of particular interest to him and to the army. With Craig and Simonds running the army, the college was well connected as war clouds gathered. Craig's three successors, with one unhappy exception, failed to become household names.

Craig was succeeded immediately by Walter S. Grant (AWC 1924), who ran the college until June 1937.[37] Grant's successor, John L. DeWitt, was commandant from June 1937 until November 1939. DeWitt (AWC 1920) was one of the thirteen officers assigned to the first post–World War I War Plans Division on the General Staff, where he served from September 1921 until July 1924 as a colonel.[38] From July 1928 until February 1930 he had been deputy commandant at the Army War College, so he was thoroughly familiar with the college.[39] Between his tours at the college he was quartermaster general (1930–34) and later commanded the Philippine Division. Upon departing the college in November 1939, he became the senior army commander on the West Coast and in that capacity supervised the internment of Japanese and Japanese-Americans after war broke out.[40] He was also commandant of the Army and Navy Staff College for its entire wartime existence (1943–45) and retired with four stars.[41] Philip B. Peyton (AWC 1931) followed DeWitt as commandant from December 1939 until the college was closed in June 1940.[42]

Almost all of the officers who served in the War Plans Division of the War Department General Staff during the interwar period were graduates of the Army War College. Simonds, Craig, Grant, and DeWitt had also served on the college faculty, as had Stanley D. Embick, Walter Krueger, William H. Simpson, Joseph T. McNarney, Charles L. Bolte, and J. Lawton Collins. Embick (twice), Krueger (twice), DeWitt, Simonds, and McNarney also served in WPD—Embick, Simonds, and Krueger as the boss, the assistant chief of staff. The key officers in WPD/OPD during World War II came from the classes of the late 1930s. This was to be expected. The college prepared officers for war planning. The number of key officers who served both in WPD and on the faculty of AWC—including as chiefs of WPD and commandants of AWC—illustrates the strong connection between the college and the staff, especially the WPD connection.[43]

Considerations of age and unreadiness to handle stress weeded out some older men, making room for the graduates of the 1930s in command and staff positions of great influence and responsibility during World War II. Some of them became famous and were household names into the 1960s. Many served faithfully and well in anonymity.

# 13

★ ★ ★

# AWC Graduates in the
# Transition from Peace to War

Until Hitler really got acting up in Europe we were not confronted
with any threat. People are not going to pay for an Army if they
haven't got any use for it or can't see any use for it.
—**GEN. THOMAS T. HANDY,** AWC, 1935

During World War II Jacob L. Devers (AWC 1933) and Omar N. Bradley
(1934) would command army groups. Courtney Hodges (1934) would command First Army. Bradley would serve after the war as army chief of staff
and during the Korean War as chairman of the Joint Chiefs of Staff. Jonathan
M. Wainwright (1934) had the unhappy task of surrendering American
troops in the Philippines in 1942. Lewis B. Hershey (1934) would direct the
Selective Service System through three wars. In the Pacific theater, William
F. Halsey (1934) would become an admiral of the fleet, and George C. Ken-
ney (1933) would lead the Fifth Air Force. John R. Hodge (1935) would command the American military occupation of Korea after World War II.[1] And
there were the stars, the household names of World War II: Marshall, Leahy,
Nimitz, Patton, Halsey, Eisenhower, King, Arnold, and Spruance lead the list.
A much longer list would include the later graduates who commanded corps
and divisions.[2] Younger men, headed for peacetime obscurity in the 1930s,
made their mark, among them Collins, Gavin, Taylor, and Ridgway. Combat
command is what the soldiers wanted and what the public understood.

Others, working in bureaucratic anonymity, did the staff work that prepared the vastly expanded U.S. forces and guided them to victory in World
War II. Their careers provide useful insights into how the Army War College prepared a generation of professional soldiers for the unglamorous but

necessary quill pushing. They link the War College students of 1934–40 to the Rainbow planners on the eve of war.

Thomas T. Handy (AWC 1935) deserves close attention. He provided unheard-of continuity in the War Plans Division/Operations Division, serving from August 1936 until October 1944 except for one year with troops (June 1940–June 1941). Only Carl A. Russell, Jr. (1 July 1939–28 November 1944), John E. Hull (2 December 1941–2 September 1945), and John E. Upston (27 January 1941–27 February 1944) come close to Handy in length of service in WPD/OPD.[3] These men link the War College of the 1930s to the transition to war and its conduct.

Handy joined WPD for his first tour as a major after completing the Naval War College in 1936; left WPD as a lieutenant general in 1944; succeeded Eisenhower as chief of the Operations Division when Ike was sent to command troops in Europe; and worked with Marshall on an almost daily basis as the chief of Marshall's wartime command post.[4] He was deputy chief of staff, U.S. Army, from 1945 to 1947 and held top command and staff jobs in the army until he retired in 1954. His distinguished service in the center of historic events entitles him to pontificate, but he doesn't. His folksy style, humor, and commonsense reflections shed light on war planning, particularly for the transition from peace to war.[5]

Handy understood the tentative and complex nature of war planning, the need for constant adjustment as circumstances change, and how much easier it is to plan once friends and enemies have been identified. It was also much easier to plan when the United States had a real army on the ground rather than one on paper that had to be raised before operations could be seriously considered. Speaking about the Color Plans as part of his oral history interview, Handy said,

> I don't think that as a practical matter from the planning standpoint they had a great deal of value because they all depended essentially (we didn't have any Army to amount to anything then) on mobilization. . . . [After] you got to D+180 you'd probably be all right. . . . But, I think they had a great deal of value from a training viewpoint because each one of us [in WPD] had [was responsible for] a plan, and it taught you a lot of things you had to think about in war planning.[6]

Handy touches on three important points. First, had his interviewer asked whether the Orange Plans were useful, he doubtless would have said they were the basis for the Pacific portions of Rainbow 5. Second, American planners considered the first six to twelve months of war critical, after which the United States would mobilize so many resources that victory would be almost certain. Third, the training value of the Color Plans should not be underestimated. Planning for Green (a small war) or Red/Crimson (an unlikely war) required the collection of mountains of data later useful in hemispheric defense and cooperation with Britain and Canada. And the staff techniques used in WPD and the rest of the General Staff were those taught at the college. Perhaps the greatest benefit of college war planning was the mind-expanding habit of thinking in strategic and global terms.

Handy often returned to the difficulty of planning for big wars when planners were fully aware of the inadequacy of the tiny U.S. Army, pointing out, "We didn't have really any Army. The Navy had a Navy all the time. They had people commanding ships and they had maneuvers and everything else. We really didn't have an Army. You'd call a thing a division, it would be like the 1st Division scattered all over the Northeast and they never saw each other."[7] This difference between the navy's readiness to go to war from a standing start and the army's need for time to mobilize, train, equip, concentrate, and deploy a vastly expanded force caused army and navy planners to see the transition to war differently.

Only three of the thirty-four American corps commanders of World War II had commanded divisions before the war: Oscar Griswald, George S. Patton, Jr., and Innis Smith. Handy marveled at how well army leaders did during World War II in commanding large formations, considering their limited opportunities to command war-strength units between the wars.[8] "In the first place there weren't really any divisions to command and very few regiments ... it was quite discouraging."[9] Even at much lower levels it was discouraging to find limited opportunity to train because of shortages of men and equipment. Only one in five eligible peacetime officers, according to Handy's reckoning, would command a battalion, and "lots of times when you got one it wasn't much of a battalion. . . . The main thing that saved the Army was the school system. Theory is a wonderful thing," the general concluded, "but you've got to get down to cases where you see and do the actual thing. No guy ever got to be an expert mechanic reading a book."[10]

Some command opportunities overseas, for example in Panama or Hawaii, meant command of a war-strength unit, but in the United States it was only at the schools that things were done right: "I know I was impressed when I went to the War College. . . . Hardly any subject came up that there wasn't somebody there, and it was in the students as often as in the faculty, who really knew a lot about it or was an expert in it."[11] Similarly, at Leavenworth the school battalion was maintained at war strength so that students could get a sense of being a "real" battalion commander one day and, for example, communications officer the next. Such opportunities, Handy commented, made the Leavenworth experience "a very valuable and very pleasant year."[12]

Comparing the Naval War College (1936) to the Army War College (1935), Handy thought that NWC was more like the Leavenworth experience. William F. Halsey (NWC 1933 and AWC 1934) agreed that there was a significant difference, saying that at Newport he studied "the strategy and tactics of naval campaigns with emphasis on logistics." At the Army War College in Washington he studied "on a large scale—wars, not campaigns—and from the viewpoint of the top echelon."[13] Handy says of his Newport experience, "We spent weeks playing games on the floor up there. We had a big room and you maneuvered the ships and flew the airplanes. . . . So I'd say it was more on the type of Leavenworth. . . . They weren't studying the broad questions that they studied at the AWC as a whole."[14]

Scholars corroborate the firsthand impressions of Handy and Halsey. In a 1969 article in the *Naval War College Review,* Gerald E. Wheeler writes, "War planning requires a clear picture of the ends or goals to be achieved by a plan. The ORANGE plan of the 1920s and 1930s was more of an operational plan than a plan to meet the ends of national strategy."[15] Historian Robert G. Albion, in a book published in 1980 by the Naval Institute Press, describes the addition of an advanced course to the Naval War College in 1933 "which will cover the drafting of war plans and advanced phases of naval campaigns." The existing senior course, he says, "barely touched on the conduct of war as a whole, or on the political, economic, social and other factors that initially affect the strategy of war." He goes on to say that intellectual achievement had become not only respectable but "highly useful." The priority attached to seamanship and contempt for intellect in the navy is suggested by Albion's humorous reference to a comment made by an officer passed over for promotion: "I cannot understand why I wasn't selected; I've never run a ship aground; I've never insulted a superior officer; and I've never contributed to the Institute Proceedings."[16]

The "advanced course," added in 1934 to the junior and senior courses at the Naval War College, in which selected officers would study "on the large scale" described by Halsey, proved unsatisfactory. The college blamed the Navy Department for not sending the right officers. Interestingly, the history of the Naval War College marks the summer of 1934 as "the beginning of the transition from a peacetime fleet to one in which men were mentally and emotionally prepared for a future war."[17]

Saying that the course at Newport was not conducted at the strategic level, Handy was nevertheless impressed by the imaginative president of NWC, saying, "Admiral [Edward C.] Kalbfus . . . an old Pennsylvania Dutchman and quite a fellow," wanted to show the class two sides of an issue:

> This was in the '30s and Hitler had a start then and all that. [Kalbfus] got a young German who was in this country as a professor at some university, who'd served in the German Army . . . at the end of World War I, to present the German side. Then he got a Frenchman who was also a professor in one of our universities to present the French side of the situation in Europe. . . . The German was really up against the bit and driving ahead, and the Frenchman was all depressed which was very much the way it worked out, certainly initially in World War II.[18]

In response to a question asking if AWC prepared officers for the General Staff and WPD/OPD, Handy replied, "I'd say yes but not directly. . . . General McNair used to call these guys the Ph.D.s of the Army, the ones that had gone through the War College. . . . As I said, anything that came up, there was some guy who just knew a hell of a lot about it. . . . It was the one place where you could sit down and think."[19] The time to sit and think had to be defended in an action-oriented profession that often confuses motion with progress: "There were people, including some of them pretty high up, [who] tried to get the War College off the 'gentlemen of leisure' foot, but they never did succeed. They had too much resistance from faculty and student."[20]

Handy was at the Naval War College when the Germans remilitarized the Rhineland in March 1936: "There was a feeling . . . that that was the time to stop Hitler. The French could have stopped him, but they didn't do anything." Handy recalled that later, when he was in WPD, Albert C. Wedemeyer was particularly well informed about Germany after his studies at the Kriegsakademie. Handy also recalled that while in WPD he received the reports of the U.S. military attaché in Berlin, Truman Smith (AWC 1933): "[Smith] told about what the Germans were doing, but he kind of missed the biggest picture of all. . . . After every one of these moves, like into Austria and so on, Truman indicated that that was about the last thing they'd do because it would take them four or five years to digest what they had."[21]

Handy's comment demonstrates ironically just how well informed Smith was.[22] His sources were excellent. The problem was that the German military professionals, Smith's best sources, were telling their Führer precisely what Smith was reporting: the Wehrmacht needed time to train, equip, absorb, and integrate masses of new soldiers into an army that had expanded too rapidly from the one hundred thousand men prescribed by the Treaty of Versailles. This was neither the first nor the last time that Hitler would confound military professionals, German and foreign. Col. Jacob W. S. Wuest (AWC 1923), recently returned from four years as military attaché in Germany, addressed the officers of the War Department about conditions in Germany on 10 May 1935. He estimated, "It would take several years [for Germany] to properly organize, train and equip." He also said that the German people were strongly for Hitler; German despair had given way to hope; no European nation was willing to risk antagonizing Germany; the French were very defensive; the Czechs were afraid; and Germany and Japan were trying to get together.[23]

Responding to a question about the quality of planning, Handy observed, "There's hardly ever a time that any plan is carried out in detail. We had those Green, Red, and Orange colored plans and one man was in charge of each one." But plans provided only a starting point for operations, since the actual circumstances were never precisely what the plans had anticipated. Further, the heavy workload in WPD must be considered. Officers assigned there were busy men who might not have been attentive enough to all their responsibilities. As has been noted, there were eleven officers in WPD when Handy joined in 1936 and in most of the interwar years. Those numbers would swell as the WPD planning cell became OPD, Marshall's command post, the planning and operations brain of the army during World War II. In the period from 1 January to 6 December 1941, sixty-six officers served in WPD/OPD. During the war the numbers were as follows:

| | |
|---|---|
| 7 December to 8 March 1942: | 93 |
| 9 March to 31 December 1942: | 204 |
| 1 January 1943 to 21 October 1944: | 319 |
| 22 October 1944 to 2 September 1945: | 310[24] |

Handy puts war plans and their use in perspective by describing some dramatic events in which he played a part. He was the WPD duty officer on 1 September 1939 when Gen. George Strong, chief of war plans, called sometime in the night and said, "All hell's broken loose. The Germans are bombing Warsaw." Handy went to WPD to pull out a recently completed contingency plan that had been approved by the chief of staff:

> It wasn't just a theoretical plan. . . . Hell, we got the plan out and had it all polished up and ready for General Gasser [deputy chief of staff] to look at when he arrived at about 7:30. Hell, the very first thing, he

was suggesting changes. "We don't want to move this outfit," etc. But I think that's perfectly natural and to be expected, but it was rather amusing. Now, had it been a theoretical plan like the Color Plans, way ahead of time, but this was a plan for a particular event or happening or contingency that actually occurred and the very first attitude was to change it. . . . Well, anyhow I go back to it, that the principal value in our planning was to train people in a lot of things you had to think about.[25]

Handy suggests that war studies and imaginative scenarios—while not formal war plans that needed updating in any event—shaped the thinking of professionals who would lead during World War II. For one thing, studies and college exercises are not limited by means available. They allow a freedom whose only limits are the degree to which professional judgment prevents imagination from becoming fantasy out of touch with the existential world. Those responsible to political authority for the General Staff war plans during the interwar period were necessarily inhibited by the political and material limitations of the day, not to mention the fear of leaks to the press or the public. "War planning" had a nefarious ring to it, perhaps akin to reading someone else's mail. The formal planning process required a product from WPD, concurrence by the army staff, coordination with the navy in the Joint Planning Committee and the Joint Board, and approval by the secretaries of war and the navy. A college and its students could rush in where responsible officials feared to tread. Historian Stetson Conn said that the distancing of AWC from the day-to-day business of the General Staff after World War I had the beneficial effect of divorcing college work from the inhibitions of isolationism.[26]

That explains in part why the uninhibited studies at the War College were five or six years ahead of the General Staff in coalition war planning. If some offensive or contentious contents of the studies were made public, they could be explained away as no more than schoolboy exercises. In the public opinion climate of the 1930s, the president had to move cautiously. Even on the eve of Pearl Harbor the leaked "Victory Plan" caused a furor about the president's leading the nation to war like a Pied Piper.

Handy understood the political constraints under which the president had to function, but he was also sympathetic to the military's need for clear guidance regarding what later came to be called "the rules of engagement." He recalled that the president always said that "the first aggressive act must come from the other fellow," but Handy also made this observation about the "undeclared war" in the Atlantic:

There was quite a bit of shooting and so on going on in the North
Atlantic before we got into the war. The Navy had a hell of a time.
They would have a conference in the White House and think they
had the dope. Well, that's got to be translated into orders for those
poor bastards out there with the destroyers. They have got to know
whether they can shoot and when. It's got to be very definite. Well,
that's awful hard to get across with the other side, the civilian side of
our government.[27]

He notes some of the means used to bridge the gap between the military
and the civilian leadership as war drew near. General Marshall, for instance,
worked hard to get Adm. William D. Leahy to be the president's chief of
staff so that the military would have a direct line to the president. Handy
liked Leahy. The army and the navy wanted to be sure that FDR had their
views, especially before he would meet with Churchill, who knew just what
he wanted. Handy shows no concern that Leahy, the former chief of naval
operations, might do some special pleading for the navy. He was confident
that Leahy would represent the military point of view to the president.[28]

Another ally of the soldiers with a need for access to FDR was his confi-
dant, Harry L. Hopkins: "Harry Hopkins was a hell of an asset. General
Marshall used to use Harry Hopkins. If you had to get something to the
President right now and it was really critical, he was pretty good."[29]

American soldiers believed that Churchill always had the benefit of
British military opinion, and Handy, as a result of his close cooperation with
British planners, held them in very high regard: "We were more or less
babes in the wood on this planning and joint business with the British.
They'd been doing it for years. They were experts at it, and we were just
starting. . . . The British planners were just smarter than hell."[30] Handy and
his American colleagues regarded Churchill as a clever fox keenly aware of
the connection linking military and political issues. They wanted their
secretive and freewheeling president to be similarly prepared for his face-to-
face and private meetings with the prime minister.

Responding to a question about army-navy cooperation, Handy says
again how much easier it was to address short-term operational issues than
midterm planning several years into the future:

With operational questions, you generally don't have much trouble,
but when you get into the future . . . some guy would picture what
might happen, and [it] might be embarrassing or disadvantageous
to his service. . . . Instead of taking a definite statement, there would

be a weasel put in or a thing that could in the future be subject to different interpretations. That was the great difficulty.[31]

Immediate operational problems made service cooperation easy; fires must be doused. Solutions to indeterminate problems reaching into the misty future caused soldiers and sailors to hedge their bets. And Handy believed that the navy played the Washington bureaucratic game better than the army. The reason he offers is ironic. Since the navy had no General Staff, it was not subject to the so-called Manchu Act, which sent army officers away after four years on the General Staff and limited the number of General Staff officers in Washington. Each year the assistant chief of staff, War Plans Division, was notified which of his officers, by name, had to leave the General Staff: "Now, the Navy had this system . . . most of their people in War Plans were repeaters, and practically none of ours were. In other words, they'd served one tour there and gone off to sea or wherever it was and come back again. So, they were quite a jump ahead of us. They knew all the canned language and techniques and all that. It was new to us and we were just country boys."[32]

Ruminating on the question of why army planning was not better than it was, Handy noted that the American geopolitical situation, in most ways a blessing, creates a unique feeling of well-being antithetical to military preparedness:

> The trouble with the Army is that we didn't have any live frontier [as Germany and France do]. Well, for years we were not confronted by any real threat. There was some from Japan, the Navy built it up very strongly and all that, but until Hitler really got acting up in Europe we were not confronted with any threat. People are not going to pay for an Army if they haven't got any use for it or can't see any use for it.[33]

Japan was the navy's problem. Hitler's "acting up in Europe" was recognized by the American people as a reason to pay for an army. Speaking as an elder statesman in an interview in 1972–73, Handy was prepared to see events through Japanese eyes (one suspects that he was less understanding in 1942):

> If you look at it from their viewpoint, they didn't have much choice . . . if they had to jump us, what could have been a better time? You see, the war in Europe was going very well for the Germans. . . . We practically told the Japs to give up their ambitions in Asia, just like if

somebody told us to give up ours in America. They had all this expansion on the Asiatic continent and we told them to pull back. It meant that if they had done everything we said they'd [have] given up some of their aims and objectives, fundamental ones.[34]

It is striking how close this remark comes to the Tasker Bliss 10 June 1904 paper prepared for the Joint Board (described in chapter 2). Bliss says, "We may yet find ourselves fighting for our Monroe Doctrine on one side of the world and against somebody else's Monroe Doctrine on the other side of the world."

Handy's personal experience as an insider—from the Army War College, the Naval War College, and seven years in WPD/OPD, and from the key national security positions he occupied until his retirement in 1954—underscores the value of his remarks. His unpretentiousness makes them a delight to read.

Thompson Lawrence's personal experience links AWC prewar exercises to the planning of WPD in the transition to war. Lawrence (AWC 1933) was selected to teach at the college in 1938. He had earlier taught at the U.S. Military Academy at West Point and at Fort Leavenworth.[35] In 1940 he was one of the key people from the group of students and faculty directed to temporary duty with the War Plans Division. His specific assignment was to work on War Plan Rainbow.[36] Other AWC officers, including one naval officer and one Marine Corps officer, worked with representatives of the staff on concentration and operational plans. The group was called WCG, for War College Group. Their efforts were coordinated by WPD. Lawrence became deeply involved in several aspects of Rainbow 4, all pertaining to hemispheric defense.

There was some logic to his assignment. While a student at the Army War College in 1932 and 1933, Lawrence had served on committees focusing on War Reserves and General Mobilization; Joint Operations Overseas; Expedition to Seize and Hold Halifax; War Plans (Red Coalition); and Eight Requirements/Map Problems, Southern Theater (Green). This kind of academic work has been called unrealistic and out of touch with contemporary international affairs, but it was excellent preparation for what Lawrence had to do in 1940 as he worked on Rainbow 4.[37]

Lawrence's signature is on the "Covering Memorandum for the Draft of the War Department Operations and Concentration Plans—Rainbow 4," dated 23 October 1940.[38] This document transmitted the "revised War Department Operations and Concentration Plan Rainbow 4, prepared originally by the WPD of the WDGS and revised during Oct. 1940, by the group of officers on War Plans, at the AWC." Among other things, the plan addressed command and control exercised by the General Headquarters (GHQ), established at AWC as of July 1940, and the deployment of troops to Brazil. Lawrence's contributions flowed from his teaching at AWC and his work as a student. His students had worked out Plan Purple, the American expeditionary force to Brazil, in both 1938 and 1939. The work on Rainbow 4 in 1940 refined previous planning as events forced new thinking about old themes:

> When the [Joint Army and Navy] basic plan was drawn up it was not contemplated that American forces would occupy outposts in British possessions in Newfoundland, Bermuda, and the Caribbean area under peacetime arrangements. . . . Should the American occupation of the British possessions become a fact prior to the initiation of Rainbow 4, then the plans should be revised to fit the new situation.[39]

Earlier plans maintained a sharp distinction between war and peace. The shooting peace between German submarines and American ships in the Atlantic had not been foreseen. Lawrence's experiences in dealing with mobilization and the seemingly provincial Red and Green war plans as a student in 1932 and 1933 and as a faculty member since 1938 took him to *terra cognita* in 1940 and 1941 as he wrestled with the problems of hemispheric defense. Further, WPD's 1938 request that the college "specify by name and location . . . the critical points . . . which if occupied by US naval or land forces would . . . delay the advance of enemy forces" had rehearsed both the college and WPD for very similar planning in 1940, this time for real. The homework of the 1930s was excellent preparation for the tests of 1941–45.

Lawrence was the senior officer responsible for several projects for which documentation exists. It was over his signature that plans, amendments to plans, and comments on plans—most notably Rainbow 4—were transmitted to the assistant chief of staff, War Plans Division, from the War College Group. His work ranged from review and commentary on broad topics to determining the cost of reproduction of strategic studies. His geographic responsibilities stretched from northeastern Brazil and "other parts of South America" through Mexico, Bermuda, and the Bahama Islands to Newfoundland and Greenland.[40] The "Data Re Plan for US Participation in the Defense of Newfoundland and Greenland" was forwarded along with a memo from Lawrence, an "Estimate of the Situation," an "Operations Plan," and an enclosure from the Joint Planning Committee to the Joint Board

dated 8 January 1941. The formats and language used are those used in
AWC and in WPD throughout the 1930s. The students of 1940 stepped into
their planning jobs to do what they had been prepared to do.

The September 1941 plan prepared by a committee of Brazilian and
American officers to support the Brazilian government against rebels was
very detailed. It proceeded from broad concept to the very specific in
annexes. Air and engineer operations were particularly detailed. The U.S.
and Brazilian contributions to the joint effort were spelled out in detail.[41]
Memories of the unpaid World War I debts of allies to the United States are
suggested in the plans involving "Participation with Allies." Planners, condi-
tioned to frugality in the lean years, often seem to have had one eye on the
strategic situation and one eye on the cash box.

It will be recalled that "Participation with Allies"—Purple—prepared by
the AWC committee in 1939, addressed a situation in which Germany, Italy,
and Argentina involved themselves in supporting rebels in Brazil. The
United States supported the government and enforced the Monroe Doctrine by sending an army expeditionary force to Brazil, while the U.S. Navy
prevented German and Italian support of the rebels.[42] The exercises of the
earlier years at AWC anticipated the 1941 plan to defend Brazil. Thompson
Lawrence played a major role in hemispheric defense as a student in 1932
and 1933, as a faculty member responsible for Purple from 1938 to 1940, and
as a team leader in the official Rainbow 4 planning in 1940 and 1941.

In his presentation to the AWC class on 31 March 1939, Assistant Chief of
Staff General Strong mentioned Rainbow for the first time, lamenting the
mismatch between assets on hand and requirements.[43] During the question
period he was asked about interagency cooperation for national defense and
answered that the Treasury Department cooperated 100 percent, the others almost zero. Therefore, the army and navy took the initiative, preparing
draft legislation and draft documents, including executive orders, for the
Joint Board. The documents were available to the president for emergencies. Strong said the army and the navy were way ahead of the others. They
prepared neutrality proclamations covering certain contingencies, many of
which had been drafted by the Joint Planning Committee, tentatively
approved by the Joint Board, and, said Strong, "put on ice, to be shoved up
when the emergency arises. . . . The only thing left to us is to put down on
paper what we want and trust we will get the President to get out an Executive Order when the bell rings."[44]

Despite keen awareness of the weaknesses in the American security situation, U.S. officers between the wars showed consistent deference to civilian authority. They wanted to prepare the United States for the coming war, but they respected civilian ascendancy in the American system of government, even when the civilians were slow to react as war drew near. The officers of that generation have been accused of being too self-effacing—or too fearful of career damage—to tell the emperor when he had no clothes. The fate of the American garrison in the Philippines might have been different had high-ranking army and navy officers sacrificed themselves in Washington by emphatically notifying civilian authority that the Philippines and Guam would be lost if the Japanese chose to take them. These charges will not be answered here, but the opposing views of two distinguished historians should be noted.

Russell F. Weigley took the U.S. Army to task for not fully informing civilian authority just how ill-prepared the United States was for war in the Pacific before World War II. The army knew that the Philippines could not be defended with the means available, but it "had nurtured . . . a tradition of armed forces so monastically divorced from politics and policy that Army leaders never clearly presented to the civil government their misgivings about challenging Japan in the Western Pacific until the course of challenge was already firmly set." American policy set a course for which American forces were not ready.[45] But Martin Blumenson absolves the military of Weigley's charge: "The military had repeatedly informed the political authorities of the needs for growth and modernization and had just as repeatedly requested funds to initiate the twin process." The villain of the piece, according to Blumenson, was isolationist American society.[46] In any event, resignation of senior officers in protest is exceedingly rare in the American military experience. The U.S. Army's officers of the 1930s were even more docile than top military leadership during the war in Vietnam.

Charles L. Bolte (AWC 1937), another key player in the transition to war, clarifies the rationale for planning for war against Britain and Canada when such a war was highly unlikely: it was training.[47] The expected war was with Japan: "When I was on the [AWC] faculty . . . Orange was the premier problem plan. We had to have a plan for the contiguous theater, in which you could have a war with Mexico or a war with Canada or Britain or something, just to get a scenario to set it up. But the Orange Plan was the one that got the most attention from the students and from the faculty who were guiding the course." He added that even "after the basic decision was made by the political heads, Mr. Churchill and Mr. Roosevelt, that we would win in

Europe first and then turn to the Pacific . . . our Navy was always reluctant as to Europe."[48]

Bolte joined the AWC faculty after he completed the course in 1937. He said that General Marshall closed the college in 1940 because "there were presumably good officers being students at the War College, and on the faculty, so he . . . scattered us around."[49] Bolte at first assisted the chief of the Air Corps. Then he joined the War College Group before going to London as a member of the "special observer group" for the ABC (American-British Staff Conversations). He was close to the centers of power in the critical period just before the United States entered the war, and he would end his career with four stars. Experience as a student and teacher at the college from 1936 to 1940 was a recent memory as he rose quickly in power and influence.

Bolte's recollections are confirmed by those of his friend, John E. Hull (AWC 1938).[50] Hull confirmed that before the war, everyone looked to Japan when war was considered. It is not clear in the documents whether it was the German invasion of Poland in September 1939 or the shocking German successes of May–June 1940 in Western Europe that placed Germany ahead of Japan as the chief concern of American war planners. Hull said that it was generally assumed that in a war with Germany, Italy, and Japan, the United States would go on the strategic defensive in the Pacific and put the main effort in Europe to defeat Germany and Italy.[51] The predisposition then and later was to defeat Germany first.

Hull, like Handy—whom Hull succeeded as assistant chief of staff, Operations Division, when Handy moved up to become deputy chief of staff, U.S. Army—held British planners in high regard and admired General Marshall, calling him "a great man."[52] Hull joined WPD/OPD as a lieutenant colonel on 2 December 1941 and departed a lieutenant general on 2 December 1945. He said of top leadership that Henry L. Stimson, Robert P. Patterson, John J. McCloy, and Robert A. Lovett were an ideal civilian leadership team: "It was a pleasure to work with them because they were not there to gain personal promotion or publicity; they were there to fight a war and they fought it."[53]

Russell Maxwell (AWC 1934) also found himself in the midst of planning for the defense of the Western Hemisphere at the end of the decade in the transition to war. He served as the special assistant to the secretary of war in

1938 as an expert logistician. The *Philadelphia Inquirer* in 1945 credited him with coining the expression "Hemisphere Defense" in a February 1939 report.[54] His papers include correspondence, official papers, and newspaper clippings showing interest in German, Japanese, and Italian penetration of Latin America from 1938 to 1941; American logistical support to Britain and the nations of the hemisphere; bases in Newfoundland and Bermuda; congressional authorization to the secretaries of war and the navy "to assist the governments of American republics to increase their military and naval establishments"; aviation capabilities in Latin America; and a copy of President Roosevelt's 14 April 1939 speech on Pan-America Day before the Governing Board of the Pan-American Union, in which the president both woos and warns the nations of the hemisphere to stay out of European affairs. (It appears that Maxwell contributed to the speech, but the basis for that suspicion is circumstantial, based on the organization of his papers.)

Maxwell's work from 1939 onward brought him into close contact with George Marshall, George Strong of WPD, and Assistant Secretary of War Louis Johnson. When the shooting war in Europe broke out he was named administrator of export control. Later he would ply his trade as a logistical planner by heading up the U.S. Military Mission to the Middle East. Two weeks before Pearl Harbor he was in Cairo, and he remained in the region until 1943. In 1944 he headed the Supply Division in the Office of the Assistant Chief of Staff, G-4. Recall that it was Maxwell's class of 1934 at the Army War College that first dedicated a committee during the War Plans Period of the course to "Participation with Allies." Within four years of his graduation, Maxwell was working with allies in Latin America, and his later work in the Middle East found him the senior American working with the British in the region.

The class of 1934 heard the following remarks from Maj. Gen. Fox Connor during the War Plans Period of the course. They were based on his World War I experience with allies: "Dealing with an enemy is a simple and straightforward matter when contrasted with securing close cooperation with an ally." Connor, Dwight D. Eisenhower's mentor, continued: "I would rather fight an alliance than a single nation and an alliance of three than an alliance of two enemies." Here was a soldier-to-soldier warning about the problems inherent in waging coalition warfare.[55]

As early as 1934, the committee addressing "Participation with Allies" set up what it called the Inter-Allied War Council to coordinate the alliance. It was based on the Supreme War Council of the world war and anticipated the political and military command and control of an alliance in a single theater.[56] Seven graduating classes of the Army War College had been thinking through the nuances of coalition warfare when the college closed its doors in 1940. Their preparation caused the State Department's Robert Murphy, political adviser to Eisenhower during the war, to remark that the senior military "had the benefit of previous instruction in political problems, such as the excellent course given at the Army War College," but Murphy had no equivalent training in military matters.[57]

Improved communications and the increasing importance of public opinion would further compound the complexities inherent in alliances. Hitler used radio and film to influence German popular opinion, and Roosevelt's radio talks were used to influence American opinion, both in "real time." The public relations aspect of wartime leadership was not lost on the students at the Army War College, nor were they naive waifs regarding the complexities of interalliance cooperation. Forcing thought about the problems of coalition warfare was, after all, the purpose of installing "Participation with Allies" in the college curriculum. Mass communication and public relations were taken into consideration in college war planning.

Student committees also gave a great deal of thought to war aims and to war termination. A group of students from the 1934 committee insisted upon producing—at some cost to themselves in time and effort—a minority report, reflecting awareness of the danger of imposing a vindictive peace that would eventually result in the vanquished demanding revision of an unfair treaty. One can almost see them tracking events in Germany as Hitler's name became known in 1933.[58]

Student officers of the class of 1934 were confronted with problems in an academic setting that many of them would see again as they led troops in the field or as they served on high-level staffs. In addition to Maxwell, at least four others from that class would serve in WPD: Leslie L. MacDill, 1935–38; Clayton L. Bissell, 1939–42; Charles W. Bundy, 1941; and Ernest N. Harmon, 1941.[59] Maxwell, Bissell, and Harmon would retire as major generals.

The record shows close and constant formal and informal contact between the Army War College and the General Staff. The assistant chief of staff, War Plans Division, and his colleagues, the principals on the War Department General Staff, addressed the students each year and tapped the college to work on problems of professional interest to them. Key officers went from college to General Staff assignments and back to the college to teach or to command the college. Former commandants and deputy commandants served as the chief of staff of the army and as the deputy chief of staff. The army and the navy invested two years of the careers of handpicked officers, like Halsey and Handy, to attend both the Army and Naval War Colleges (so that the services understood each other), and had the good sense to use their skills in the crisis to come. The small American army between the wars was enlightened in developing carefully selected people and in assigning them to key jobs in the transition to war. The informed creativity of students was exploited by the more cautious General Staff.

# 14

# Conclusions

> The facts of history never come to us "pure," since they
> do not and cannot exist in a pure form: they are always
> refracted through the mind of the recorder.
> —**E. H. CARR,** *WHAT IS HISTORY?*

Playing armchair strategist allows the reader to simulate the way army war planners looked at the world. Hindsight permits the illusion of authority as we pronounce on the might-have-beens of a past we think we understand.

For example, had Hitler expected the rapidity and scale of the German victories of the spring of 1940, he might have crushed the British forces at Dunkirk and followed with a hasty invasion of Britain. The Royal Air Force and Royal Navy would have exacted a price, but consider for a moment Hitler's readiness to roll the dice before and after June 1940. His professional soldiers advised against remilitarization of the Rhineland in 1936, against rushing events in Middle Europe in 1937–38 (his demand for the Sudetenland and his insistence upon the union of Germany and Austria), against the attack on Poland in 1939 and on France in 1940. His generals reasoned that the transition from the Reichswehr—the "treaty army" of one hundred thousand—to the Wehrmacht would take time. Integrating millions of men, masses of equipment, and new doctrine was no small matter. But Hitler would not wait. Again and again the soldiers urged caution. Again and again Hitler was bold, and right—always. Similarly, in 1941 the German professional soldiers advised against Barbarossa, the invasion of the Soviet Union.

Hitler was a risktaker. He might have been able to pull off a hasty invasion of a Britain that had just taken some hard knocks on the Continent.

Britain was suffering increasingly heavy losses at sea to German U-boats and was about to fight the Battle of Britain in the air. Britain stood alone. Invasion of Britain made more operational and strategic sense than attacking the Soviet Union before Britain was knocked out of the war. Defeating Britain would have permitted Hitler to turn against the Soviet Union in a one-front war.

However, the Germans having decided to strike east, one marvels that Germany could not work out with Japan a coordinated campaign to knock the Soviet Union out of the war. It was, after all, a near-run thing in 1941–42 with the Germans attacking alone. A little patience on the part of the Japanese in picking up the European possessions in the Far East might have avoided the near-suicidal war with the United States. Attacking Pearl Harbor was necessary to protect the Japanese flank exposed to the United States as Japan moved to the Dutch East Indies, French Indochina, and British Singapore-Malaysia-Burma, and perhaps India. Concerned about the U.S. Navy in a strike to the south, Japan was in for a penny, in for a pound. That is, if there was to be war with the United States, then go for the jugular: the U.S. fleet at Pearl Harbor. But had the Japanese move to the south taken place after the Soviet Union was out of the war—and when Britain was isolated—Japan might have negotiated with the United States for a Japanese Monroe Doctrine in its own neighborhood, the main objective of Japanese policy.

What would U.S. policy have been in 1942–43 in a world in which the attack on Pearl Harbor had not taken place; with the Soviet Union divided between Germany and Japan (a Brest-Litovsk on a grander scale); with Germany in control of Europe from the white snows of the Urals to the White Cliffs of Dover (or including the United Kingdom with a Vichy-style government); and with Manchuria and Chinese coastal cities under Japanese control as the Communists and Chiang Kai-shek continued their civil war in the Chinese interior?

Japan's barbarous conduct in China; the *Panay* incident of 1937, in which Japan sank a U.S. warship in China; Hitler's unilateral revisions of the Treaty of Versailles, invasion of Poland in 1939, and invasion of France in 1940—none of these events brought the United States into the war as a belligerent. The American inclination was to view Versailles as a vindictive peace. Too bad about China, but it was far away. U.S. territories had not been violated. Best to tend one's own garden.

The Japanese might have proposed Japanese-American cooperation in the Pacific and in the Far East to address the anarchy in the former European possessions, whose mother countries, now occupied by Germany, were unable to administer colonies. Perhaps Japanese mandates in the East Indies, Indochina, Singapore, Malaysia, and Burma and independence for India would be acceptable. Perhaps there would be a north-south line of demarcation through Midway, assigning Japanese and American spheres of interest in the Pacific.

Given German and Japanese control of Europe, Asia, and half of the Pacific, the United States would look to its own security. Western Hemispheric solidarity from Newfoundland or Iceland through the Caribbean to South America, and from Alaska to Midway to South America, might be about right in the new world order of 1943.

This excursion, based on actual historical events, is like the strategic ruminations that went into war planning in the 1930s. War planning proceeded from geopolitical and economic realities, professional evaluations of social and cultural factors, military estimates of capabilities, and the weighing of intangibles like morale, public opinion, and propaganda—all in the future. There is something surreal in a third-rate military thinking first-rate global schemes.

Planning for war is more than preparing formal documents for approval by duly constituted authority and filing them in a secure container in a war ministry. In the United States between the world wars it was a process at the Army War College and at the War Department General Staff that shaped the way a generation of military professionals thought about future wars of all kinds at the national level. That generation provided the nation with combat leaders and strategic planners in World War II; military governors; leaders in the Korean War, the Cold War, and Vietnam; presidential advisers, cabinet secretaries, and a president of the United States.

Soldiers at the Army War College planned for a two-ocean war from 1934 onward. The principal foes from 1934 onward were Germany and Japan. All officers who passed through the college knew that at least one committee each year addressed "Participation with Allies" during the War Plans Period of the course of instruction. Each class from 1934 to 1940 heard what their classmates had to say about the United States fighting as a part of an alliance: in the Pacific in 1934, in the Pacific and in Europe in 1935, 1936, and 1937, and in South America in 1938, 1939, and 1940. In the spring of 1940 the students worked on Rainbow X, in immediate response to the new circumstances presented to the world by German military successes in Western Europe.

In each of the scenarios from 1934 to 1940, students assigned to "Participation with Allies" found themselves scanning the horizon for other enemies even while planning for the specific theater assigned. While planning for war with Japan in 1934, they tracked events in Europe carefully. Conversely, engaged in an alliance fighting a Nazi-led coalition in 1935, 1936, and 1937, planners kept a sharp eye on Japan and events in the Pacific and Asia. Assigned in 1938 and 1939 to support Brazil against German and Italian infiltration into the Western Hemisphere, planners expressed concern for a Japanese threat to U.S. possessions and interests in the Pacific and wondered if they should confront Germany and Italy in Europe instead of in Brazil. Knowledge of contemporary international relations forced planners to consider the possibility that the United States could make a serious mistake in committing initially scarce resources to the wrong theater. Global war was much on their minds in the mid-1930s. So was the realization that transition to war and its early stages would be critical. The degree to which Army War College planners were convinced that American material strength ensured ultimate victory is striking. That conclusion was not chauvinistic. Events would demonstrate that American material resources would smother Germany and Japan while simultaneously providing masses of materiel to keep Britain, the Soviet Union, and China in the war.

Synchronizing means, ways, and ends is what strategists do for the nations they serve. Time was needed to transform American potential into actual military power. Fortunately, industrial mobilization for war was one of the lessons learned in the Great War. Legislation, organization, massive productive capacity, and a ready work force were the means. They were available before the war, as was presidential leadership. Industrial mobilization began two to three years before the attack on Pearl Harbor. The first peacetime draft in American history was also in place before the attack. After a decade at about 140,000 men, U.S. Army strength increased to 179,968 men in 1937 and to 1.5 million in 1941. And the United States was fighting an undeclared war in the Atlantic. All before Pearl Harbor. Japan's attack on Pearl Harbor was an operational surprise. The coming of war was not.

The ends of war with Germany and Japan were spelled out in Army War College planning, and they were the ends the United States and its allies chose. Germany would be defeated and occupied so that there would be no doubt in the future about what had happened. No claim of a stab in the back would be possible. The Japanese would be driven back to their home islands after the expected successes of their early offensives. Then Japan would be blockaded by sea and air and would be invaded, if necessary.

With the means in place that would allow the United States and its allies to grind down inexorably any foe or combination of foes, and with the ends clearly stated, it remained for planners to decide the ways to use the means to arrive at the desired ends.

In chapters 4–10 we have seen the realism of the planning conducted at the Army War College from 1934 to 1940. The Color Plans were continued after 1934, but the introduction of "Participation with Allies" in that year produced the plans that anticipated the course of World War II in the Atlantic and in the Pacific. Assuming superior French and British capabilities in a 1935 war with a German-led coalition, planners dedicated a modest American force to the European theater, saving most of the American strength for the war against Japan. However, when German superiority in Europe was assumed in later iterations, the AWC planners decided that Germany must be defeated first. The actual circumstances after Germany's defeat of France in 1940 affirmed the Germany-first decision.

Similarly, in both coalition planning for a war with Japan in 1934 and in the pure one-on-one Orange planning throughout the interwar period, the AWC planners thought through the course of war with Japan under various assumptions. A key consideration was what one assumed regarding the fate of the American naval base in the Philippines. Retention of the base in Manila would permit a swift projection of American power into the western Pacific. Early loss of the Philippines would rule out a long thrust as too risky and dictate a deliberate campaign to establish aviation and logistics support bases en route. A two-ocean war with alliances arrayed on both the friendly and enemy sides demanded a basic decision regarding priority of American effort.

The various scenarios the Army War College faculty presented to the students resulted in various plans. When it seemed that war was inevitable, planners turned to a conservative strategy that was initially defensive. In 1938, 1939, and 1940 the AWC planners focused on defense of the continental United States, American overseas possessions, Orange, and the Western Hemisphere, coupled with mobilization planning. This was explicit recognition that the United States needed to buy time. There would be no bold adventures abroad until America had transformed its vast potential in men and materiel into actual power available to the policymaker and strategist. The so-called strategic triangle, represented by drawing lines from Alaska to Hawaii to the Panama Canal Zone, was neither the concept of simple-minded provincials nor the longing of isolationists for some Golden Age. It was a practical first phase of a strategy well suited to national needs.

The temptation to dissipate U.S. strength by sending armed forces every-where at once had to be resisted. In the late 1930s danger to the United States was visible in the Atlantic, in the Pacific, and in the Western Hemi-sphere. The turn inward to hemispheric defense was not a reflexive retreat from reality. It was sound strategic planning. If national strategy is seen as the reconciliation of ways, means, and ends to improve a state's security, the most obvious American shortcomings in 1938 and 1939 were the means necessary for waging simultaneous war with Japan (long regarded as in-evitable), a war in Europe (increasingly possible), and a war to defend the Western Hemisphere (where significant numbers of Germans, Italians, and Japanese could be found). Time was needed to prepare for an increasingly likely big war. Defense of the strategic triangle made sense for at least two reasons: it was something the United States *could* do with the modest means available; and it would buy time during which the nation would mobilize without taking big risks. Running like a red thread through all of the plan-ning at the college was complete confidence that the next war would be a long war of materiel during which America would grow stronger as its ene-mies grew weaker. A modest strategy in the first phase of war made good sense and matched the modest means immediately available.

The college plans were lucid about the ends of war with Germany and Japan. In both cases decisive military victory was intended and expected. If Japan did not surrender as a consequence of bombardment and blockade, invasion was planned. There was no doubt that war would be brought to Germany. The political objective of the United States was imposition of its will—a clear end.

The ways, the concepts guiding strategy, were also in place, but specifics necessarily had to await the unfolding of a number of variables. Membership in the contesting alliances did not hold still until 1936. Italy, it might be recalled, was an ally of the United States in the 1935 scenario but was assigned to the enemy camp in 1936. After 1936 the German-Italian-Japanese lineup remained fixed, as did the American-British-French-Chi-nese alliance. (The Russians were assumed to be allies in an American war with Germany and/or Japan, but Russian reliability was questionable.) The kind and degree of American participation in the war in Europe depended upon the esti-mates of the relative strengths of the competing forces in Europe. When the scenario indicated that the British and French could con-tain Germany, America's military efforts were weighted toward the war with Japan. When Germany was assumed to dominate in Europe, the United States weighted its military efforts toward Europe.

The ends of strategy were clear: to impose American will on Germany and Japan. The means were mobilization of millions of American men and the industrial mobilization that would make the United States the "arsenal of democracy." The ways of the strategic concept had to remain flexible, a list of options, until the composition and relative strengths of the contending coalitions were known. German dominance of Middle and Western Europe in June 1940 settled the matter for American strategists. It would be "Germany first," as it had been in the 1936 and 1937 AWC planning.

The work at the Army War College responded to the concerns of the War Department General Staff and to Rainbow planning. Evidence linking the AWC plans of 1934–40 to General Staff planning is direct. Correspondence between the General Staff and the college is on file at the Military History Institute as the "-0" (zero) and "flat" files. That correspondence shows that the college routinely responded to staff needs by directing students toward projects desired by the General Staff. Malin Craig asked the college to study mobilization, and it did. The college was asked to study Purple, the defense of Brazil, and it did. In 1940 the college was asked to study Rainbow X, and it did. That the college would shift its attention to the Western Hemisphere after 1938 as General Marshall and the General Staff did the same was not a coincidence. The college was doing what the army thought needed to be done. The rotation of key people from the college to the General Staff and back kept the school in the army mainstream. Commandant Simonds, for example, ran the War Plans Division of the War Department General Staff and the Army War College before serving as MacArthur's deputy chief of staff, and each year from 1934 to 1940 several AWC graduates were assigned to WPD.

Many less-famous officers performed well in key jobs in the transition from peace to war. Thomas T. Handy provided unprecedented continuity in the War Plans Division/Operations Division, serving from 1936 until 1944 (except for June 1940 to June 1941, when he was with troops). Thompson Lawrence taught at the college from 1938 to 1940 and in 1940 continued his work on Rainbow 4 for WPD as a leader in the so-called War College Group. Charles Bolte joined the faculty upon his graduation in 1937. He later served as a member of the special observer group for the ABC conversations after working for WPD as a member of the War College Group in 1940. John E. Hull (1938) succeeded Handy (who succeeded Eisenhower) as assistant chief of staff, OPD, and worked closely with General Marshall throughout the war. Russell Maxwell (1934) also planned for hemispheric defense at the end of the 1930s before serving as the administrator of export control. He was later chief of the U.S. Military Mission to the Middle East and head of the Supply Division, G-4. The point is that many important but unglamorous jobs in the transition to war were done by men who passed through the Army War College between 1934 and 1940.

There were certain constants in the planning done at AWC that became a part of the collective belief system of the officers who attended the college and served in key positions. Some of the beliefs were constraints. In good times and in bad, the U.S. Army of the 1920s and 1930s was starved thin. Army leaders knew that until there was a crisis, the army would remain weak. They also understood—and fully accepted—that they were to execute policy determined by political authority. It was not for the military to make policy. Institutional constraints caused the officers of the 1930s to be more passive than their heirs. Organizational constraints can also be found in the State Department's prewar unwillingness to involve itself in war planning and in the inability of the army and navy to accept unity of command. "Cooperation" was the best the army and navy could do. It was not good enough.

Constraints demanded careful analysis and imaginative solutions to prepare the sleeping giant for the transition to war. The result was sound planning. American professional soldiers were convinced that a major war would be a long war of materiel, and they were confident that the United States would win that war against any enemy and against any combination of enemies. The United States needed something less than a year to prepare civilians to be soldiers in modern war and more than a year, probably two years, to convert to a war economy. Given a year or two to prepare, and resisting the temptation to dissipate resources by trying to do too many things at once, the United States would, in due course, crush its enemies. That is what happened.

Seven years before the United States declared war, and with increasing certainty as time passed, planners at the Army War College sorted out friend from foe. The United States would ally with Britain and its dominions, France, China, and probably Russia against Germany, Austria, Hungary, Italy, and Japan. The scenarios changed, but it was generally assumed that Germany would be the toughest enemy and the Japanese would go on the defensive after grabbing resource-rich Southeast Asia. Germany had to be defeated first, requiring ground combat on the Continent after weakening Germany with bombardment and blockade. Planners hoped that blockade from the sea and bombardment from the air could force a Japanese surrender without invasion, but they were prepared to conduct a bloody invasion, if necessary.

The nations involved made it clear that the issue was total and world war. The phrases "total victory" and "unconditional surrender" were not used in AWC planning—that would come later—but "imposition of will" was. The assumptions of ground combat in Germany and occupation of Germany made the step to demand unconditional surrender a short one. There would be no "stab in the back" theory and no "shame of Versailles" after World War II. Defeat of Germany would be unambiguous.

The students, faculty, and commandants of the Army War College and the General Staff officers constituted a nucleus, the insiders who ran the army in peacetime, planned for war at the college and in the War Plans Division, and led during World War II. "Participation with Allies," coalition plans produced at the college between 1934 and 1940, became the Rainbow Plans whose options guided the transition to war and the course of World War II.

The college had done its job well. The data produced in considering the strengths and weaknesses of potential friend and foe across the full spectrum of national power—political, economic, psychosociological, and military—was voluminous and useful in real-world planning. But the process was even more useful. Continuous reconsideration of plans, and the rationale for them, was important in forming a habit of mind critical to strategists. The professionals of the small army did the mechanics of planning at the Army War College as it was done in the War Plans Division, and they made it a habit to think about war at the level of national strategy. That habit, formed at the college, explains in part how American officers, whose command experience of skeletal units was typically at lower levels, were capable of stepping into key positions near the apex of political power and into high command with a great degree of confidence and competence. They were dedicated professionals well schooled in tactics, operations, and staff work at Leavenworth and, as General Handy put it, "the Ph.D.s of the Army" because of the Army War College experience. A third-rate army educated first-rate strategists. It was an education that would serve them and the nation conspicuously well.

# Appendix A

## AWC Graduates 1934–1940 Who Served in WPD 1935–1945

| Name | AWC Year | Tour at WPD |
|---|---|---|
| MacDill, L. | 1934 | 18 Aug. 1935–9 Nov. 1938 |
| Bissell, C. L. | 1934 | 28 Jun. 1939–15 Feb. 1942 |
| Bundy, C. W. | 1934 | 16 Mar. 1941–12 Dec. 1941 |
| Harmon, E. N. | 1934 | 26 May 1941–18 Jun. 1941 |
| Streett, St. C. | 1935 | 20 Aug. 1935–26 Jun. 1939 |
| Perkins, R. M. | 1935 | 1 Jul. 1936–27 Jun. 1939 |
| Handy, T. T. | 1935 | 14 Aug. 1936–25 Jul. 1940 and 2 Aug. 1941–21 Oct. 1944 |
| Allen, L. C. | 1935 | 28 May 1941–10 Feb. 1942 |
| McKee, J. L. | 1935 | 20 Jul. 1941–20 Aug. 1942 |
| Greely, J. N. | 1936 | 1 Jul. 1936–22 Aug. 1937 |
| Walker, W. H. | 1936 | 5 Aug. 1937–1 Apr. 1941 |
| Crawford, R. W. | 1936 | 14 Mar. 1939–22 Jun. 1942 |
| Russell, C. A. | 1936 | 1 Jul. 1939–28 Nov. 1944 |
| MacKelvie, J. W. | 1936 | 10 Feb. 1941–13 Apr. 1942 |
| Malony, H. J. | 1936 | 26 Apr. 1941–18 Jun. 1941 |
| Nevins, A. S. | 1936 | 12 May 1941–2 Aug. 1942 |
| Irvine, W. W. | 1936 | 21 May 1941–17 Apr. 1942 |
| Carrington, G. deL. | 1936 | 7 Jun. 1941–18 Jun. 1941 |
| Ridgway, M. B. | 1937 | 30 Sep. 1939–24 Jan. 1942 |
| Kilburn, C. S. | 1937 | 12 May 1941–16 Aug. 1941 |
| Barber, H. A. | 1937 | 12 Jul. 1941–16 May 1943 |
| Kibler, A. F. | 1938 | 1 Mar. 1939–13 Jul. 1942 |
| Harrison, W. K. | 1938 | 16 Aug. 1939–13 Jul. 1942 |
| Scobey, W. P. | 1938 | 16 May 1940–9 May 1942 |
| Slocum, LeC. H. | 1938 | 1 Feb. 1941–29 Dec. 1941 |
| Davis, T. D. | 1938 | 17 Jul. 1941–6 Feb. 1943 |
| Hull, J. E. | 1938 | 2 Dec. 1941–2 Sep. 1945 |
| Zellars, J. T. | 1938 | 7 Feb. 1942–15 May 1942 |
| Loomis, H. F. | 1939 | 21 Jun. 1939–1 Dec. 1941 |
| Sherrill, S. H. | 1939 | 21 Jun. 1939–12 Aug. 1942 |

| Name | AWC Year | Tour at WPD |
|------|----------|-------------|
| Gerow, L. S. | 1939 | 5 Jun. 1940–14 May 1942 |
| Upston, J. E. | 1939 | 27 Jan. 1941–27 Feb. 1944 |
| Gruenther, A. M. | 1939 | 1 May 1941–18 Jun. 1941 |
| Jaynes, L. C. | 1939 | 21 Jul. 1941–10 Mar. 1942 |
| Balmer, J. D. | 1939 | 6 Dec. 1941–16 Jun. 1942 |
| Gallagher, P. E. | 1939 | 5 Jan. 1942–4 Feb. 1942 |
| Pierce, J. R. | 1940 | 22 May 1940–31 Dec. 1940 |
| Johnston, O. R. | 1940 | 22 May 1940–15 Feb. 1941 |
| Hays, G. P. | 1940 | 22 May 1941–18 Jun. 1941 |
| Lemnitzer, L. L. | 1940 | 28 May 1941–18 Jun. 1941 |

*Source:* Compiled by cross-referencing HRC 321, WPD, appendix D, "Master Personnel List, Arrivals and Departures," 1 September 1921 to 2 September 1945, Center for Military History, and *Directory of U.S. Army War College Graduates* (Carlisle, Pa.: Alumni Association, USAWC, 2000).

# Appendix **B**

## AWC Graduates 1934–1939 in High-Level Staff Jobs, March 1940

*See page 162.*

**APPENDIX B ★ AWC Graduates 1934–1939 in High-Level Staff Jobs, March 1940**

| Year | No. of AWC Grads | No. in WD, 1940 | G-1 | G-2 | G-3 | G-4 | WPD | ODCS | OASW | AWC | ENG | CAC | FA | INF | AC | SC | CAV | AG | QM | ORD | AIC | Other |
|---|---|---|---|---|---|---|---|---|---|---|---|---|---|---|---|---|---|---|---|---|---|---|
| 1939 | 96 | 26 | 3 | 1 | 2 | 5 | 2 | | | 2 | | 2 | 1 | | 4 | 1 | | | 1 | | | 2 |
| 1938 | 93 | 21 | 3 | 2 | 3 | 1 | 2 | 2 | | 1 | | 1 | | | 3 | | | | | 1 | 1 | 1 |
| 1937 | 95 | 27 | 2 | 3 | 3 | 2 | 1 | 1 | 2 | 2 | 1 | | | | 1 | 1 | 2 | 2 | 1 | 1 | 1 | 2 |
| 1936 | 95 | 25 | 1 | | 3 | 3 | 3 | 1 | | 3 | | 1 | 2 | | 3 | | 3 | 1 | | | | |
| 1935 | 82 | 13 | 1 | 1 | 3 | 1 | 1 | 1 | 1 | 2 | | 1 | | 2 | | | | | | | | 1 |
| 1934 | 84 | 15 | 2 | 1 | 1 | 1 | 1 | | 2 | 1 | | | | | | | | 1 | | 2 | | 1 |
| Total | 545 | 127* | 12 | 8 | 15 | 13 | 10 | 5 | 5 | 11 | 1 | 5 | 3 | 2 | 11 | 2 | 5 | 4 | 2 | 4 | 2 | 7 |

*Source:* Compiled by cross-referencing *AWC Directory,* 2000, and *War Department Telephone Directory,* 1 March 1940.

*In March 1940, 23 percent of AWC graduates 1934–39 were in Washington, most of them in key staff jobs.

*Note:* The "Other" category refers to National Guard Bureau, Headquarters Washington Provisional Brigade, General Staff (without further description), Federal Security Agency, Inspector General, Secretary General Staff, and Surgeon General.

*Abbreviations:*

| | |
|---|---|
| WPD | War Plans Division |
| ODCS | Office of Deputy Chief of Staff |
| OASW | Office of Assistant Secretary of War |
| AWC | Army War College |
| ENG | Engineers |
| CAC | Coast Artillery Corps |
| FA | Field Artillery |
| INF | Infantry |
| AC | Air Corps |
| SC | Signal Corps |
| CAV | Cavalry |
| AG | Adjutant General |
| QM | Quartermaster |
| ORD | Ordnance |
| AIC | Army Industrial College |

# Appendix **C**

## AWC Graduates 1934–1940 in High-Level Staff Jobs, November 1941

*See page 164.*

**APPENDIX C ★ AWC Graduates 1934–1940 in High-Level Staff Jobs, November 1941**

| Year | No. of AWC Grads | No. in WD, 1941 | G-1 | G-2 | G-3 | G-4 | WPD | GHQ | AAF | GS | BPR | ODCS | ENG | CAC | FA | INF | AC | SC | CAV | AG | QM | ORD | Other |
|---|---|---|---|---|---|---|---|---|---|---|---|---|---|---|---|---|---|---|---|---|---|---|---|
| 1940* | 100 | 44 | 4 | 5 | 4 | 5 |  | 7 | 2 | 7 | 1 |  |  | 1 |  |  |  |  | 2 | 1 | 3 |  | 2 |
| 1939 | 96 | 42 | 1 |  | 1 | 8 | 4 | 5 | 4 | 3 | 1 | 1 | 1 | 3 |  | 1 | 2 |  |  |  | 2 | 2 | 2 |
| 1938 | 93 | 37 | 3 | 2 | 8 | 2 | 4 | 3 | 1 | 4 |  | 1 | 1 | 1 |  |  | 3 | 1 |  |  |  | 1 | 3 |
| 1937 | 95 | 32 | 1 | 1 | 1 | 3 | 1 | 5 | 4 | 4 |  | 1 |  | 1 |  | 1 | 1 | 1 |  | 1 | 2 | 2 | 2 |
| 1936 | 95 | 21 | 1 | 1 | 2 | 3 | 3 | 3 | 1 | 2 |  |  |  |  |  | 1 | 1 |  |  | 1 |  |  | 2 |
| 1935 | 82 | 19 |  | 1 | 1 | 1 | 2 |  | 1 | 2 | 2 |  | 1 |  | 1 | 1 | 1 | 2 |  |  | 1 | 2 | 4 |
| 1934 | 84 | 20 | 1 |  | 2 |  | 2 | 1 |  | 1 | 1 |  |  |  | 1 | 1 |  |  | 3 |  | 2 | 1 | 2 |
| Total | 645 | 215** | 11 | 10 | 19 | 22 | 16 | 24 | 13 | 23 | 5 | 3 | 3 | 6 | 2 | 5 | 8 | 4 | 5 | 3 | 10 | 8 | 17 |

*Source:* Compiled by cross-referencing *AWC Directory, 2000,* and *War Department Telephone Directory,* 15 November 1941.

*A third of this class, the last until 1951, was ordered to special duty in the War Department on 6 June 1940. The remainder of the class conducted studies for the WDGS (MH1, file 1-105, 1939–40, 4).

**In November 1941, 33 percent of AWC graduates 1934–40 were in Washington, most in key staff positions.

*Notes:* The "Other" category refers to Judge Advocate General, Inspector General, Executive Officer to President, Chemical Warfare, Selective Service, Chief of Finance, Surgeon General, and Office of the Undersecretary of War.

The following positions were in the 1941 *War Department Telephone Directory* but not in the 1940 version:

a. BPR (Bureau of Public Relations).

b. AAF Staff. In 1940, Air Corps had more than twice as many officers as any other branch. (Coast Artillery and Cavalry had five each.) By 1941 there is an Army Air Force with staff sections (A-1, A-2, A-3, A-4, etc.).

Obviously Air Corps officers were stockpiled to form AAF staff.

| *Abbreviations:* | | | |
|---|---|---|---|
| WPD | War Plans Division | FA | Field Artillery |
| GHQ | General Headquarters | INF | Infantry |
| AAF | Army Air Force | AC | Air Corps |
| GS | General Staff | SC | Signal Corps |
| BPR | Bureau of Public Relations | CAV | Cavalry |
| ODCS | Office of Deputy Chief of Staff | AG | Adjutant General |
| ENG | Engineers | QM | Quartermaster |
| CAC | Coast Artillery Corps | ORD | Ordnance |

# Appendix D

## Eisenhower's OPD Roster by Rank, 3 April 1942

| Name | AWC Class | Rank | Branch | Serial No. |
|------|-----------|------|--------|------------|
| Eisenhower, Dwight D. | — | Major Gen. | — | 03822 |
| Miller, Lehman W. | 1940 | Brig. Gen. | — | 03773 |
| Crawford, Robert W. | 1936 | " | — | 03667 |
| MacKelvie, Jay W. | 1936 | " | — | 05476 |
| Townsend, James R. | — | " | — | 06357 |
| Handy, Thomas T. | 1935 | " | — | 04665 |
| Streett, St. Clair | 1935 | " | — | 09619 |
| Scobey, William P. | 1938 | Colonel | INF | 04898 |
| Russell, Carl A., Jr. | 1936 | " | INF | 05144 |
| Sherrill, Stephen H. | 1939 | " | SC | 05258 |
| Harrison, William K., Jr. | 1938 | " | CAV | 05279 |
| McKee, John L. | 1935 | " | INF | 05613 |
| Irvine, Willard W. | 1936 | " | CAC | 05838 |
| Kibler, A. Franklin | 1938 | " | FA | 06668 |
| Wiggins, Porter P. | — | " | INF | 07052 |
| Zellars, John T. | 1938 | " | INF | 07056 |
| Nevins, Arthur S. | 1936 | " | INF | 07110 |
| Maddocks, Ray T. | — | " | CAV | 07291 |
| Hull, John E. | 1938 | " | INF | 07377 |
| Blizzard, John C., Jr. | — | " | INF | 07581 |
| Davis, Thomas D. | 1938 | " | INF | 08223 |
| Barber, Henry A., Jr. | 1937 | " | INF | 08576 |
| Upston, John E. | 1939 | " | AC | 010595 |
| Webster, Robert M. | — | " | AC | 011946 |
| Walker, Kenneth N. | — | " | AC | 012510 |
| Douglass, Robert W., Jr. | — | " | AC | 014972 |

*Source:* File "Officers, War Department General Staff, Operations Division," in MHI, Biography Room, *DOD Telephone Directories.*

*Note:* Five of the six brigadier generals are AWC 1935–40 graduates. Thirteen of the nineteen colonels are AWC 1935–39 graduates. Nine of the thirteen AWC 1935–39 graduates listed as colonels were later generals.

| *Abbreviations:* | AC | Air Corps | FA | Field Artillery |
|---|---|---|---|---|
| | CAC | Coast Artillery Corps | INF | Infantry |
| | CAV | Cavalry | SC | Signal Corps |

# Appendix E

### ★ ★ ★

## Colors, War Plans

| Color | Country | Color | Country |
|-------|---------|-------|---------|
| Black | Germany | Green | Mexico |
| Blue | United States | Maroon | Italy |
| Brown | Philippines | Olive | Dutch Indies |
| Carnation | Manchukuo | Orange | Japan |
| Cerise | British India | Pink | Russia |
| Crimson | Canada | Rainbow | League of Nations |
| Gold | France | Red | Great Britain |
| Gray | *One or more Caribbean countries:* | Scarlet | Australia |
| | Guatemala | Tan | Cuba |
| | Honduras | Violet* | Intervention—Latin America |
| | Nicaragua | White | Internal disturbances |
| | Costa Rica | Yellow | China |
| | El Salvador | | |
| | Haiti | | |
| | Dominican Republic | | |

*Source:* MHI, WP 1A, 1939, card showing color codes by country.

*"Purple" was for Brazil after 1938.

*Note:* There were changes in color codes over the years, but the colors used in the text come from this list.

# Appendix F

## The War Planning Process

Brig. Gen. Walter Krueger, assistant chief of staff, WPD, WDGS, began student war planning on 1 March 1938 with an annual presentation called "The War Plans Division, War Department General Staff." The presentation can be found at MHI in the curricular files, War Plans Course No. 5, 1937–38. For the sake of brevity, this appendix includes two charts: "Organization Chart, War Plans Division" (p. 15), and "Position of War Plans Division in the General Set-up" (p. 16).

Organization Chart, War Plans Division, War Department General Staff

**Assistant Chief of Staff, War Plans Division**

Functions

1. Chief of Division.
2. Member of the Joint Board.

**Executive, War Plans Division**

Functions

1. Administrative matters.
2. Collaboration with State Department on matters pertaining to international conferences and other international subjects.

**Operations Section**

Personnel

Five (5) Officers of the Regular Army

Functions

1. Matters pertaining to Joint Army and Navy Plans.
2. Strategical Plans.
3. Organizational and Mobilization Problems affecting War Plans.
4. Matters pertaining to Joint Army and Navy Exercises.
5. Maneuvers, CPX, Terrain Exercises, and Staff Rides involving units higher than the Army.
6. Exercises involving tests of War Plans.
7. Unit Mobilization Plan, GHQ.
8. Special studies of broad problems of National Defense.

**Supplies and Projects Section**

Personnel

Four (4) Officers of the Regular Army and one (1) Officer of the National Guard

Functions

1. Defense Projects and Defense Plans of Overseas Departments.
2. Harbor Defense Projects.
3. Antiaircraft Defense.
4. Strategic Highway Projects.
5. Supply Problems affecting War Plans.
6. Budgetary matters.
7. Special studies of broad problems of National Defense.

**Joint Planning Committee**

Personnel

Four (4) Officers selected from the personnel of WPD

Functions

1. Joint Army and Navy Plans.
2. Joint Army and Navy Exercises.
3. Other matters pertaining to National Defense and involving action of the Joint Board.

**The Aeronautical Board**

One (1) Officer of War Plans Division serves as a member of this Board.

APPROVED:
OCT. 20, 1937

W. KRUEGER,
Brigadier General,
Asst. Chief of Staff

The Position of the War Plans Division, War Department General Staff, in the General Set-up

# Appendix G

## AWC Graduates 1934–1940, by Year

### CLASS OF 1934, RESIDENT

| Name | Rank | Branch/Service | Name | Rank | Branch/Service |
|------|------|----------------|------|------|----------------|
| Abbott, J. S. | CAPT | USN | Harding, Edwin F. | MG | GO |
| Almond, Edward M. | LTG | GO | Harmon, Ernest N. | MG | GO |
| Amsden, William F. | CAPT | USN | Henry, Stephen G. R. | MG | GO |
| Andrus, Clift | MG | GO | Hershey, Lewis B. | GEN | GO |
| Beasley, Rex W. | MG | GO | Hibbs, Louis E. | MG | GO |
| Bingham, Sidney V. | COL | CAV | Hinman, Dale D. | BG | GO |
| Bissell, Clayton L. | MG | USAF | Hodges, Courtney H. | GEN | GO |
| Bradley, Omar N. | GA | GO | Hurdis, Charles E. | MG | GO |
| Brett, Sereno E. | BG | GO | Jarman, Sanderford | MG | GO |
| Brock, Arthur W., Jr. | COL | AC | Jones, Roy M. | COL | AC |
| Bundy, Charles W. | COL | CAC | Kelton, Edwin C. | COL | ENG |
| Cauldwell, Oscar R. | MG | USMC | Kimball, Allen R. | BG | GO |
| Chambers, William E. | BG | GO | Kimberly, Allen | COL | CAC |
| Christian, Thomas J. J. | BG | GO | Kingman, Allen F. | BG | GO |
| Clarkson, Percy W. | MG | GO | Kirk, James | MG | GO |
| Conklin, John F. | BG | GO | Lawes, Herbert J. | BG | GO |
| Davidson, Lewis C. | COL | INF | Lindroth, Elmer G. | COL | INF |
| Davis, Louis P. | CAPT | USN | Lindt, John H. | COL | CAC |
| Dawley, Ernest J. | MG | GO | Lynd, William E. | MG | USAF |
| Duenner, Robert H. | COL | MC | MacDill, Leslie | COL | AC |
| Eastwold, Oscar A. | COL | CM | Macon, Robert C. | MG | GO |
| Erickson, Sidney | BG | GO | Maxwell, Russell L. | MG | GO |
| Faymonville, Philip R. | BG | GO | McCoy, Gordon H. | COL | FA |
| Fitzgerald, Francis V. | COL | QM | McFarland, Earl | BG | GO |
| Gibson, Samuel A. | COL | INF | McMahon, John E., Jr. | BG | GO |
| Gill, Isaac, Jr. | COL | INF | Moore, George F. | MG | GO |
| Glasgow, Lawrence B. | COL | INF | Nalle, William | COL | CAV |
| Glover, Hamilton F. | CAPT | USN | Olmstead, Dawson | MG | GO |
| Grant, Ulysses S., III | MG | GO | Osmun, Russell A. | BG | GO |
| Greene, Douglass T. | MG | GO | Peale, James N. | COL | INF |
| Halsey, William F., Jr. | FAD | USN | Pirie, John H. | COL | AC |

## CLASS OF 1934, RESIDENT, CONTINUED

| Name | Rank | Branch/Service | Name | Rank | Branch/Service |
|------|------|----------------|------|------|----------------|
| Porterfield, Herbert D. | COL | MC | Strong, Robert W. | BG | GO |
| Pratt, John S. | COL | CAC | Taylor, Thomas F. | COL | INF |
| Randall, David M. | COL | USMC | Thomas, Charles W., Jr. | COL | INF |
| Richardson, Robert C., Jr. | GEN | GO | Ulio, James A. | MG | GO |
| Royce, Ralph | MG | GO | Vanhook, Clifford E. | RADM | USN |
| Rumbough, William S. | MG | GO | Vanvliet, John H. | COL | INF |
| Rustemeyer, Joseph H. | COL | INF | Wainwright Jonathan M. | GEN | GO |
| Ryder, Charles W. | MG | GO | Waltz, Floyd R. | COL | INF |
| Sadtler, Otis K. | COL | SC | Watson, Leroy H. | MG | GO |
| Sasse, Ralph I. | COL | CAV | Weems, George H. | BG | GO |
| Stadtman, Claud E. | COL | INF | Wyche, Ira T. | MG | GO |

## CLASS OF 1935, RESIDENT

| Name | Rank | Branch/Service | Name | Rank | Branch/Service |
|------|------|----------------|------|------|----------------|
| Adler, Elmer E. | MG | USAF | Fuller, Francis R. | COL | INF |
| Allen, Leven C. | MG | GO | Garcin, Frederick R. | COL | CM |
| Allen, Roderick R. | MG | GO | Garrett, Robert C. | BG | GO |
| Allen, Terry DeL. M. | MG | GO | Handy, Thomas T. | GEN | GO |
| Arnold, Archibald V. | MG | GO | Heard, Falkner | COL | FA |
| Benson, Howard H. J. | COMO | USN | Hobbs, Leland S. | MG | GO |
| Bonham, Francis G. | MAJ | INF | Hobson, William H. | BG | GO |
| Bowley, Freeman W. | COL | FA | Hocker, Carl E. | COL | CA |
| Brown, Homer C. | BG | GO | Hodge, John R. | GEN | GO |
| Burns, John H. | COL | INF | Irwin, Constant L. | BG | GO |
| Burress, Withers A. | LTG | GO | Johnston, Edward S. | COL | INF |
| Cain, David E. | COL | FA | Kraus, Walter F. | MG | USAF |
| Chambliss, Turner M. | COL | INF | Kuegle, Albert S. | COL | INF |
| Chase, William C. | MG | GO | Layman, Walter G. | BG | GO |
| Christmas, John K. | MG | GO | Lennon, Bert M. | COL | INF |
| Coles, Roy H. | LTC | SC | Lindsey, Malcolm F. | BG | GO |
| Collins, Harry J. | MG | GO | Longino, Olin H. | BG | GO |
| Cumming, Samuel C. | MG | USMC | Lutes, Leroy | LTG | GO |
| Dessez, John H. S. | CAPT | USN | Malven, Henry H., Jr. | LTC | AG |
| Dougherty, Louis R. | COL | FA | Martin, Frederick L. | MG | USAF |
| Eberle, George L. | MG | GO | Matejka, Jerry V. | MG | GO |
| Finan, Bernard J. | COL | QM | McKee, John L. | MG | GO |
| Finley, Thomas D. | MG | GO | Metzger, Earl H. | BG | GO |
| Fletcher, Robert H. | COL | INF | Meyer, George R. | MG | GO |
| Ford, Louis P. | COL | INF | Moore, Charles B. | COL | INF |
| Fowler, Raymond F. | BG | GO | Mullenix, John C. | COL | CAV |

## CLASS OF 1935, RESIDENT, CONTINUED

| Name | Rank | Branch/Service | Name | Rank | Branch/Service |
|------|------|---------|------|------|---------|
| Myers, Donald J. | BG | GO | Spencer, Earl W., Jr. | CDR | USN |
| Parsons, Harold L. | COL | USMC | Streett, St. Clair | MG | USAF |
| Patch, Joseph D. | MG | GO | Stuart, David H. | CAPT | USN |
| Peabody, Hume | BG | USAF | Surles, Alexander D. | MG | GO |
| Perkins, Robert M. | BG | GO | Swing, Joseph M. | LTG | GO |
| Peyton, Thomas G. | LTC | FA | Vanderveer, Harold C. | BG | GO |
| Powell, Ralph E. | COL | INF | Weaver, Theron D. | BG | GO |
| Ransom, Paul L. | MG | GO | Welch, Gordon B. | COL | ORD |
| Robins, Augustine W. | COL | AC | Wilbur, William H. | BG | GO |
| Rudolph, Jacob H. | BG | USAF | Williams, Robert P. | BG | GO |
| Scowden, Frank F. | MG | GO | Willis, John M. | MG | GO |
| Selleck, Clyde A. | COL | FA | Wilson, Arthur R. | MG | GO |
| Smith, Charles C. | LTC | CAV | Woodberry, John H. | BG | GO |
| Smith, Ralph C. | MG | GO | Young, Gordon R. | BG | GO |
| Sparks, Leonard C. | COL | FA | Zeidner, Samuel I. | COL | QM |

## CLASS OF 1936, RESIDENT

| Name | Rank | Branch/Service | Name | Rank | Branch/Service |
|------|------|---------|------|------|---------|
| Akin, Spencer B. | MG | GO | Dahlquist, John E. | GEN | GO |
| Atkins, Layson E. | LTC | ENG | Daley, Edmund L. | MG | GO |
| Avery, Ray L. | BG | GO | Davis, George A. | BG | GO |
| Baldwin, Karl F. | COL | CAC | Davison, Paul R. | COL | CAV |
| Baldwin, Ross O. | COL | INF | Denit, Guy B. | MG | GO |
| Blakelock, David H. | BG | GO | Doll, Frederick S. | COL | INF |
| Blesse, Frederick A. | BG | GO | Drysdale, Walter S. | COL | INF |
| Blood, Kenneth T. | MG | GO | Duff, Robinson E. | MG | GO |
| Bourke, Thomas E. | LTG | USMC | Dumas, Walter A. | BG | GO |
| Brady, Francis M. | BG | USAF | Eager, Howard | COL | FA |
| Brett, George H. | LTG | USAF | Ferris, Benjamin G. | BG | GO |
| Bruce, Andrew D. | LTG | GO | Fortier, Louis J. | BG | GO |
| Burr, William E. | COL | FA | Gere, Edwin C. | COL | QM |
| Buse, Karl I. | COL | USMC | Goodman, William M. | MG | GO |
| Candee, Robert C. | BG | USAF | Greely, John N. | BG | GO |
| Carrington, Gordon D. | COL | CAC | Greer, Frank U. | BG | GO |
| Considine, John A. | COL | CAV | Griffin, Virgil C., Jr. | CAPT | USN |
| Cota, Norman | MG | GO | Grow, Robert W. | MG | GO |
| Cramer, Raymond V. | LTC | CAC | Hardaway, Francis P. | BG | GO |
| Crawford, Robert W. | MG | GO | Hearn, Thomas G. | MG | GO |
| Curry, John F. | MG | USAF | Henderson, Harry M. | COL | INF |
| Dager, Holmes E. | MG | GO | Herwig, Hans R. W. | COL | QM |

## CLASS OF 1936, RESIDENT, CONTINUED

| Name | Rank | Branch/Service | Name | Rank | Branch/Service |
|---|---|---|---|---|---|
| Hinckley, Robert M. | CAPT | USN | Nisley, Harold A. | BG | GO |
| Hodgson, Paul A. | COL | ENG | Pendergrast, Grady H. | MAJ | INF |
| Holmes, Henry B., Jr. | BG | GO | Pendleton, Alan | MAJ | INF |
| Houghton, Charles F. | COL | CAV | Perry, Basil H. | BG | GO |
| Hueper, Remi P. | BG | GO | Reinhart, Stanley E. | MG | GO |
| Irvine, Willard W. | MG | GO | Ritchie, Scott B. | COL | ORD |
| Jay, Henry D. | BG | GO | Rose, William C. | MG | GO |
| Jones, Charles H. | COL | INF | Ross, Frank S. | MG | GO |
| Karlstad, Charles H. | BG | GO | Rudelius, Ernest A. | COL | INF |
| Kilner, Walter G. | BG | GO | Russell, Carl A., Jr. | COL | INF |
| Landrum, Eugene M. | MG | GO | Smith, Henry J. M. | COL | CAV |
| Legge, Barnwell R. | BG | GO | Spalding, Sidney P. | MG | GO |
| Lucas, Chauncey A. | CAPT | USN | Stivers, Charles P. | MG | GO |
| Lyman, Charles B. | BG | GO | Stone, Laurence F. | LTC | AC |
| MacKelvie, Jay W. | BG | GO | Stuart, Alexander J. | COL | ORD |
| Malony, Harry J. | MG | GO | Taulbee, Edgar W. | COL | CAV |
| Mandell, Harold C. | BG | GO | Trammell, Webb | CAPT | USN |
| Marshall, Richard J. | MG | GO | Vandeusen, George L. | MG | GO |
| McBride, Horace L. | LTG | GO | Walker, Walton H. | GEN | GO |
| McClure, Robert A. | MG | GO | Wallace, Fred C. | MG | GO |
| McFarland, Andrew J. | BG | GO | Ward, Orlando | MG | GO |
| McMahon, William C. | MG | GO | Whittaker, Frank L. | COL | CAV |
| McMurray, Clarence M. | COL | INF | Willoughby, Charles A. | MG | GO |
| Miller, Lester T. | MG | USAF | Wilson, John H. | BG | GO |
| Netherwood, Douglas B. | COL | AC | Yount, Barton K. | LTG | GO |
| Nevins, Arthur S. | BG | GO | | | |

## CLASS OF 1937, RESIDENT

| Name | Rank | Branch/Service | Name | Rank | Branch/Service |
|---|---|---|---|---|---|
| Barber, Henry A., Jr. | BG | GO | Clark, Mark W. | GEN | GO |
| Barnett, James W. | BG | GO | Clemenson, Wendell L. | COL | INF |
| Bobrink, Henry W. | COL | QM | Collier, William A. | BG | GO |
| Bolte, Charles L. | GEN | GO | Connell, Carl W. | COL | AC |
| Bradford, Karl S. | BG | GO | Coughlan, Joseph D. | COL | CM |
| Brooks, Edward H. | LTG | GO | Cousins, Ralph P. | MG | USAF |
| Brown, Philip E. | MG | GO | Cummings, Robert E. | COL | AG |
| Bullard, Peter C. | COL | INF | Cureton, William H. | COL | FA |
| Campbell, William A. | BG | GO | Davison, Donald A. | MG | GO |
| Case, Homer | BG | GO | Ellis, E. Detreville | COL | QM |
| Chandler, William D., Jr. | CAPT | USN | Ewert, Earl C. | COL | FA |

## CLASS OF 1937, RESIDENT, CONTINUED

| Name | Rank | Branch/ Service | Name | Rank | Branch/ Service |
|------|------|------|------|------|------|
| Fairchild, Muir S. | GEN | USAF | Milliken, Charles M. | BG | GO |
| Farthing, William E. | MG | USAF | Noce, Daniel | LTG | GO |
| Franke, Gustav H. | MG | GO | Parker, Edwin P. | MG | GO |
| Gatchell, Oscar J. | BG | GO | Patrick, Edwin D. | MG | GO |
| Gregory, Edmund B. | LTG | GO | Paul, Willard S. | LTG | GO |
| Gurney, Augustus M. | BG | GO | Pierce, John T. | BG | GO |
| Hale, Willis H. | MG | USAF | Porter, Ray E. | MG | GO |
| Hamblen, Archelaus L. | BG | GO | Pratt, Don F. | BG | GO |
| Hasbrouck, Robert W. | MG | GO | Price, Xenophon H. | COL | ENG |
| Heffner, Pete T., Jr. | COL | INF | Rayner, Harold M. | COL | CAV |
| Hickok, Monte J. | COL | CAC | Rice, George W. | MG | GO |
| Hines, Charles | BG | GO | Ricker, George W. | COL | CAC |
| Hoover, John H. | ADM | USN | Ridgway, Matthew B. | GEN | GO |
| Hough, Romeyn B., Jr. | LTC | AC | Riefkohl, Rudolf W. | COL | QM |
| Howard, Clinton W. | BG | GO | Robinett, Paul M. | BG | GO |
| Irwin, Stafford L. | LTG | GO | Roesch, Herbert O. | CAPT | USN |
| Johnson, Frank M. S. | COL | ENG | Roffe, A. Worrell | COL | CAV |
| Kane, Paul V. | BG | GO | Rooks, Lowell W. | MG | GO |
| Keyes, Geoffrey | LTG | GO | Sawbridge, Ben M. | MG | GO |
| Kilburn, Charles S. | BG | GO | Schmidt, Feodor | COL | INF |
| King, George L. | COL | INF | Shepard, Whitfield P. | MG | GO |
| King, Henry L. P. | BG | GO | Skelton, Robert | COL | MC |
| Koenig, William C. | COL | CAC | Smith, Walter B. | GEN | GO |
| Kraft, George L. | COL | INF | Stroh, Donald A. | MG | GO |
| Kresge, Miles W. | COL | ORD | Summers, Iverson B. | COL | MP |
| Kron, Philip H. | COL | INF | Sweet, Joseph B. | BG | GO |
| Kutschko, Emerick | BG | GO | Taylor, James | BG | GO |
| Leiber, Paul E. | COL | INF | Thomas, Charles E., Jr. | MG | USAF |
| Loder, Ames | CAPT | USN | Thomason, John W., Jr. | COL | USMC |
| Lopez, Andres | COL | INF | Vanaman, Arthur W. | MG | USAF |
| Maris, Ward H. | MG | GO | Waldron, Albert W. | MG | GO |
| Matthews, Frederick S. | COL | INF | Warnock, Alan D. | BG | GO |
| McSherry, Frank J. | BG | GO | Wells, Gordon M. | BG | GO |
| Melasky, Harris M | MG | GO | Wharton, James E. | BG | GO |
| Meyer, Vincent | BG | GO | Wheeler, Raymond A. | LTG | GO |
| Milbuiln, Bryan L. | MG | GO | Wooten, Ralph H. | MG | USAF |
| Miller, Eugene L. | COL | INF | | | |

## CLASS OF 1938, RESIDENT

| Name | Rank | Branch/Service | Name | Rank | Branch/Service |
|---|---|---|---|---|---|
| Alfonte, James R. | BG | GO | Hogg, William S., Jr. | CAPT | USN |
| Arnold, Calvert H. | BG | GO | Hull, John E. | GEN | GO |
| Barker, John De F. | MG | USAF | Jenkins, Reuben E. | LTG | GO |
| Barnes, Gladeon M. | MG | GO | Johns, Dwight F. | BG | GO |
| Bledsoe, William P. | BG | GO | Johnson, Harry A. | MG | USAF |
| Bolling, Alexander R. | LTG | GO | Jones, Alan W. | MG | GO |
| Boyd, Leonard R. | BG | GO | Kibler, A. Franklin | MG | GO |
| Brann, Donald W. | MG | GO | Ladd, Jesse A. | BG | GO |
| Brougher, William E. | BG | GO | Larkin, Thomas B. | LTG | GO |
| Brown, Robert D. | COL | CAC | Lewis, John E. | BG | GO |
| Bryan, Hamilton V. | CDR | USN | Lewis, John T. | LTG | GO |
| Carter, Warren R. | MG | USAF | Lucas, Burton L. | COL | INF |
| Caygill, Harry W. | LTC | INF | Lyon, Alfred J. | BG | GO |
| Collins, J. Lawton | GEN | GO | Maguire, Hamilton E. | BG | GO |
| Colton, Roger B. | MG | GO | Martenstein, Austin W. | BG | USAF |
| Compton, Louis J. | COL | FA | McCunniff, Dennis E. | BG | GO |
| Cotter, Clarence E. | COL | CAC | McDonnell, Paul J. | COL | INF |
| Cranston, Joseph A. | BG | GO | Mickelsen, Stanley R. | LTG | GO |
| Cushman, Horace O. | BG | GO | Middleswart, William H. | MG | GO |
| Danielson, Clarence H. | MG | GO | Miller, Charles S. | COL | CAV |
| Davis, Thomas D. | COL | INF | Miller, Robert S. | COL | INF |
| Delvalle, Pedro A. | LTG | USMC | Moore, Cecil R. | MG | GO |
| DeWitt, Calvin, Jr. | BG | GO | Morgan, Clyde H. | COL | ORD |
| Dunckel, William C. | MG | GO | Morrison, Charles H. | CAPT | USN |
| Dunn, Beverly C. | BG | GO | Oliver, Lunsford E. | MG | GO |
| Dunn, Walter K. | COL | CAC | Ott, Edward S. | BG | GO |
| Edward, Harvey | COL | QM | Porter, William N. | MG | GO |
| Edwards, Idwal H. | LTG | USAF | Ramey, Rufus S. | BG | GO |
| Forster, George J. | BG | GO | Rayens, Charles E. | COL | INF |
| Foster, Ivan L. | BG | GO | Richart, Duncan G. | BG | GO |
| Futch, Theodore L. | BG | GO | Rogers, Fred B. | COL | INF |
| Gorlinski, Joseph S. | COL | ENG | Rogers, Pleas B. | BG | GO |
| Gridley, Cecil J. | COL | INF | Scobey, William P. | COL | INF |
| Hamilton, Raymond C. | COL | INF | Shambora, William E. | MG | GO |
| Harmon, Hubert R. | LTG | USAF | Short, James C. | COL | CAV |
| Harms, Henry W. | BG | GO | Slocum, LeCount H. | BG | GO |
| Harrison, William K., Jr. | LTG | GO | Stuart, LaRhett L. | BG | GO |
| Heidner, Samuel J. | COL | INF | Tate, Foster J. | BG | GO |
| Henning, Frank A. | BG | GO | Thayer, Arthur P. | COL | CAV |
| Hickey, Lawrence P. | COL | USAF | Thompson, John B. | BG | GO |
| Hinemon, John H., Jr. | COL | SC | Tilton, Rollin L. | BG | GO |

### CLASS OF 1938, RESIDENT, CONTINUED

| Name | Rank | Branch/ Service | Name | Rank | Branch/ Service |
|---|---|---|---|---|---|
| Umsted, Scott. | RADM | USN | Wickert, Howard T. | COL | MC |
| Vance, Preston T. | COL | FA | Williams, Samuel T. | LTG | GO |
| Walker, William G. | BG | GO | Woolfley, Francis A. | BG | GO |
| Wallace, John H. | LTC | FA | York, John Y., Jr. | MG | USAF |
| Watson, Thomas E. | LTG | USMC | Zellars, John T. | COL | INF |
| Weible, Walter L. | LTG | GO | | | |

### CLASS OF 1939, RESIDENT

| Name | Rank | Branch/ Service | Name | Rank | Branch/ Service |
|---|---|---|---|---|---|
| Adcock, Clarence L. | MG | GO | Goode, Paul R. | COL | INF |
| Alexander, Boyd R. | CAPT | USN | Griner, George W., Jr. | MG | GO |
| Archer, Waine | COL | INF | Groves, Leslie R. | LTG | GO |
| Argo, Edwin Y. | COL | FA | Gruenther, Alfred M. | GEN | GO |
| Balmer, Jesmond D. | BG | GO | Haines, Oliver L. | BG | GO |
| Barr, David G. | MG | GO | Harriman, Joseph E. | BG | GO |
| Beebe, Lewis C. | BG | GO | Hart, Franklin A. | GEN | USMC |
| Billick, Eugene W. | COL | MC | Hawley, Paul R. | MG | GO |
| Blakeley, Harold W. | MG | GO | Hermle, Leo D. | LTG | USMC |
| Brower, Gerald E. | COL | AC | Hewett, Hobart | MG | GO |
| Campbell, Boniface | MG | GO | Hill, Edmund W. | MG | USAF |
| Carmody, Robert E. | COL | CAV | Hinds, John H. | MG | GO |
| Carpenter, Giles R. | COL | FA | Hodnette, Lovic P. | COL | INF |
| Cooke, Elliot D. | BG | GO | Homer, John L. | MG | GO |
| Cooney, Harold A. | COL | FA | Humphries, Otho W. | COL | QM |
| Copthorne, William A. | COL | CM | Hutt, William C. | COL | QM |
| Craig, Louis A. | MG | GO | Jaynes, Lawrence C. | MG | GO |
| Cress, Erle F. | COL | CAV | Killmaster, Benjamin S. | CAPT | USN |
| Daly, Cornelius M. | BG | GO | Kurtz, Guy O. | BG | GO |
| Daly, John C. | COL | CAV | Lewis, Burton O. | BG | GO |
| Deane, John R. | MG | GO | Loomis, Harold F. | BG | GO |
| Dodge, Frank R. | RADM | USN | Maertens, Kameil | COL | INF |
| Donovan, Leo | MG | GO | Magruder, Carter B. | GEN | GO |
| Echols, Oliver P. | MG | USAF | Malin, Howard A. | COL | INF |
| Ennis, Riley F. | MG | GO | Marston, Morrill W. | BG | GO |
| Faith, Don C. | BG | GO | Martin, Thomas L. | BG | GO |
| Fellers, Bonner F. | BG | GO | McClure, Robert B. | MG | GO |
| Foster, Eugene M. | MG | GO | McDaniel, Arthur B. | BG | GO |
| Gallagher, Philip E. | MG | GO | McFadyen, Bernice M. | MG | GO |
| Geiselman, Ellis H. | CAPT | USN | McKinley, Edward B. | BG | GO |
| Gerow, Lee S. | BG | GO | McKinnon, Morton H. | COL | USAF |

## CLASS OF 1939, RESIDENT, CONTINUED

| Name | Rank | Branch/ Service | Name | Rank | Branch/ Service |
|---|---|---|---|---|---|
| Mehaffery, Joseph C. | MG | GO | Sherrill, Stephen H. | BG | GO |
| Moran, Richard B. | BG | GO | Sibert, Edwin L. | MG | GO |
| Morse, William P. | COL | INF | Starr, Rupert E. | BG | GO |
| Mullins, Charles L., Jr. | MG | GO | Strahm, Victor H. | BG | USAF |
| Niles, Wallace E. | COL | ORD | Stratemeyer, George E. | LTG | USAF |
| Ostrom, Charles D. Y. | BG | GO | Summers, Owen | BG | GO |
| Palmer, Williston B. | GEN | GO | Swift, Ira P. | MG | GO |
| Pick, Lewis A. | LTG | GO | Tate, Ralph H. | BG | GO |
| Ready, Joseph L. | BG | GO | Taylor, Victor V. | BG | GO |
| Rehm, George A. | BG | GO | Upston, John E. | MG | USAF |
| Ryan, William O. | MG | USAF | Vandenberg, Hoyt S. | GEN | USAF |
| Sandlin, Erle O. | COL | INF | Vonholtzendorff, John D. | COL | FA |
| Schlieker, Grant A. | COL | INF | Walk, Arthur R. | BG | GO |
| Schneider, Max F. | BG | USAF | Walker, Samuel P., Jr. | COL | CAV |
| Schow, Robert A. | MG | GO | Wallis, Luther D. | COL | INF |
| Searcy, Cyrus H. | BG | GO | Weart, Douglas L. | MG | GO |
| Sheetz, Josef R. | MG | GO | Weeks, Lawrence B. | BG | GO |

## CLASS OF 1940, RESIDENT

| Name | Rank | Branch/ Service | Name | Rank | Branch/ Service |
|---|---|---|---|---|---|
| Allen, Frank A., Jr. | MG | GO | Clarke, Carter W. | BG | GO |
| Bacon, Robert L. | COL | INF | Coffey, John W. | BG | GO |
| Badger, George M. | BG | GO | Cook, Lloyd H. | COL | INF |
| Bandholtz, Cleveland H. | COL | ORD | Copeland, John E. | BG | GO |
| Banfill, Charles Y. | BG | USAF | Crawford, David M. | BG | GO |
| Barber, Edward | BG | USAF | Culin, Frank L., Jr. | MG | GO |
| Barker, Ray W. | MG | GO | Davidson, Howard C. | MG | USAF |
| Beall, Burns | COL | INF | Dean, William F. | MG | GO |
| Beckley, Stuart A. | COL | FA | Dunkelberg, Wilbur E. | BG | GO |
| Bissell, John T. B. | BG | GO | Easley, Claudius M. | BG | GO |
| Blanchard, Charles C. | BG | GO | Fenn, Clarence C. | BG | GO |
| Bryan, Blackshear M. | LTG | GO | Ferenbaugh, Claude B. | LTG | GO |
| Bullene, Egbert F. | MG | GO | Fitts, William T., Jr. | BG | GO |
| Bultman, Herbert F. E. | MAJ | CAC | Flory, Lester D. | BG | GO |
| Burnell, Nathaniel A., II | MG | GO | Foote, William C. | COL | CAC |
| Burney, Joel R. | COL | INF | Galloway, Floyd E. | BG | USAF |
| Burt, Ernest H. | BG | GO | Goodman, John F. | COL | INF |
| Byers, Clovis E. | LTG | GO | Grogan, Stanley J. | COL | INF |
| Cates, Clifton B. | GEN | USMC | Handwerk, Morris C. | BG | GO |
| Christiansen, James G. | MG | GO | Hays, George P. | LTG | GO |

**CLASS OF 1940, RESIDENT,** CONTINUED

| Name | Rank | Branch/ Service | Name | Rank | Branch/ Service |
|------|------|---------|------|------|---------|
| Heileman, Frank A. | MG | GO | Newcomer, Francis K. | BG | GO |
| Hodes, Henry I. | GEN | GO | Nicholas, Richard U. | BG | GO |
| Holbrook, Willard A., Jr. | BG | GO | Parks, Floyd L. | LTG | GO |
| Howell, Reese M. | BG | GO | Pearson, Frank J. | COL | INF |
| Hudnutt, Dean | COL | FA | Pearson, Madison | BG | GO |
| Jackson, Stonewall | MG | GO | Pierce, James R. | MG | GO |
| Jefferson, Leslie W. | COL | CAC | Pierson, Albert | MG | GO |
| Johnston, Oscar R. | COL | INF | Prichard, Vernon E. | MG | GO |
| Kendall, Donald J. | COL | USMC | Ramsey, Thomas H. | BG | GO |
| Kiel, Emil C. | BG | USAF | Refs, Thomas H. | COL | CAV |
| Kurtz, Maurice K. | COL | FA | Ridings, Eugene W. | MG | GO |
| Lafferty, Frederick R. | COL | USAF | Rodes, Peter P. | BG | GO |
| Lange, Otto F. | BG | GO | Rogers, Arthur H. | BG | GO |
| Lawhon, Zim E. | COL | FA | Ruddell, James C. | COL | CAC |
| Lemnitzer, Lyman L. | GEN | GO | Sherman, John B. | COL | INF |
| Lentz, John M. | MG | GO | Shingler, Don G. | BG | GO |
| Lester, James A. | MG | GO | Shoe, Robert O. | MG | GO |
| Longino, James C. | COL | QM | Smith, George I. | COL | CAV |
| Martin, Clarence A. | MG | GO | Sturgis, Samuel D., Jr. | LTG | GO |
| Martin, Joseph I. | MG | GO | Taylor, Maxwell D. | GEN | GO |
| Martin, Louis LeR. | COL | CAV | Thompson, Harry F. | BG | GO |
| Matchett, Henry J. | BG | GO | Tindall, Richard G. | BG | GO |
| May, Edwin T. | COL | INF | Tompkins, Francis P. | COL | CAV |
| McAabe, Frederick | BG | GO | Vinson, Wilbur H. | COL | INF |
| McAuliffe, Anthony C. | GEN | GO | Walsh, Robert LeG. | MG | USAF |
| McGaw, Edward J. | MG | GO | Warren, Webster H. | LTC | CAC |
| Mickle, Gerald St. C. | BG | GO | Williamson, Raymond E. S. | BG | GO |
| Miller, Fred W. | MG | GO | Wilson, Milton E. | COL | DO |
| Miller, Lehman W. | BG | GO | Wilson, William | BG | GO |
| Mudge, Verne D. | MG | GO | Wood, Philip S. | COL | INF |

Source: AWC Directory, 2000.

Note: The rank indicated is the rank at the time of separation from the service.

| Abbreviations: | AC | Air Corps | | COL | Colonel |
|---|---|---|---|---|---|
| | ADM | Admiral | | COMO | Commodore |
| | AG | Adjutant General | | ENG | Engineers |
| | BG | Brigadier General | | FA | Field Artillery |
| | CAC | Coast Artillery Corps | | FAD | Fleet Admiral |
| | CAPT | Captain | | GA | General of the Army |
| | CAV | Cavalry | | GEN | General |
| | CDR | Commander | | GO | General Officer |
| | CM | Chemical Corps | | INF | Infantry |

| LTC | Lieutenant Colonel | QM | Quartermaster |
| LTG | Lieutenant General | RADM | Rear Admiral |
| MAJ | Major | SC | Signal Corps |
| MC | Medical Corps | USAF | U.S. Air Force |
| MG | Major General | USMC | U.S. Marine Corps |
| MP | Military Police | USN | U.S. Navy |
| ORD | Ordnance | | |

# Appendix H

## AWC Graduates 1934–1940 Who Attained Flag Rank

| Year | Number of Graduates | Number Who Attained Flag Rank |
|------|---------------------|-------------------------------|
| 1934 | 84 | 48 |
| 1935 | 82 | 50 |
| 1936 | 95 | 61 |
| 1937 | 95 | 61 |
| 1938 | 93 | 63 |
| 1939 | 96 | 69 |
| 1940 | 100 | 70 |
| Total | 645 | 422 |
| Percentage attaining flag rank | 65 | |

*Source: AWC Directory, 2000.*

# Appendix ▌

★  ★  ★

## Maps

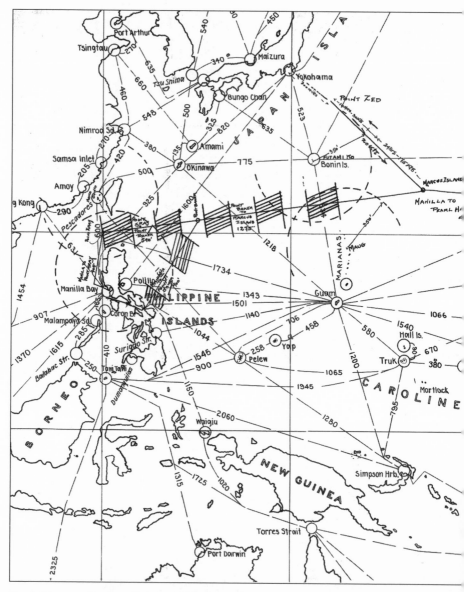

**Map 1.** This strategic chart accompanied Cdr. John H. Dessez's presentation of the Naval basic Plan to the Army War College on 13 April 1935. AWC planners considered coalition vs. coalition war. Japan and a Nazi confederation were the enemies of the United States and its allies. (The hatched areas depict night runs from Marcus Island.)

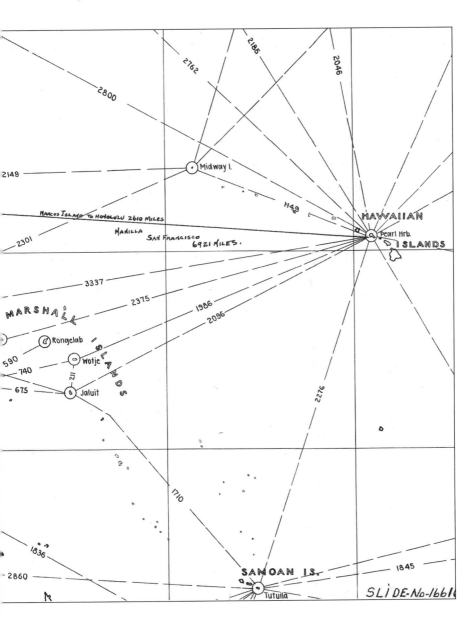

2762
2185
2046
2800
2149
MARCUS ISLAND TO HONOLULU 2610 MILES
MANILLA SAN FRANCISCO 6921 MILES.
H49
HAWAIIAN
Pearl Hrb.
ISLANDS
Midway I.
2301
3337
2375
1986
2096
MARSHALL
Rongelab
Wotje
590
740
211
675
Jaluit
ISLANDS
2276
1710
1836
2860
SAMOAN IS.
1845
Tutuila
SLIDE-No-1661

**Map 2.** The Army War College scenario posited in 1937 versus real world events of 1939–1940

# Notes

## Abbreviations

| | |
|---|---|
| AWC | U.S. Army War College, Carlisle Barracks, Pa. |
| CMH | U.S. Army Center of Military History, Washington, D.C. |
| HMC | Historical Manuscripts Collection, CMH |
| HRC | Historical Records Collection, CMH |
| MHI | U.S. Army Military History Institute, AWC |
| NA | National Archives, Washington, D.C. |
| NHC | Naval Historical Collection, U.S. Naval War College, Newport, R.I. |
| RG | Record Group |
| WDGS | War Department General Staff |
| WP | War Plan |
| WPD | War Plans Division |

## Introduction

1. Peyton C. Marsh, *The Nation at War* (Garden City, N.Y.: Doubleday, 1932), 341.

2. The WPD study citing the numbers of divisions is found in Marvin A. Kreidberg and Merton G. Henry, *History of Military Mobilization in the United States Army, 1775–1945,* Department of the Army Pamphlet no. 20-212 (Washington, D.C.: U.S. Government Printing Office, November 1955), 547.

3. Historian Richard M. Ketchum refers to "the pitiable state of the United States Army" inherited by George C. Marshall on 1 September 1939. Ketchum, *The Borrowed Years, 1938–1941: America on the Way to War* (New York: Random House, 1989), 537.

4. *Annual Reports, War Department. Fiscal Year Ended June 30, 1941* (Washington, D.C.: U.S. Government Printing Office, 1941), 48.

5. Stephen E. Ambrose began his review of Jean Edward Smith's *Lucius D. Clay: An American Life* (New York: Henry Holt, 1990) with these words. See *New York Times Book Review,* 29 July 1990, 13.

6. Dan Beaver, "The Industrial-Military Complex in Historical Perspective," *Journal of American History* 56 (March 1970): 819–39.

7. Mark Watson, "First Vigorous Steps in Re-arming, 1938–39," *Military Affairs* 12 (Summer 1948): 65–78.

8. MHI, Thomas T. Handy Papers, "Transcripts of the Debriefing of General Handy" by Lt. Col. Edward M. Knoff, Jr., 1973–74, 51–52.

9. See Alfred Vagts, "Hopes and Fears of an American-German War, 1870–1915," *Political Science Quarterly* 54 (December 1939) and 55 (March 1940).

10. Michael Vlahos, *The Blue Sword: The Naval War College and the American Mission, 1919–1941* (Washington, D.C.: U.S. Government Printing Office; Newport, R.I.: Naval War College Press, 1980).

11. Maurice Matloff, "Prewar Military Plans and Preparations, 1939–41," *U.S. Naval Institute Proceedings* 79 (July 1953): 741. See the preface of this book for more detail on this issue.

### Chapter 1. American Military Preparedness between the World Wars

1. Harry Kessler, *Berlin in Lights: The Diaries of Count Harry Kessler, 1918–1937,* translated and edited by Charles Kessler (New York: Grove Press, 2000).

2. For army strength 1919–46, see Kreidberg and Henry, *History of Military Mobilization,* 379. For expenditures of the War Department and the Department of the Army since 1789, see Russell F. Weigley, *History of the United States Army* (New York: Macmillan, 1967), 560–61. For annual naval appropriations, see George T. Davis, *A Navy Second to None* (Westport, Conn.: Greenwood Press, 1940), 473–74.

3. Russell F. Weigley, *The American Way of War: A History of United States Military Strategy and Policy* (New York: Macmillan, 1973).

4. Kreidberg and Henry, *History of Military Mobilization,* 461–63.

5. For concise one-chapter descriptions of the U.S. Navy in the interwar period, see Samuel Eliot Morison, *The Two-Ocean War: A Short History of the United States Navy in the Second World War* (Boston: Little, Brown, 1963), chap. 1, "The Twenty Years' Peace, 1919–1939," and Nathan Miller, *The U.S. Navy: A History* (New York: Quill, William Morrow, 1990), chap. 8, "The Long Armistice."

6. For a detailed account of the evolution of planning for the war with Japan, see Edward S. Miller, *War Plan Orange: The U.S. Strategy to Defeat Japan, 1897–1945* (Annapolis, Md.: Naval Institute Press, 1991). For development of amphibious assault capability, see Allan R. Millett, *Semper Fidelis: The History of the United States Marine Corps,* rev. and expanded ed. (New York: Free Press; Toronto: Maxwell Macmillan Canada, 1991), esp. chap. 12, 319–43.

7. There is a vast literature describing President Roosevelt's decision making and leadership, but the following essay is particularly good on his management of public opinion in the years before American entry into World War II: Calvin L. Christman, "Franklin Delano Roosevelt and the Craft of Strategic Assessment," in *Calculations: Net Assessment and the Coming of World War II,* edited by Williamson Murray and Allan R. Millett (New York: Free Press; Toronto: Maxwell Macmillan Canada, 1992).

### Chapter 2. The Army War College, Strategic Continuity, and Service Preferences

1. CMH, HRC 352, Army War College. Stetson Conn, "The Army War College, 1899–1940: Mission, Purpose, Objectives. A Study Prepared for the Commandant," Army War College, December 1964, 1.

2. Ibid., 2.

3. See John B. Hattendorf, B. Mitchell Simpson III, and John R. Wadleigh, *Sailors and Scholars* (Newport, R.I.: Naval War College Press, 1984), chap. 1.

4. Conn, "Army War College," 2–4.

5. Ibid., 8–12.

6. NA, RG 225, letter from Chaffee to the secretary of war, 22 April 1904.

7. NA, RG 225, on first endorsement to Chaffee letter. Endorsement is dated 23 April 1904 and refers Chaffee letter to the Joint Board.

8. NA, RG 225, Bliss paper to the secretary of the Joint Board, 21 pp., 10 June 1904, and letter of transmittal, Bliss to Dewey, 17 June 1904.

9. The Naval War College, established in 1884, was already twenty years old. Tasker H. Bliss had been assigned to the faculty of the Naval War College in 1885 and therefore had some insights into that interesting subculture called the U.S. Navy.

10. See Paul M. Kennedy, ed., *The War Plans of the Great Powers, 1880–1914* (Boston: Allen and Unwin, 1979), 5. Kennedy's introduction, 1–22, puts the strategic planning of the Great Powers prior to 1914 in perspective. In that same volume, see also J. A. S. Grenville, "Diplomacy and War Plans in the United States, 1890–1917," 23–38, and H. H. Hervig and D. F. Trask, "Naval Operations Plans between Germany and the USA, 1898–1913," 39–74, for an early strategic appreciation of the U.S. geopolitical position with respect to the Atlantic (Germany), the Pacific (Japan), and Latin America (the Monroe Doctrine). The reflections of strategic thinkers in the United States from 1898 to 1917 are strikingly similar to those found in curricular materials in the archives of both the Army War College and the Naval War College for the 1930s.

11. Bliss paper, 10 June 1904, 5–6. This formulation in 1904 by Bliss recalls a remark made by Gen. Thomas T. Handy after World War II as he reflected on the Japanese position on the eve of war: "We practically told the Japs to give up their ambitions in Asia, just like somebody told us to give up ours in America." MHI, Thomas T. Handy Papers, "Transcripts of the Debriefing of General Handy" by Lt. Col. Edward M. Knoff, Jr., 1973–74, section 3, 24. Even more explicit is George H. Blakeslee, "The Japanese Monroe Doctrine," *Foreign Affairs* 11 (July 1933): 671–81.

12. Bliss paper, 6.

13. Ibid., 11.

14. MHI, 7-1938-0, correspondence, includes a request by WPD that AWC examine the "Strategy of a Blue–South American combine against a German-Italian challenge to the Monroe Doctrine." See also MHI, 111-41/16, for comments and corrections regarding WPD, WDOP-R-40 (Rainbow 4), 17 September 1940, and MHI, 111-41/13 and /14, "Troop Strengths, Deployments in W. Hemisphere."

15. Bliss paper, 20–21.

16. NA, RG 225, serial 634 dated 21 April 1939.

17. Paul M. Kennedy, *The Samoan Tangle: A Study in Anglo-German-American Relations, 1878–1900* (New York: Barnes and Noble, 1974), and Thomas A. Bailey, "Dewey and the Germans at Manila Bay," *American Historical Review* 45 (October 1939): 59–81. Kennedy shows that tension between Germany and America grew as Anglo-American relations became congenial. He calls the latter development "one of the most important in the world history of the past hundred years" (137). For early U.S. war planning, see also William R. Braisted, *The United States Navy in the Pacific, 1897–1909* (Austin: University of Texas Press, 1958), 21. See also Seward W. Livermore, "The American Navy as a Factor in World Politics, 1903–1913," *American Historical Review* 63 (July 1958): 863–79. Livermore cites the *New York Times* of May 1903 (day not specified): "When we contemplate the actual employment in war of our navy, Germany is the power which we naturally associate with the notion of such employment" (867).

18. Vlahos, *Blue Sword,* 123. See also Louis Morton, "Military and Naval Preparations for the Defense of the Philippines during the War Scare of 1907," *Military Affairs* 13 (Summer 1949): 95–104, for the emergence of Japan as a likely foe. The war scare flowed out of the Japanese victory over Russia in 1905 and the San Francisco School Board segregation order of 1906 that ordered "all Chinese and Japanese pupils transferred to the Oriental Public School together with 'children of filthy or vicious habits or children suffering from contagious or infectious diseases.'" On 14 June 1907 President Theodore Roosevelt asked Assistant Secretary of War Robert S. Oliver what plans had been made by the Joint Army and Navy Board "in case of trouble arising between the United States and Japan." Morton concludes that the decision to fortify Corregidor and the surrounding islands and to concentrate on the defense of Manila was the direct result of the 1907 war scare (104).

19. NA, RG 225, 31 May 1904, revised draft as read to the Joint Board by Rear Admiral Taylor, 10 June 1904, 7 pp.

20. It is "the American mission" in the subtitle of Vlahos's *The Blue Sword.*

21. Thirty-five years later Charles L. Bolte noted the navy preference. Even after the "Germany-first" decision by Winston Churchill and Roosevelt, he said, "Our Navy was always reluctant as to Europe." MHI, Bolte interview with Arthur J. Zoebelin, AWC, 1971–72, 7–8.

22. Kennedy, *War Plans,* 5.

## Chapter 3. Plans and Planning

1. See appendix F of this book for notes on war planning in WPD, including an organization chart and a description of the position of WPD in WDGS. Students at AWC followed WPD methods.

2. Mark Skinner Watson, *Chief of Staff: Prewar Plans and Preparations,* United States Army in World War II: The War Department (Washington, D.C.: Office of the Chief of Military History, Department of the Army, 1950), 30.

3. Annual report of chief of staff, 30 June 1939, in ibid., 30.

4. HRC 321, WPD, appendix D, "Master Personnel List, Arrivals and Departures," last (unnumbered) page.

5. See appendix F of this book. See also Watson, *Chief of Staff,* 74.

6. Watson, *Chief of Staff,* 75.

7. Robert H. Ferrell, ed., *The Eisenhower Diaries* (New York: Norton, 1981), 44, 50, and 40.

8. MHI, Course at the AWC, 1933–34, Preparation for War Course, 2d Part, War Plans Period, War Plans Group 4, "Participation with Allies," tab 3, 15.

9. James E. Hewes, Jr., *From Root to McNamara: Army Organization and Administration, 1900–1963,* Special Studies Series (Washington, D.C.: Center of Military History, United States Army, 1975), 74 and 104.

10. See appendix A of this book.

11. *Directory of U.S. Army War College Graduates* (Carlisle, Pa.: Alumni Association, USAWC, 2000) (hereafter cited as *AWC Directory*) lists students by name and year group, and indicates USN and USMC for officers of the maritime services. See appendix G of this book for a complete listing of graduates 1934–40.

12. MHI, Course at the AWC, 1933–34, Preparation for War Course, 2d Part, War Plans Period, War Plans Group 4, "Participation with Allies." See also "Participation with Allies" in each of the courses from 1935 to 1940.

13. Planners at AWC spoke of "Russia," not the "Soviet Union."

14. MHI, file 1-105, Summary of the Courses at the AWC since the World War, 1919–40. See p. 7 of the 1922–23 course summary.

15. Ibid., 1924–25 course summary, 10.

16. Ibid., 1939–40 course summary, 31.

17. See Morton, "Military and Naval Preparations," 22–42, for a crisp and comprehensive summary of Orange Plans from 1906 to 1938.

18. MHI, file 1-105, Summary of the Courses at the AWC since the World War, 1919–40, 2.

19. Ibid. See esp. the summary of the 1936–37 course, 3.

20. To appreciate public opinion in the United States from 1935 onward, see George H. Gallup, *The Gallup Poll: Public Opinion, 1935–1971,* 3 vols. (New York: Random House, 1972). Vol. 1, *1935–1948,* is most relevant to opinion on neutrality, likely friends and foes, the need to rearm, and other issues bearing on American security. See also Hadley Cantril, *Public Opinion, 1935–1946* (Princeton: Princeton University Press, 1951). The Cantril volume also covers surveys beginning in 1935 and is organized alphabetically so that the researcher can turn directly to "Military," "Defenses," "War," or "Germany," for example. The Gallup book is organized chronologically. Both Gallup and Cantril trace opinion as Americans by degrees realized that however much they craved neutrality, it was likely that the United States would be drawn into the coming war. For example, in July 1937, 56 percent of the sample thought America could stay out of the war (*Gallup Poll,* 65); by March 1939, 58 percent thought America would be drawn in (150); by July 1939, 76 percent thought America would be drawn in (175).

21. Kreidberg and Henry, *History of Military Mobilization,* 547.

22. The evolution of thinking that went into the plans year by year can be tracked in the data, analyses, and plans, and in the question-and-answer sessions that followed student presentations available in the MHI files. See records of the curriculum at the Army War College between the world wars. The War Plans Period files, esp. "Participation with Allies" from 1934 to 1940, provide the detailed plans most pertinent to the current study.

## Chapter 4. 1934: War with Japan

1. MHI, Course at the AWC, 1933–34, Preparation for War Course, 2d Part, War Plans Period, War Plans Group 4, "Participation with Allies." Except where noted otherwise, the substance of the 1934 plan comes from this file.

2. See Adm. Sir Herbert Richmond's "Immediate Problems of Naval Reduction," *Foreign Affairs* 9 (April 1931): 371–88, and "Naval Problems of 1935," *Foreign Affairs* 13 (October 1934): 45–58. Adm. William V. Pratt, USN (president of the Naval War College, 1925–27; CINC U.S. Fleet, 1929–30; naval adviser to the American delegation at the London Conference, 1930; and CNO, 1930–33), took the opportunity of the Japanese denunciation of the Five-Power Treaty of 6 February 1922 to join in the debate with British and Japanese admirals with "The Setting for the 1935 Naval Conference," *Foreign Affairs* 12 (July 1934): 541–52, and "Pending Naval Questions," *Foreign Affairs* 13 (April 1935): 409–19. Adm. Kichisaburo Nomura pitched in with "Japan's Demand for Naval Equality," *Foreign Affairs* 13 (January 1935): 196–203.

3. Faymonville served as military attaché in Moscow from July 1934 to January 1939. See David M. Glantz, "Observing the Soviets: Army Attaches in Eastern Europe during the 1930s," Soviet Army Studies Office, U.S. Army Combined Arms Center, Fort Leavenworth, Kansas, 1990. Glantz presented this paper at the Conference of Army Historians, Washington, D.C., 26–29 March 1990. He praises Faymonville's reporting. Wainwright led the American forces into captivity in the Philippines and was a prisoner of war from 1942 to 1945. Olmstead was chief signal officer from 1941 to 1943. He retired a major general.

4. NHC, RG 4, 2261-BB, Joint Problem I, 1926, 12. In 1933 both students and faculty in Newport were very dubious. Boldly reaching from Hawaii to Manila was just too risky. (See NHC, RG 4, 2261-1, enclosure "T" for summarized data regarding losses and damage and enclosure "P" for how damage was inflicted. See RG 4, 2261-AA for a faculty critique of Ops. Prob. IV-33.) Without a forward fortified base, estimated Japanese damage to the U.S. fleet so far from Pearl Harbor made a bold offensive unacceptable. Bases had to be established, requiring a deliberate strategy in the Pacific. At the Naval War College in 1933–34 were also Ernest J. King, student commander of Blue, and Raymond A. Spruance. See Vlahos, *Blue Sword,* 93. See also MHI, 1933–34, War Plans Group 4, tab 5, appendix 2, 30.

5. MHI, 1933–34, War Plans Group 4, tab 3.

6. Morton, "Military and Naval Preparations," 24, 25, 33, 35, 38, and 39.

7. See question-and-answer period following the presentation by the 1934 committee. The Q&A sessions following all war plans presentations at AWC clarify what planners were thinking and do so in clear language. See also Clark G. Reynolds, "MacArthur as Maritime Strategist," *Naval War College Review* 33 (March–April 1980): 79–90. The MacArthur strategy in the Pacific in World War II was in accordance with the classic formula propounded by Sir Julian Corbett in 1911 and called the "indirect approach" by Sir Basil Liddell Hart in the period between the wars. Reynolds says, "History would not be far wrong in remembering him also as Admiral Douglas MacArthur" (!) (89).

8. MHI, 1933–34, War Plans Group 4, tab 4, 44.

9. The Gallup and Cantril polls suggest a grudging realization that war might come to Americans. A Gallup question: "In order to declare war, should Congress be required to obtain the approval of the people by means of a national vote?" Response:

| Page | Date | Yes |
|------|------|-----|
| (3) | 9/18–23/1935 | 75% |
| (35) | 8/17–22/1936 | 71% |
| (71) | 9/9–14/1937 | 73% |
| (120) | 9/15–20/1938 | 68% |
| (144) | 2/18–23/1939 | 58% |
| (178) | 9/1–6/1939 | 51% |

Cantril (*Public Opinion,* 458–59) asked from December 1938 to November 1946, "Should every able-bodied American boy twenty years old be required to go into the Army or Navy for one year?" The affirmative response was 37 percent to 39 percent in 1938 and 1939. In 1940, eight surveys showed the affirmative response ranging from 50 percent in May to 71 percent in August (probably a response to the German offensive in Western Europe). From 1940 until 1946 the affirmative response ranged from 62 percent to 75 percent. America wanted to avoid war; a Gallup poll of January 1937 found that 70 percent of the sample regarded American entry into World War I as "a mistake." But prudent measures to prepare for war were generally accepted by the public.

10. MHI, 1933–34, War Plans Group 4, tab 4, bibliography.

11. Ibid., tab 5, 1–3. Edwin F. Harding, William E. Chambers, Lewis B. Hershey, William E. Lynd, Clift Andrus, and Stephen G. Henry were the dissenters.

12. General Simonds, while chief of WPD, suggested in 1931 that an AWC student examine the possibility that England trade possessions in the Western Hemisphere "to the United States in consideration of the cancellation of all debts." MHI, 387 flat. See also the question-and-answer period after the committee report in MHI, 5-1936-2, report of War Plans Group 4, "Participation with Allies."

13. MHI, 1933–34, War Plans Group 4, tab 5, 17.

14. Ibid., tab 10, 11.

15. Ibid., tab 4, 2, regarding mobilization and conscription.

16. Ibid., tab 5, appendix 2, 38. See also NA, RG 165, file 3500 for an after-action report on Grand Joint Exercise 4 dated February 1932. The consideration of an

attack on Pearl Harbor analyzes the capabilities and likely missions of aviation, air-craft carriers, and submarines. It also explores once more the issue of a single com-mander at Pearl Harbor. Gen. Malin Craig was the army commander and chief umpire; Adm. Frank H. Schofield was the navy chief umpire; and Maj. Carl Spatz was the aviation umpire.

17. MHI, 1933–34, War Plans Group 4, tab 7.

18. Ibid., tab 10, 11. The question-and-answer periods following student presen-tations were sometimes verbatim accounts, and speakers were often named. Appar-ently during heated discussions the stenographer focused on the comment, failing to identify the speaker. Such seems to have been the case here.

19. At end of question-and-answer period, MHI, 1933–34, War Plans Group 4.

## Chapter 5. 1935: The Nazi Confederation

1. Except where otherwise noted, the source of the scenario presented to the committee and the committee's reaction is MHI, 5-1935-20, Course at the AWC, 1934–35, War Plans Course, report of War Plans Group 4, "Participation with Allies," oral presentation.

2. Those officials were the U.S. representative to the Inter-Allied Council, the commander of the U.S. expeditionary force destined for Europe, and the com-mander of the U.S. fleet.

3. The planners referred to these officials as "the Mr. House, the General Persh-ing, and the Admiral Mayo of today."

4. MHI, 5-1935-20, 97, appendix 1 to tab 4.

5. Ibid.

6. Ibid., tab 7.

7. See tabs attached to ibid., esp. tab 7.

8. The army had recently discovered public opinion and sought means to shape it. See ibid., appendix C. Also note that the Bureau of Public Relations appears in the 1941 *War Department Telephone Directory* for the first time. Gallup polling began in 1935.

9. Ibid., tab 12, "Political Estimate of the United States."

10. *Gallup Poll,* October 1937, 72 and 160.

11. MHI, 5-1935-10, tab 12.

12. Ibid.

13. Ibid., tab 4.

14. This is the first time in the War Plans Period files that the expression "First" World War is used. Previous references to the 1914–18 war had been to the Great War or the World War.

15. MHI, 5-1935-20, appendix 2, "An Estimate of the Naval Situation."

16. Ibid.

## Chapter 6. 1936: The Central Coalition

1. MHI, file 1-105, Summary of the Courses at the AWC since the World War, 1919–40, 1935–36, 1–3.

2. MHI, 5-1936-21, Course at the AWC, 1935–36, Preparation for War Course, 2d Part, War Plans Period, report of War Plans Group 4, "Participation with Allies." Except where noted, citations that follow are from this report by War Plans Group 4.

3. Ibid., 88. "Czechoslovakia will be quickly overrun by Germany and her strength discounted because of her weak geographic position" (98).

4. See p. 16 of the question-and-answer session following the 31 March 1939 lecture by Brig. Gen. George V. Strong in MHI, WP 13, 1939, "The War Plans Division, War Department General Staff." Asked about how the various departments and agencies of government cooperated in emergency planning, Strong said that only the army and navy think in emergency terms.

5. MHI, 5-1936-21, War Plans Group 4, oral presentation.

6. Ibid., question-and-answer session.

7. Emphasis added.

8. Ibid., question-and-answer session.

9. The others are John N. Greely, Walton H. Walker, Jay W. MacKelvie, Harry J. Malony, Arthur S. Nevins, Willard W. Irvine, and Gordon deL. Carrington. Compiled by cross-referencing two documents: HRC 321, WPD, appendix D, "Master Personnel List, Arrivals and Departures," and the *AWC Directory.*

## Chapter 7. 1937: Europe and the Pacific

1. MHI, file 1-105, Summary of the Courses at the AWC since the World War, 1919–40, 1936–37, 1 and 5.

2. Ibid., 3.

3. Ibid., 4.

4. MHI, 5-1937-24B, Course at the AWC, 1936–37, Preparation for War Course, 2d Part, War Plans Period, supplement 3 to the report of Committee 6, "Subject: War Plan—Participation with Allies, Joint Plan with Appendices, Date of Conference 8 May 1937," 2–3.

5. Edward J. Drea, *Nomonhan: Japanese-Soviet Tactical Combat, 1939,* Leavenworth Papers no. 2, Combat Studies Institute, United States Army Command and General Staff College, Fort Leavenworth, Kans., 1981. The AWC plans refer to the Soviet Union as "Russia."

6. See MHI, 5-1937-24A, memorandum for the chairman, Committee 6, 10 April 1937, for the complete situation given to the work group.

7. MHI, 5-1937-24A, Course at the AWC, 1936–37, oral presentation with supplements 1 and 2, report of Committee 6, "Subject: War Plan, Participation with Allies—European." Note that a file 5-1937-24B contains a supplement 3 from the same Committee 6. Supplement 3 contains the Joint Plan with Appendices and is dated 8 May 1937. It appears that a clean copy of the report including all supporting documents

was submitted a month after the oral presentation on 10 April 1937. Unless specified otherwise, the page references that follow are to 5-1937-24A.

8. Ibid., 50. See 50–55 for a detailed rationale.

9. Ibid., 74.

10. Ibid., 73.

11. These estimates were confirmed after the war. The lead times for industrial processes "were usually estimated to require eighteen months to two years." Richard M. Leighton and Robert W. Coakley, *Global Logistics and Strategy, 1940–1943,* United States Army in World War II: The War Department (Washington, D.C.: Office of the Chief of Military History, Department of the Army, 1955), 709.

12. Ibid., 54, 709.

13. MHI, 5-1937-24B, supplement 3, 2.

14. Ibid., 42.

15. Ibid., 37.

16. See ibid., 41–49, for a political tour of the horizon.

17. Ibid., 72.

18. Ibid., 38.

19. Ibid., 2.

20. Ibid., 46.

21. Ibid., 5.

22. See ibid., 56–71, for observations regarding armies and navies.

23. Ibid., 47ff.

24. Ibid., 43.

25. Ibid., 45.

26. Ibid., 78.

27. Ibid., 77–78.

28. Ibid., 29.

29. On "the other side of the hill" another Realpolitiker made his estimate. Hitler, at a conference at Obersalzburg on 14 August 1939, "stated categorically" that Russia would keep out of the war. He also said that "the men I got to know in Munich are not the kind that start a new World War." He went on to predict that Britain would, in the end, draw back. Without Britain, France would not move. Raymond J. Sontag, "The Last Months of Peace, 1939," *Foreign Affairs* 35 (April 1957): 521. Within three weeks Russia would be an ally, France and Britain would declare war when Germany invaded Poland, and both sides in the West would assume defensive positions in the Sitzkrieg of late 1939 and early 1940—while Hitler had his way with Poland.

30. MHI, 5-1937-24A, 78.

31. Ibid., 79.

32. Ibid., 80.

33. Ibid. See the oral presentation, 80–82.

34. Cross-reference HRC 321, WPD, appendix D, "Master Personnel List, Arrivals and Departures," and *AWC Directory.*

## Chapter 8. 1938: Orange and Purple

1. See MHI, 7-1938-0, for correspondence between WPD, WDGS, and AWC. Orange was updated.

2. MHI, file 1-105, Summary of the Courses at the AWC since the World War, 1919–40, 1937–38, 3.

3. MHI, 5-1938-19/2, Joint Estimate, Red Coalition, 1.

4. MHI, 5-1938-20/1, War Plans—Green.

5. MHI, file 1-105, Summary of the Courses at the AWC since the World War, 1919–40, 1937–38, 2.

6. Ibid., 3–4.

7. This strategic assessment found an echo in public opinion. In a survey conducted 24–29 September 1939—that is, after the German invasion of Poland—95 percent said that America should not send our forces abroad to fight Germany. In the same survey, 73 percent said that in the event of an invasion of Canada, the United States should use its army and navy to aid Canada; 72 percent favored fighting to keep any European power from invading Cuba "or any other country within 1,500 miles of the Panama Canal"; and 53 percent thought the United States should fight to keep European powers from invading Brazil, Chile, "or any other South American country." See *Gallup Poll,* 184.

8. See Leighton and Coakley, *Global Logistics and Strategy,* 27–28. The same points are made in Stetson Conn and Byron Fairchild, *The Framework of Hemisphere Defense,* United States Army in World War II: The War Department (Washington, D.C.: Office of the Chief of Military History, Department of the Army, 1960), 2–10, and by Watson, *Chief of Staff,* 95–96 and 104–7.

9. Donald Cameron Watt, *How War Came: The Immediate Origins of the Second World War* (New York: Pantheon, 1989), 133 and 135. For a thorough military analysis of how the defeat of Britain and France would affect the security of the United States, see also the response to a congressman prepared by WPD dated 17 November 1939, "Subject: Information request as to what extent our national defense is involved in the defeat of Hitler—Congressman Vorys," in NA, RG 225, 3793-80, box 153. The seven-page analysis is tightly written and holds up very well after sixty years.

10. MHI, Course at the AWC, 1937–38, WPD, Notes on War Planning, WP 31, 1938.

11. For a discussion of Malin Craig's 16 December 1936 directive that WDGS begin work at once on a practical "protective mobilization plan," see Kreidberg and Henry, *History of Military Mobilization,* 474–92. For industrial mobilization planning, see ibid., 493–540. WPD was working this out in 1937 and 1938 when AWC was asked to consider Purple with a large-scale troop deployment.

12. Leslie Anders, *Gentle Knight: The Life and Times of Major General Edwin Forrest Harding* (Kent, Ohio: Kent State University Press, 1985), 122.

13. Larry I. Bland and Sharon R. Ritenour, eds., *The Papers of George Catlett Mar-*

*shall,* 3 vols. to date (Baltimore: Johns Hopkins University Press, 1981– ), vol. 1, *The Soldierly Spirit, December 1880–June 1939,* 533.

14. Ibid., 707–8.

15. WP 4, 1938, War Plans Period, 28 February–30 March 1938, Information Period.

16. The official history of economic mobilization for World War II says that "America's outpouring of war materiel, rather than an allied preponderance of manpower, was the dominant factor in winning the war." R. Elberton Smith, *The Army and Economic Mobilization,* United States Army in World War II: The War Department (Washington, D.C.: Office of the Chief of Military History, Department of the Army, 1959), 706. Smith also called the army's prewar plans for industrial preparedness to meet a war emergency "realistic and thorough." There was little of the "floundering, delay, and confusion apparent at the beginning of World War I" (705).

17. MHI, 5-1938-21/2, 88–89. See 83–99 for a detailed analysis of the courses of action available to Japan and the work group's conclusions and decisions.

18. Ibid., 22, 33–44, 71–73, 79–82.

19. MHI, 5-1938-21/5, Navy Basic Plan, 6.

20. MHI, 5-1938-21/3, Joint Plan. Group 3 made supporting plans in accordance with the way the General Staff would have done them. MHI, 5-1938-21/2 is the Joint Estimate of the Situation; 21/4 is the War Department Plan; 21/5 is the Navy Basic Plan; 21/6 is the Joint Pacific Theater Plan; 21/6B is the Operations Plan; 21/6C and 21/6D contain the annexes to the plans. Estimates of the duration of the war came from such realistic planning.

21. MHI, 5-1938-21/2, 11.

22. MHI, 5-1938-21/5, 15.

23. MHI, 5-1938-21/1, 62. Emphasis added.

24. See box 21 in MHI, Hugh A. Drum Papers, for a letter dated 25 July 1936, MacArthur to Drum (p. 2). Drum's response of 4 September 1936 is to "Dear Mac," but the address is "Field Marshal Douglas MacArthur." Drum expected to be appointed Craig's successor as army chief of staff. Despite Drum's seniority and custom, George C. Marshall got that appointment. The Wainwright letter is in MHI, Jonathan M. Wainwright Papers, box 2, Pre–World War II Papers. See also Bradford Grethen Chynoweth, *Bellamy Park: A Memoir* (Hicksville, N.Y.: Exposition Press, 1975), 192–97.

25. MHI, 5-1938-20, oral presentation, 71.

26. Ibid., 73.

27. Ibid., 74.

28. Ibid., 76.

29. See ibid., 76–80, for the lively discussion following the oral presentation. On 27 February 1934 the president of the Naval War College "took the unusual step of sending an unsolicited letter" to the CNO saying it was "highly questionable" that the United States with its "treaty Navy" could accomplish its strategic mission against determined Orange opposition. On 21 March 1933, Capt. Adolphus Andrews, chief

of staff at the Naval War College, responded to the request of Capt. J. D. Wainwright, USN, then a student at AWC (class of 1933), for data on Orange. Andrews provided the data and told Wainwright that any naval officer arguing optimistically would be guilty of "giving a very false impression of what we could actually do." See Michael K. Doyle, "The U.S. Navy and War Plan Orange, 1933–1940: Making Necessity a Virtue," *Naval War College Review,* May–June 1980, 49–63, esp. 54 and 55.

30. MHI, 5-1938-20, oral presentation, 81.

31. Ibid., 82–83.

32. MHI, 7-1935-0, correspondence between AWC and General Staff regarding student work.

33. MHI, 5-1938-22/2, Joint Estimate of the Situation, 6–8.

34. See MHI, 5-1938-22/1, Purple, for the concept and details of the plan.

35. "I think the committee has done a really good job. It is a new study and I must say that I think you have made a very good start." Ibid., 31.

36. In 1938 the total strength of the U.S. Army was 184,126. Kreidberg and Henry, *History of Military Mobilization,* 379.

37. MHI, 5-1938-22/1, Purple, 35–36.

38. See MHI, Hull interviews with Lt. Col. James W. Wurman, October–April 1973. See also Ray S. Cline, *Washington Command Post: The Operations Division;* Maurice Matloff, *Strategic Planning for Coalition Warfare, 1943–1944;* Maurice Matloff and Edwin M. Snell, *Strategic Planning for Coalition Warfare, 1941–1942;* Richard M. Leighton and Robert W. Coakley, *Global Logistics and Strategy, 1940–1943;* and Louis Morton, *Strategy and Command: The First Two Years.* All of the listed books are in the United States Army in World War II series; all are in the War Department subseries, except for Morton's volume, which is in the War in the Pacific subseries. See also MHI, Thomas T. Handy Papers, including "Transcripts of the Debriefing of General Handy" by Lt. Col. Edward M. Knoff, Jr., 1973–74, and the oral history: Gen. Thomas T. Handy, USA, Ret., Floyd J. Davis. The other members of the class of 1938 who served in WPD/OPD are A. Franklin Kibler (1 March 1939–13 July 1942); William K. Harrison (16 August 1939–13 July 1942); William P. Scobey (16 May 1940–9 May 1942); LeCount H. Slocum (1 February 1941–29 December 1941); Thomas D. Davis (17 July 1941–6 February 1943); and John T. Zellars (7 February 1942–15 May 1942). All but Slocum served in Eisenhower's OPD. (See appendix D of this book.) Harrison retired with three stars, Kibler with two, and Slocum with one. Zellars, Scobey, and Davis retired as colonels. (See appendix G of this book.)

39. MHI, file 7-1938-0, correspondence regarding Individual Staff Memoranda (ISM).

40. The MHI "-0" files (7-1935-0, 7-1936-0, 7-1938-0, and 7-1939-0) and "flat" files (407 flat, 387 flat, and 397 flat) contain correspondence between the college and the various sections of the General Staff. They show how the college responded to the staff with individual studies, group projects, and war plans such as Purple in 1938 and 1939. See also MHI, "Misc. #3," 1938, for student work sent to the War Department.

It contains an April 1938 exchange of letters between the assistant commandant, Col. Ned B. Rehkopf, and Robert L. Eichelberger, secretary to the army chief of staff. Rehkopf wanted to be sure that student work was realistic and in tune with the actual needs of the army. Eichelberger was a busy man and very responsive to the college, suggesting the importance of AWC.

### Chapter 9. 1939: Orange and Purple Again

1. MHI, file 1-105, Summary of the Courses at the AWC since the World War, 1919–40, 1938–39, 2.

2. Ibid., 5.

3. MHI, "Misc. #3," War Plans Course Orientation, 1939. See also MHI, WP 16, 1939, a lecture by Admiral Ghormley.

4. MHI, WP 18, 1939, 4–5.

5. MHI, 5-1939-2A, Course at the AWC, War Plans, Hawaiian Department, 8.

6. Ibid., 11. Unity of command is one of the principles of war memorized, if not learned, by many generations of officers. In Ray S. Cline and Maurice Matloff, "Developments of War Department Views on Unification," *Military Affairs* 13 (Summer 1949): 65–74, we see that the army feared "ponderous bureaucratic control." See also NA, RG 165, file 635 for documentation considering the establishment of a Department of National Defense. File 635-3 contains General Orders no. 94, an agreement between the secretaries of war and navy establishing the organization and procedures of the Joint Army and Navy Board and the Joint Army and Navy Planning Committee dated 25 July 1919. A memo for the chief of staff of the army dated 21 April 1922 states that "adequate and efficient machinery already exists." The chief objection to consolidating the War and Navy Departments is "interposing the head of this department between the services concerned and the President." File 635-2 contains correspondence between AWC and WPD and WPD's reaction to the student study of consolidation: Wells to McGlacklin, 28 February 1923; Wells memo, 28 December 1922; Wells memo, 26 February 1923. File 635-16 is a 140-page typescript entitled "The Question of the Creation of a Department of National Defense" by George V. Strong, dated 1927 with a January 1932 revision. Also in file 635-16 see Embick study, January 1928. Various reasons for rejecting the unification of the War and Navy Departments in a Department of National Defense are raised, but at root one suspects that soldiers did not want sailors to command soldiers, and sailors quaked at the prospect of soldiers commanding fleets.

7. MHI, 5-1939-2A, Course at the AWC, War Plans, Hawaiian Department, 12.

8. MHI, 5-1939-4, Philippine Department, tab 1, 1–2.

9. Ibid., tab 3, 1–2.

10. Ibid. The minority report is tab 3 and is dated 7 April 1939.

11. MHI, 5-1939-6/1, Orange, discussion following the student presentation, 62. Collins (AWC 1937) joined the faculty upon graduation.

12. Ibid., 63–64.

13. MHI, 5-1939-6/2, War Plan Orange.

14. Ibid., 20.

15. Ibid., 22.

16. Ibid., 52.

17. Ibid., 48.

18. Ibid., 76.

19. Ibid., 79. The navy deserves credit for educating the army's student-officers. Orange was exercised every year at Newport. The exercises from 1926 through the 1930s reveal that in 1926 the navy's sober estimate was that Japan would be defeated in a Trafalgar-like battle. By 1933 the after-action comments by students and faculty made it clear that without a forward base, the Philippines were not expected to hold out very long. Seeking an early decision would be irresponsible. See NHC, RG 4, Joint Problem 1-1926, 2261-BB, for cautious optimism, and RG 4, Ops. Prob. IV-33, Critique, 2261 AA, for glum comments. See also 2261-1K, 2261-10, and 2261-1Q in the 1933 Ops. Prob. IV for the analysis leading to pessimism.

20. MHI, 5-1939-6/2, War Plan Orange, 82. For details on the Joint Army and Navy Basic War Plan, see MHI, 5-1939-6/3, and for the Navy Basic Plan (Orange), see also 5-1939-6/5.

21. The AWC Plan Orange, 1939, is much like the 1933 version of Orange at the Naval War College. See NHC, RG 4, 2261-1, enclosures "T" and "P." See same file, "AA," for faculty critique of Ops. Prob. IV-33.

22. MHI, WP 16, 1939, lecture by Admiral Ghormley, 2–3.

23. Ibid., 4.

24. Ibid., 16.

25. Ibid., discussion, 7.

26. Ibid., 7–8.

27. See John Ferris, "A British Unofficial Aviation Mission and Japanese Naval Developments, 1919–1929," *Journal of Strategic Studies* 5 (September 1982): 416–39, esp. 422–24.

28. MHI, 5-1939-8/1, Purple, 26.

29. Ibid., 38. See also Gerald E. Wheeler, "National Policy Planning between the World Wars: Conflict between Ends and Means," *Naval War College Review* 21 (February 1969): 54–69. Wheeler describes army-navy differences right to the eve of World War II. The army saw a need to fall back to the "strategic triangle" for a period of preparation before engaging in offensive war. The "long-legged" and heavily gunned U.S. Navy was not interested in giving up on the Philippines, nor was it much interested in hemispheric defense (63–65). Wheeler does not mention the strategic continuity and service preferences described in chap. 1 of the present work, but his analysis recalls Rear Adm. Henry C. Taylor's memorandum to the Joint Board in 1904.

30. MHI, 5-1939-8/1, Purple, 39.

31. Ibid. See 30–39 for the usual lively discussion following the student oral report.

32. MHI, WP 13, 1939, 13.

33. In addition to the correspondence between AWC and WPD found in MHI files 7-1935-0 to 7-1939-0 and "flat" files 407, 397, and 387, see also appendix A of this book.

34. See Kreidberg and Henry, *History of Military Mobilization,* esp. table 54 after 484.

## Chapter 10. 1940: School's Out

1. A new organization not listed in 1940 appears in the *War Department Telephone Directory,* 15 November 1941: the Bureau of Public Relations.

2. MHI, file 1-105, Summary of the Courses at the AWC since the World War, 1919–40, 1939–40, 4.

3. Ibid., 3.

4. MHI, 5-1940-7/1, Orange, oral presentation, 33. See also 5-1940-7/6, Joint Plan for Overseas Expedition for Capture of Truk.

5. MHI, 5-1940-7/1, Orange, oral presentation, 32.

6. Ibid., 86.

7. Ibid., 77.

8. MHI, 5-1940-7/3, Orange, Joint Plan, 36.

9. Ibid., 41.

10. MHI, 5-1940-9/2, Joint Estimate of Rainbow X.

11. Ibid., 35–36.

12. MHI, 5-1940-9/3, Joint Army and Navy Basic Plan, Rainbow X, 6.

13. In the discussion following the Rainbow X oral presentation on 21 May 1940, MHI, 5-1940-9/1, 7.

## Chapter 11. War College Plans and "Official" Plans

1. WPD had eleven officers in 1936. In the period 1 January–6 December 1941, sixty-six officers were assigned. Late in the war, 310 officers were assigned. See HRC 321, WPD, appendix D, "Master Personnel List, Arrivals and Departures." For the heavy responsibilities carried by WPD, see Watson, *Chief of Staff,* 74–75.

2. See Matloff and Snell, *Strategic Planning for Coalition Warfare,* for concise summary and commentary on Plan Dog, 25–31. See also Hattendorf, Simpson, and Wadleigh, *Sailors and Scholars,* 166.

3. Kent Roberts Greenfield, *American Strategy in World War II: A Reconsideration* (Westport, Conn.: Greenwood Press, 1963), 3–10.

4. MHI, 5-1940-9/2, 38.

5. MHI, 5-1940-9/1, Rainbow X, oral presentation, 21 May 1940.

6. Ibid. The pages in the oral presentation are not numbered.

7. Ibid.

8. Ibid., discussion, 8.

9. Ibid., 3.

10. Matloff and Snell, *Strategic Planning for Coalition Warfare,* 5. For U.S. war planning in the 1930s leading to the Rainbow Plans, see also 4–10.

11. Ibid., 6.

12. MHI, "Participation with Allies," 1934.

13. MHI, 5-1938-21/1, oral presentation and question-and-answer period. See also "Orange Revisited, 1938" in chap. 8 of this book.

14. MHI, 5-1935-20, oral report of War Plans Group 4.

15. Matloff and Snell, *Strategic Planning for Coalition Warfare,* 8.

16. MHI, 5-1936-21, report of War Plans Group 4.

17. MHI, 5-1937-24A.

## Chapter 12. Professionals in a Small Army

1. MHI, WP 5, 1938, 2, and WP 5, 1937.

2. See David Brinkley, *Washington Goes to War* (New York: Alfred A. Knopf, 1988), for an account of the transformation of that city from a provincial capital to a world center. See also Chalmers M. Roberts, *Washington, Past and Present* (Washington, D.C.: Public Affairs Press, 1949–50), 54, 137, and 141, and Arthur Robert Smith and Eric Sevareid, *Washington: Magnificent Capital* (Garden City, N.Y.: Doubleday, 1965), 14–15.

3. William Wallace Whitson, "The Role of the USAWC in the Preparation of Officers for National Security Policy Formulation," Ph.D. diss., Fletcher School of Law and Diplomacy, Tufts University, 1958, 158.

4. *AWC Directory.* One staff officer whose name became a household word was Lewis B. Hershey (1934). He directed the U.S. conscription system through three wars.

5. Maxwell D. Taylor, *Swords and Plowshares* (New York: Norton, 1972), 29–30.

6. Martin Blumenson, *Mark Clark* (New York: Congdon and Weed, 1984), 33–34.

7. Ibid., 29.

8. Among them were Lt. Col. Philip B. Peyton; Maj. James A. Van Fleet; Capt. Edward M. Almond; Capt. J. Lawton Collins; Capt. Charles L. Bolte; Lt. Col. Joseph W. Stilwell; Maj. Edwin F. Harding; Maj. Omar N. Bradley; and Maj. Harold R. Bull. Bland and Ritenour, *Papers of George Catlett Marshall,* vol. 1, *The Soldierly Spirit,* 320.

9. Anders, *Gentle Knight,* 120–21.

10. Robert H. Berlin, "The United States Army World War II Corps Commanders: A Composite Biography," *Journal of Military History* 53 (April 1989): 152, 158.

11. J. Lawton Collins, *Lightning Joe: An Autobiography* (Baton Rouge: Louisiana State University Press, 1979), 90–99.

12. Taylor, *Swords and Plowshares,* 29–30.

13. *AWC Directory.*

14. See appendix A of this book, compiled by cross-referencing HRC 321, WPD, appendix D, "Master Personnel List, Arrivals and Departures," and the *AWC Directory.*

15. See appendix B of this book, compiled by cross-referencing the *AWC Directory* and the *War Department Telephone Directory,* 1 March 1940.

16. See appendix C of this book, compiled by cross-referencing the *AWC Directory* and the *War Department Telephone Directory,* 15 November 1941.

17. See appendix D of this book, "Eisenhower's OPD," a roster dated 3 April 1942.

18. See MHI files for records of the curriculum at AWC. The War Plans Period files, especially "Participation with Allies" from 1934 to 1940, provide the detailed plans. From 1934 onward "Participation with Allies" was studied and briefed by at least one committee each year. Coordination between the college and the staff was continuous and extensive. See MHI "-0" files (7-1935-0, 7-1936-0, 7-1938-0, and 7-1939-0). See also "flat" files (387 flat, 397 flat, and 407 flat). These "flat" and "-0" files contain commentary on Individual Staff Memoranda and on war plans. Assignment of topics, faculty evaluations of ISM, and War Department comments on student work are included. The correspondence indicates what the General Staff wanted from AWC. See also NA, RG 165, files 998-1 to 998-7. File 998-7 shows how Malin Craig, when commander of the Panama Department, sent his plans to AWC through WPD and how Simonds, then chief of WPD, got plans from Hawaii to the commandant, AWC. File 998-7 covers the period 10 November 1922 to 23 May 1930.

19. MHI, Orientation, 1936, ISM 1, in 407 flat.

20. MHI, 387 flat.

21. See Martin Blumenson, "George S. Patton's Student Days at the Army War College," *Parameters* 5, no. 2 (1976): 25–32. Investment in professional education and training was essential for an army in which a relative handful of professional officers was the cadre for millions of amateur American soldiers.

22. MHI, 387 flat, 1931 file, esp. red pencil note. See also the Gallup poll conducted just a few days before the deal. It reveals popular approval (60–40) of the sale of the destroyers to Britain without reference to swapping them for bases. The careful pacing of the president's decisions to favorable public opinion is suggested. See *Gallup Poll,* 240. The poll was conducted in the period 24–29 August 1940.

23. See MHI, 387 flat, memo, 20 June 1931, Simonds, WPD, to commandant, AWC, "Suggestions for Theses." Topics on the list are marked up with comments like these: "No. Not general enough in scope." "Yes. Should be combined with [another topic]."

24. MHI, 407 flat.

25. Ibid., correspondence regarding Individual Staff Memoranda, 1933–34. See memo, 20 October 1934, "AWC Studies," from the Military Intelligence Division to AWC.

26. Ibid., letter dated 1 October 1931, "List of Subjects for Individual Studies Requested by WDGS to AWC."

27. MHI, 7-1935-0, roster dated 20 November 1934, four pages marked 33–139.

28. Ibid., letters, Craig to Lincoln, 5 March 1935, and response, 7 March 1935.

29. MHI, file 7-1938-0, correspondence regarding ISM.

30. MHI, file marked "Misc. #3," 1938.

31. Ibid. See letters dated 18, 20, 22, and 23 April 1938 between Rehkopf and Eichelberger. Six members of this class were serving in WPD, WDGS, when Pearl Harbor was bombed. They were A. F. Kibler (1 March 1939–13 July 1942); W. K. Harrison (16 August 1939–13 July 1942); W. P. Scobey (16 May 1940–9 May 1942); LeC. H. Slocum (1 February 1941–29 December 1941); T. D. Davis (17 July 1941–46 February 1943); and J. E. Hull (2 December 1941–42 September 1945). See HRC 321, WPD, appendix D, "Master Personnel List, Arrivals and Departures."

32. MHI, 7-1935-0, letters, Reardon to Simonds, 8 December 1934, and Simonds to Reardon, 10 December 1934.

33. *AWC Directory.*

34. Harry P. Ball, *Of Responsible Command: A History of the U.S. Army War College,* rev. ed. (Carlisle: Alumni Association of the United States Army War College, 1994), 194–98.

35. Ibid., 228.

36. Ibid., 225–26.

37. From 1938 until 1940 Grant commanded the Philippine Division and retired a major general. Ibid., 203, 233.

38. HRC 321, WPD, appendix D, "Master Personnel List, Arrivals and Departures."

39. *AWC Directory.*

40. Obituary, *New York Times,* 22 June 1962.

41. Ball, *Of Responsible Command,* 257–58.

42. Peyton later commanded the 8th Division and retired a major general. Ibid., 233, 249.

43. Ibid., 252, and HRC 321, WPD, appendix D, "Master Personnel List." See appendices A, B, C, and D of this book for details regarding AWC graduates of the post-1934 classes and where they were during the transition to war.

## Chapter 13. AWC Graduates in the Transition from Peace to War

1. Ball, *Of Responsible Command,* 229–30.

2. Robert H. Berlin lists the corps commanders (p. 157) in his previously cited "Composite Biography."

3. See appendix A of this book.

4. MHI, Thomas T. Handy Papers, including "Transcripts of the Debriefing of General Handy" by Lt. Col. Edward M. Knoff, Jr., 1973–74.

5. MHI, oral history: Gen. Thomas T. Handy, USA, Ret., Maj. Floyd J. Davis, Summer 1981.

6. Ibid., 1.

7. Knoff, "Debriefing of Handy," 11–12.

8. Berlin, "Composite Biography," 161.

9. Knoff, "Debriefing of Handy," 12.

10. Ibid., 8.

11. Ibid., 12.

12. Ibid., section 2, 30.

13. Hattendorf, Simpson, and Wadleigh, *Sailors and Scholars,* 146–48 and 152.

14. Knoff, "Debriefing of Handy," 13–14.

15. Wheeler, "National Policy Planning between the World Wars," 69.

16. Robert Greenhalgh Albion, *Makers of Naval Policy, 1798–1947* (Annapolis, Md.: Naval Institute Press, 1980), 91, 73.

17. Hattendorf, Simpson, and Wadleigh, *Sailors and Scholars,* 152.

18. Knoff, "Debriefing of Handy," 16.

19. Ibid., 51–52.

20. Ibid., 52. Maxwell D. Taylor also appreciated the time for introspection, the lack of competition, and the collegiality at AWC. *Swords and Plowshares,* 37.

21. Knoff, "Debriefing of Handy," section 3, 1–3.

22. MHI, Truman Smith Papers. Smith was highly regarded by his peers. His papers are extensive and, with his wife's papers, provide fascinating insights into Nazi Germany before World War II.

23. MHI, 132-18, "An Address by Colonel Jacob W. S. Wuest, A.C., to Officers of the War Department on May 10, 1935 Relative to Conditions in Germany," 1–6.

24. From HRC 321, WPD, appendix D, "Master Personnel List, Arrivals and Departures."

25. Knoff, "Debriefing of Handy," 6.

26. Conn, "Army War College," 11.

27. Knoff, "Debriefing of Handy," 32–35.

28. Ibid., 36–37.

29. Ibid., 37.

30. Ibid., 41–42.

31. Ibid., section 3, 6.

32. Ibid., section 3, 8–9. See also NA, RG 165, files 3354-1 to 3354-19 for a selection process that attempted to get the best and the brightest officers to WPD, including a memo signed by the chief, WPD, General Kilbourne, 16 October 1933, in which he states WPD's need for a graduate of the Naval War College.

33. Knoff, "Debriefing of Handy," section 5, 16.

34. Ibid., section 3, 24.

35. He would retire a major general. *AWC Directory.*

36. MHI, 111-41/20, TAG 6-21-40 and 6-22-40, "Secretary of War dirs. folwg. ofcrs. rept. to ACofS, WPD at AWC folwg. temp. duty. (i/c/w/War Plan Rainbow)." See also in MHI, 111-41/20, memo for ACS G-1, G-2, G-3, G-4, "Subject: Color Plans, Rainbow," 17 June 1940, with enclosure 1, same subject, 14 June 1940, signed by George V. Strong, ACS, WPD, WDGS, a detailed directive to the staff.

37. MHI, Lawrence Family Papers, Maj. Gen. Thompson Lawrence, 201 file.

38. MHI, 111-41/17.

39. Ibid., 3.

40. MHI, 111-41/16, comments and corrections regarding WPD, WDOP-R-40 (Rainbow 4), 17 September 1940, signed by Lawrence; MHI, 111-41/15, "Reproduction of Strategic Studies," 23 September 1940, signed by Lawrence; MHI, 111-41/13 and /14, "Troop Strengths, Deployments in W. Hemisphere," signed by Lawrence; 111-41/15, "Priorities of Photos in Caribbean," 14 September 1940, signed by Lawrence.

41. See MHI, 111-41 file, for U.S. unilateral and "joint plans." (Terminology has changed. The U.S. Department of Defense calls bi- or multi-national military cooperation with allies "combined." "Joint" is used to describe multi-U.S.-service staffs, plans, or operations.)

42. MHI, 5-1939-8/1, Purple.

43. MHI, WP 13, 1939, WPD, WDGS lecture by Brig. Gen. Geo. V. Strong, ACS, WPD, 31 March 1939, 13.

44. Ibid., 16.

45. Russell F. Weigley, "Military Strategy and Civilian Leadership," in *Historical Dimensions of National Security Problems,* edited by Klaus Knorr (Lawrence: University Press of Kansas, 1976), 63–64.

46. Martin Blumenson, "America's World War II Leaders in Europe: Some Thoughts," *Parameters* 19 (December 1989): 4.

47. MHI, Bolte interview with Dr. Maclyn Burg, 17 October 1973, 24.

48. MHI, Bolte interview with Arthur J. Zoebelin, AWC, 1971–72, 7–8.

49. Bolte interview with Burg, 25.

50. MHI, Hull interviews with Lt. Col. James W. Wurman, October–April 1973.

51. Ibid., section 3, 37–45.

52. Ibid., section 5, 27, and section 3, 48.

53. Ibid., section 5, 32.

54. MHI, Russell Maxwell Papers. See the *Philadelphia Inquirer,* 12 August 1945, 1 and 9, in the Maxwell boxes.

55. MHI, Course at the AWC, Preparation for War, 2d Part, War Plans Period, War Plans Group 4, "Participation with Allies," conference on 21 April 1934.

56. See the bibliography to tab 4, ibid. "America's Part in the Supreme War Council during the World War" is included.

57. Robert Murphy, *Diplomat among Warriors* (New York: Pyramid Books, 1965), 122.

58. Hitler comes to power halfway through the academic year of AWC 1933. The frequent elections in Germany before his appointment as chancellor, and the Reichstag fire and the Nazi Revolution that follow, were the backdrop to AWC 1934.

59. See appendix A of this book.

# Bibliography

## Archives

### U.S. Army Center of Military History, Washington, D.C. (CMH)

Historical Manuscripts Collection (HMC)
Historical Records Collection (HRC)

### National Archives, Washington, D.C. (NA)

Record Group 165, Name and Subject Index to the General Correspondence of the War Plans Division, 1921–42 (RG 165). Includes:
> Registers of Communications Received from Military Attaches and Other Intelligence Officers ("Dispatch List"), 1889–1941.
> Correspondence of the Military Intelligence Division Relating to General, Political, Economic, and Military Conditions in Japan, 1918–41.
> Name Index to Correspondence of the Military Intelligence Division of the War Department General Staff, 1917–41.

Record Group 225, Records of the Joint Board, 1903–47 (RG 225).

### Naval Historical Collection, U.S. Naval War College, Newport, R.I. (NHC)

Record Group 4, Publications Office, 1915–77
Record Group 8, Intelligence and Technical Archives, 1895–1948
Record Group 12, Student Problems and Solutions
Record Group 13, Student Theses and Research Papers, 1912–74

### U.S. Army Military History Institute, Carlisle Barracks, Pa. (MHI)

U.S. Army War College Curricular Archives:
> Lectures
> Student Papers
> Records

Personal Papers and Interviews:
> Tasker H. Bliss
> Charles L. Bolte
> Omar Nelson Bradley
> J. Lawton Collins

Hugh A. Drum
Thomas T. Handy
John E. Hull
Thompson Lawrence
Lyman Lemnitzer
Russell Maxwell
Matthew B. Ridgway
Truman Smith
Maxwell D. Taylor
Albert C. Wedemeyer

## Unpublished Manuscripts

Ahern, George P., ed. "A Chronicle of the Army War College." Vol. 1, 1899–1919. Washington, D.C., July 24, 1919. (See also vol. 2, 1919/20–1932/33, and vol. 3, 1933/34–1946, no editors named.) U.S. Army War College and the Military History Institute.

"Chronology, War Plans Division, 11 July 41–21 Nov 41." HRC 314.76, Historical Records Branch, Center of Military History.

Conn, Stetson. "The Army War College, 1899–1940: Mission, Purpose, Objectives. A Study Prepared for the Commandant." Army War College, December 1964. HRC 352, Historical Records Branch, Center of Military History.

Cooling, Benjamin Franklin. "A Suggested Guide to the Curricular Archives of the U.S. Army War College, 1907–1940." Carlisle Barracks, U.S. Army Military History Research Collection, May 1973.

Dewey, Edward John. "The Evolution of Rainbow 5." M.A. thesis, University of Virginia, 1973.

Killigrew, John W. "The Impact of the Great Depression on the Army, 1929–1936." Ph.D. diss., Indiana University, 1960.

Kirkpatrick, Charles E. "Filling the Gaps: Reevaluating Officer Professional Education in the Inter-war Army, 1920–1940." Paper presented at the Annual Meeting of the American Military Institute, Virginia Military Institute, Lexington, 14 April 1989.

———. "Orthodox Soldiers: Army Formal Schools between the Two World Wars." Paper presented at the Annual Meeting of the Organization of American Historians, Washington, D.C., 23–25 March 1990.

Mead, Dana George. "United States Peacetime Strategic Planning, 1920–1941: The Color Plans to the Victory Program." Ph.D. diss., Massachusetts Institute of Technology, 1960.

Morgan, Henry A. "Planning the Defeat of Japan." Washington, D.C.: Office of the Chief of Military History, n.d.

Reagan, David R. "American-British Strategic Planning for Coalition Warfare Prior to the Entrance of U.S. into World War II." Ph.D. diss., Fletcher School of Law and Diplomacy, Tufts University, 1964.

Rood, Harold W. "Strategy out of Silence: American Military Policy and Preparation for War, 1919–1940." Ph.D. diss., University of California, 1960.

Whitson, William Wallace. "The Role of the USAWC in the Preparation of Officers for National Security Policy Formulation." Ph.D. diss., Fletcher School of Law and Diplomacy, Tufts University, 1958.

## Books

Akira, Iriye. *Pacific Estrangement: Japanese and American Expansion, 1897–1911.* Cambridge, Mass.: Harvard University Press, 1972.

Albion, Robert Greenhalgh. *Makers of Naval Policy, 1798–1947.* Annapolis, Md.: Naval Institute Press, 1980.

Ambrose, Stephen E. *Eisenhower.* 2 vols. New York: Simon and Schuster, 1982–83. Vol. 1, *Soldier, General of the Army, President-Elect, 1890–1952.*

Anders, Leslie. *Gentle Knight: The Life and Times of Major General Edwin Forrest Harding.* Kent, Ohio: Kent State University Press, 1985.

*Annual Reports of the Secretary of the Navy.* Washington, D.C.: U.S. Government Printing Office, 1898–1940.

*Annual Reports, War Department. Fiscal Year Ended June 30, 1941. Report of the Secretary of War to the President, 1941.* Washington, D.C.: U.S. Government Printing Office, 1941.

Ball, Harry P. *Of Responsible Command: A History of the U.S. Army War College.* Rev. ed. Carlisle: Alumni Association of the United States Army War College, 1994.

Beard, Charles A. *American Foreign Policy, 1932–1940.* New Haven: Yale University Press, 1947.

———. *President Roosevelt and the Coming of the War, 1941.* New Haven: Yale University Press, 1948.

*Biennial Report of the Chief of Staff of the United States Army to the Secretary of War. July 1, 1939, to June 30, 1941.* Washington, D.C.: U.S. Government Printing Office, 1941.

Bland, Larry I., and Sharon R. Ritenour, eds. *The Papers of George Catlett Marshall.* 3 vols. to date. Baltimore: Johns Hopkins University Press, 1981–. Vol. 1, *The Soldierly Spirit, December 1880–June 1939.*

Blumenson, Martin. *The Patton Papers: 1885–1940.* Boston: Houghton Mifflin, 1972.

———. *Patton: The Man behind the Legend, 1885–1945.* New York: William Morrow, 1985.

Borg, Dorothy, and Shumpei Okamoto, eds., with the assistance of Dale K. A. Finlayson. *Pearl Harbor as History: Japanese-American Relations, 1931–1941.* New York: Columbia University Press, 1973.

Bradley, Omar N., with Clay Blair. *A General's Life.* New York: Simon and Schuster, 1983.

Braisted, William R. *The United States Navy in the Pacific, 1897–1909.* Austin: University of Texas Press, 1958.

Brinkley, David. *Washington Goes to War.* New York: Alfred A. Knopf, 1988.

Brown, Richard C. *Social Attitudes of American Generals, 1898–1940.* New York: Arno Press, 1979.

Buell, R. L. *The Washington Conference.* New York: Appleton, 1922.

Bywater, Hector C. *The Great Pacific War: A History of the American-Japanese Campaign of 1931–33.* Boston: Houghton Mifflin, 1925.

Cantril, Hadley, ed. *Public Opinion, 1935–1946.* Princeton: Princeton University Press, 1951.

Carroll, Eber Malcolm. *Germany and the Great Powers, 1866–1914: A Study in Public Opinion and Foreign Policy* (1938). Hamden, Conn.: Archon Books, 1966.

Challener, Richard D. *Admirals, Generals, and American Foreign Policy, 1898–1914.* Princeton: Princeton University Press, 1973.

Churchill, Winston. *The Grand Alliance.* Boston: Houghton Mifflin, 1951.

Chwialkowski, Paul. *In Caesar's Shadow: The Life of General Robert Eichelberger.* Westport, Conn.: Greenwood Press, 1993.

Chynoweth, Bradford Grethen. *Bellamy Park: A Memoir.* Hicksville, N.Y.: Exposition Press, 1975.

Cline, Ray S. *Washington Command Post: The Operations Division.* United States Army in World War II: The War Department. Washington, D.C.: Office of the Chief of Military History, Department of the Army, 1951.

Cole, Wayne S. *Roosevelt and the Isolationists, 1932–45.* Lincoln: University of Nebraska Press, 1983.

Collins, J. Lawton. *Lightning Joe: An Autobiography.* Baton Rouge: Louisiana State University Press, 1979.

Colville, John. *The Fringes of Power: 10 Downing Street Diaries, 1939–1955.* New York: Norton, 1985.

Conn, Stetson, and Byron Fairchild. *The Framework of Hemisphere Defense.* United States Army in World War II: The War Department. Washington, D.C.: Office of the Chief of Military History, Department of the Army, 1960.

Craig, Gordon. *The Diplomats, 1919–1939.* Princeton: Princeton University Press, 1953.

Craven, Wesley F., and James L. Cate, eds. *The Army Air Forces in World War II.* 7 vols. Chicago: University of Chicago Press, 1948–58. Vol. 1, *Plans and Early Operations, January 1939 to August 1942.*

Dallek, Robert. *Franklin D. Roosevelt and American Foreign Policy, 1932–45.* New York: Oxford University Press, 1983.

Daniels, Josephus. *The Wilson Era: Years of Peace, 1910–1917.* Chapel Hill: University of North Carolina Press, 1944.

Davis, Vernon E. *Origins of the Joint and Combined Chiefs of Staff.* Vol. 1. Washington, D.C.: History Division, Joint Chiefs of Staff, 1972.

DeWeerd, Maj. H. A., ed. *Selected Speeches and Statements of General of the Army George C. Marshall.* Washington, D.C.: Infantry Journal Press, 1945.

*Directory of U.S. Army War College Graduates.* Carlisle, Pa.: Alumni Association, USAWC, 2000.

Dodd, William and M., eds. *Ambassador Dodd's Diary, 1933–1938.* New York: Harcourt Brace, 1941.

Earle, Edward Mead, ed. *Makers of Modern Strategy.* Princeton: Princeton University Press, 1943.

Eisenhower, Dwight D. *At Ease: Stories I Tell to Friends.* Garden City, N.Y.: Doubleday, 1967.

Fairchild, Byron, and Jonathan Grossman. *The Army and Industrial Manpower.* United States Army in World War II: The War Department. Washington, D.C.: Office of the Chief of Military History, Department of the Army, 1959.

Feis, Herbert. *The Road to Pearl Harbor.* Princeton: Princeton University Press, 1950.

Ferrell, Robert H., ed. *The Eisenhower Diaries.* New York: Norton, 1981.

Fletcher, Marvin. *The Peacetime Army, 1900.* New York: Greenwood Press, 1988.

Gallup, George H. *The Gallup Poll: Public Opinion, 1935–1971.* 3 vols. New York: Random House, 1972.

Greenfield, Kent Roberts. *American Strategy in World War II: A Reconsideration.* Westport, Conn.: Greenwood Press, l963.

———, ed. *Command Decisions.* New York: Harcourt, Brace, 1959.

Grenville, J. A. S., and G. B. Young. *Politics, Strategy, and American Diplomacy: Studies in Foreign Policy, 1873–1917.* New Haven: Yale University Press, 1966.

Grew, Joseph C. *Ten Years in Japan.* New York: Simon and Schuster, 1944.

Hagood, Johnson. *We Can Defend America.* Garden City, N.Y.: Doubleday, 1937.

Harmon, E. N., with Milton MacKaye and William Ross MacKaye. *Combat Commander: Autobiography of a Soldier.* Englewood Cliffs, N.J.: Prentice-Hall, 1970.

Hattendorf, John B., B. Mitchell Simpson III, and John R. Wadleigh. *Sailors and Scholars.* Newport, R.I.: Naval War College Press, 1984.

Hayes, Grace P. *The History of the JCS in WWII: The War against Japan.* Annapolis: Naval Institute Press, 1982.

Heinrichs, Waldo. *Threshold of War.* New York: Oxford University Press, 1988.

Herwig, Holger H. *Politics of Frustration: The U.S. as a Factor in German Planning, 1888–1941.* Boston: Little, Brown, 1976.

Hewes, James E., Jr. *From Root to McNamara: Army Organization and Administration, 1900–1963.* Special Studies Series. Washington, D.C.: Center of Military History, U.S. Army, 1975.

Hull, Cordell. *The Memoirs of Cordell Hull,* edited by Robert E. Sherwood. New York: Macmillan, 1948.

Julia, Francis T. *Arms Staff Reorganization, 1903–1985.* Washington, D.C.: Analysis Branch, U.S. Army Center of Military History, 1987.

Keegan, John. *The Price of Admiralty.* New York: Viking, 1989.

Kennedy, David M. *Freedom from Fear: The American People in Depression and War, 1929–1945.* New York: Oxford University Press, 1999.

———. *Over Here: The First World War and American Society.* Oxford: Oxford University Press, 1980.

Kennedy, Paul M. *The Rise of the German-Anglo Antagonism.* London: Allen and Unwin, 1980.

————. *The Samoan Tangle: A Study in Anglo-German-American Relations, 1878–1900*. New York: Barnes and Noble, 1974.

————, ed. *The War Plans of the Great Powers, 1880–1914*. London: Allen and Unwin, 1979.

Ketchum, Richard M. *The Borrowed Years, 1938–1941: America on the Way to War*. New York: Random House, 1989.

King, Ernest, and Walter Muir Whitehill. *Fleet Admiral King: A Naval Record*. New York: Norton, 1952.

Knox, Dudley W., Capt. (USN). *The Eclipse of American Sea Power*. New York: American Army and Navy Journal, 1922.

Kreidberg, Marvin A., and Merton G. Henry. *History of Military Mobilization in the United States Army, 1775–1945*. Department of the Army Pamphlet no. 20-212. Washington, D.C.: U.S. Government Printing Office, November 1955.

Langer, William L., and S. Everett Gleason. *The Challenge to Isolation, 1937–1940*. New York: Harper, 1952.

————. *The Undeclared War, 1940–1941*. New York: Harper, 1953.

Larrabee, Eric. *Commander in Chief: Franklin Delano Roosevelt, His Lieutenants, and Their War*. New York: Harper and Row, 1987.

Lea, Homer. *The Day of the Saxon*. New York: Harper, 1912.

————. *The Valor of Ignorance*. New York: Harper, 1909.

Leighton, Richard M., and Robert W. Coakley. *Global Logistics and Strategy, 1940–1943*. United States Army in World War II: The War Department. Washington, D.C.: Office of the Chief of Military History, Department of the Army, 1955.

Leuchtenburg, William Edward. *The FDR Years: On Roosevelt and His Legacy*. New York: Columbia University Press, 1995.

Leutze, James R. *Bargaining for Supremacy: Anglo-American Naval Collaboration, 1937–1941*. Chapel Hill: University of North Carolina Press, 1978.

Linn, Brian McAllister. *Guardians of Empire*. Chapel Hill: University of North Carolina Press, 1997.

Low, David. *Years of Wrath*. New York: Simon and Schuster, 1946.

Masland, John W., and Laurence I. Radway. *Soldiers and Scholars: Military Education and National Policy*. Princeton: Princeton University Press, 1957.

Matloff, Maurice. *Strategic Planning for Coalition Warfare, 1943–1944*, United States Army in World War II: The War Department. Washington, D.C.: Office of the Chief of Military History, Department of the Army, 1953.

Matloff, Maurice, and Edwin M. Snell. *Strategic Planning for Coalition Warfare, 1941–1942*. United States Army in World War II: The War Department. Washington, D.C.: Office of the Chief of Military History, Department of the Army, 1953.

Miller, Edward S. *War Plan Orange: The U.S. Strategy to Defeat Japan, 1897–1945*. Annapolis, Md.: Naval Institute Press, 1991.

Miller, Merle. *Ike the Soldier: As They Knew Him*. New York: G. P. Putnam's Sons, 1987.

Miller, Nathan. *The U.S. Navy: A History.* New York: Quill, William Morrow, 1990.

Millett, Allan R. *Semper Fidelis: The History of the United States Marine Corps.* Rev. and expanded ed. New York: Free Press; Toronto: Maxwell Macmillan Canada, 1991.

Moon, John E. *Confines of Concept: Preconception of American Strategy in WWII.* New York: Garland, 1988.

Morisen, Elsing E. *Admiral Sims and the Modern American Navy.* Boston: Houghton Mifflin, 1942.

Morton, Louis. *Strategy and Command: The First Two Years.* United States Army in World War II: The War in the Pacific. Washington, D.C.: Office of the Chief of Military History, Department of the Army, 1962.

Murphy, Robert. *Diplomat among Warriors.* New York: Pyramid Books, 1965.

Murray, Williamson, and Millett, Allan R. *Calculations: Net Assessment and the Coming of World War II.* New York: Free Press; Toronto: Maxwell Macmillan Canada, 1992.

*The National Defense Act.* Approved June 3, 1916, as amended March 4, 1929. Washington, D.C.: U.S. Government Printing Office, 1929.

Nelson, Otto L., Jr. *National Security and the General Staff.* Washington, D.C.: Infantry Journal Press, 1946.

Pappas, George S. *Prudens Futuri: The U.S. Army War College, 1901–1967.* Carlisle Barracks, Pa.: Alumni Association of the U.S. Army War College, 1967.

Paret, Peter, ed. *Makers of Modern Strategy, from Machiavelli to the Nuclear Age.* Princeton: Princeton University Press, 1986.

Parrish, Thomas. *Roosevelt and Marshall, Partners in Politics and War.* New York: William Morrow, 1989.

*Peace and War—United States Foreign Policy, 1931–1941.* Washington, D.C.: U.S. Government Printing Office, 1943.

Pogue, Forrest C. *George C. Marshall: Education of a General, 1880–1939.* New York: Viking, 1963.

———. *George C. Marshall: Ordeal and Hope, 1939–1942.* New York: Viking, 1966.

Presseisen, Ernst L. *Germany and Japan: A Study in Totalitarian Diplomacy, 1933–41.* New York: Howard Fertig, 1969.

Price, Frank James. *Troy H. Middleton: A Biography.* Baton Rouge: Louisiana State University Press, 1974.

Puryear, Edgar F., Jr. *19 Stars: A Study in Military Character and Leadership.* Novato, Calif.: Presidio Press, 1981.

Reynolds, David. *The Creation of the Anglo-American Alliance, 1937–41.* Chapel Hill: University of North Carolina Press, 1982.

Richardson, James O., and George C. Dyer. *On the Treadmill to Pearl Harbor: The Memoirs of Admiral James O. Richardson.* 2 vols. Washington, D.C.: Naval History Division, 1973.

Ridgway, Matthew B., as told to Harold H. Martin. *Soldier: The Memoirs of Matthew B. Ridgway.* New York: Harper and Brothers, 1956.

Rosenmann, Samuel I., ed. *The Public Papers and Addresses of FDR.* New York: Random House, 1938.

Ross, Steven T. *American War Plans, 1941–1945.* London: Frank Cass, 1997.

Sherwood, Robert E. *Roosevelt and Hopkins: An Intimate History.* Rev. ed. New York: Harper, 1950.

Smith, R. Elberton. *The Army and Economic Mobilization.* United States Army in World War II: The War Department. Washington, D.C.: Office of the Chief of Military History, Department of the Army, 1959.

Spector, Ronald. *Professors of War.* Newport, R.I.: Naval War College Press, 1977.

Sprout, Harold and Margaret. *The Rise of American Naval Power.* Princeton: Princeton University Press, 1966.

Stoler, Mark A. *Allies and Adversaries.* Chapel Hill: University of North Carolina Press, 2000.

Taylor, Maxwell D. *Swords and Plowshares.* New York: Norton, 1972.

Toynbee, Arnold J. *Survey of International Affairs.* London: Oxford University Press, 1933.

Trask, David. *Captains and Cabinets: Anglo-American Naval Relations, 1917–1918.* Columbia: University of Missouri Press, 1972.

U.S. Congress, Joint Committee on the Investigation of the Pearl Harbor Attack. 79th Cong., 2d sess., 1946.

Vlahos, Michael. *The Blue Sword: The Naval War College and the American Mission, 1919–1941.* Washington, D.C.: U.S. Government Printing Office; Newport, R.I.: Naval War College Press, 1980.

*War Department Telephone Directories,* 1 March 1940, 1 March 1941, and 15 November 1941.

Watson, Mark Skinner. *Chief of Staff: Prewar Plans and Preparations.* United States Army in World War II: The War Department. Washington, D.C.: Office of the Chief of Military History, Department of the Army, 1950.

Watt, Donald Cameron. *How War Came: The Immediate Origins of the Second World War.* New York: Pantheon, 1989.

Wedemeyer, Albert C. *Wedemeyer Reports!* New York: Henry Holt, 1958.

Weigley, Russell F. *The American Way of War: A History of United States Military Strategy and Policy.* New York: Macmillan, 1973.

———. *History of the United States Army.* New York: Macmillan, 1967.

Weiss, Steve. *Allies in Conflict: Anglo-American Strategic Negotiations, 1938–44.* London: Macmillan, with King's College, 1996.

Wheeler-Bennett, John W., ed. *Documents on International Affairs.* London: Oxford University Press, 1933.

## Articles

Bailey, Thomas A. "Dewey and the Germans at Manila Bay." *American Historical Review* 45 (October 1939): 59–81.

Beaver, Dan. "The Industrial-Military Complex in Historical Perspective." *Journal of American History* 56 (March 1970): 819–39.

Berlin, Robert H. "The United States Army World War II Corps Commanders: A Composite Biography." *Journal of Military History* 53 (April 1989): 147–67.

Brodie, Bernard. "Strategy as a Science." *World Politics* 17 (July 1949): 467–88.

Butler, Jarvis. "The General Board of the Navy." *U.S. Naval Institute Proceedings* 56 (August 1930): 700–705.

Coffman, Edward M., and Peter F. Herrly. "The American Regular Army Officer Corps between the World Wars: A Collective Biography." *Armed Forces and Society* 3 (November 1977): 55–73.

Craig, Malin. "Our Present Military Position." *Army Ordnance,* September–October 1939, 89–90.

Doyle, Michael K. "The U.S. Navy and War Plan Orange, 1933–1940: Making Necessity a Virtue." *Naval War College Review,* May–June 1980, 49–63.

Earle, Edward Mead. "American Military Policy and National Security." *Political Science Quarterly* 53 (March 1938): 1–13.

———. "National Defense and Political Science." *Political Science Quarterly* 55 (December 1940): 481–95.

Embick, Stanley D. "Project for Coast Defenses." *Journal of the United States Artillery* 46 (September–October 1916): 151–66.

Flint, Roy K. "The United States Army on the Pacific Frontier, 1899–1939." *The American Military and the Far East.* Proceedings of the Ninth Military History Symposium, USAF Academy, 1980.

Gibbs, Norman. "The Naval Conferences of the Interwar Years: A Study in Anglo-American Relations." *Naval War College Review,* Summer 1977, 50–63.

Gole, Henry G. "War Planning at the Army War College in the Mid-1930s." *Parameters* 15 (Spring 1985): 52–64.

Greene, Fred. "The Military View of American National Policy, 1904–1940." *American Historical Review* 66 (January 1961): 354–77.

Grenville, James. "Diplomacy and War Plans in the United States, 1890–1917." In *The War Plans of the Great Powers, 1880–1914,* edited by Paul M. Kennedy, 23–38. Boston: Allen and Unwin, 1979.

Heinrichs, Waldo H., Jr. "The Role of the United States Navy." In *Pearl Harbor as History: Japanese-American Relations, 1931–1941,* edited by Dorothy Borg and Shumpei Okamoto, 197–223. New York: Columbia University Press, 1973.

Homan, Paul T. "Must It Be War with Japan?" *Political Science Quarterly* 53 (June 1938): 173–85.

James, D. Clayton. "American and Japanese Strategies in the Pacific War." In *Makers of Modern Strategy from Machiavelli to the Nuclear Age,* edited by Peter Paret, 703–32. Princeton: Princeton University Press, 1986.

Kirk, Grayson. "Philippine-American Relations: Recent Trends." *Political Science Quarterly* 54 (September 1939): 321–42.

Matloff, Maurice. "Allied Strategy in Europe, 1939–1945." In *Makers of Modern Strategy from Machiavelli to the Nuclear Age,* edited by Peter Paret, 677–702. Princeton: Princeton University Press, 1986.

———. "The American Approach to War, 1919–1945." In *The Theory and Practice of War,* edited by Michael Howard, 213–43. Bloomington: Indiana University Press, 1965.

———. "Mr. Roosevelt's Three Wars: FDR as War Leader." Harmon Memorial Lecture no. 6. USAF Academy, Colorado Springs, Colorado, 1964.

May, Ernest. "The Development of Political-Military Consultation in the United States." *Political Science Quarterly* 70 (June 1955): 161–80.

Morton, Louis. "Army and Marines on the China Station: A Study in Military and Political Rivalry." *Pacific Historical Review* 29 (February 1960): 51–73.

———. "Defense of the Philippines during the War Scare of 1907." *Military Affairs* 13 (Summer 1949): 95–104.

———. "Interservice Cooperation and Pol-Mil Collaboration." In *Total War and Cold War: Problems in Civilian Control of the Military,* edited by Harry L. Coles, 131–57. Columbus: Ohio University Press, 1959.

———. "National Policy and Military Strategy." *Virginia Quarterly Review* 36 (Winter 1960): 1–17.

———. "War Plan ORANGE: Evolution of a Strategy." *World Politics* 2 (January 1959): 221–50.

Nenninger, Timothy K. "Creating Officers: The Leavenworth Experience, 1920–1940." *Military Review* (November 1989): 58–68.

Nomura, Adm. Kichisaburo. "Japan's Demand for Naval Equality." *Foreign Affairs* 13 (January 1935): 196–203.

Peffer, Nathaniel. "Entanglement or Nonentanglement: Is There a Choice?" *Political Science Quarterly* 55 (December 1940): 522–34.

———. "The United States in the Far East." *Political Science Quarterly* 54 (March 1939): 1–14.

Pratt, Adm. William V. "Pending Naval Questions." *Foreign Affairs* 13 (April 1935): 409–19.

———. "The Setting for the 1935 Naval Conference." *Foreign Affairs* 12 (July 1934): 541–52.

Quinlan, Robert J. "The U.S. Fleet: Diplomacy, Strategy, and the Allocation of Ships (1940–41)." In *American Civil-Military Decisions,* edited by Harold Stein, 152–202. Birmingham: University of Alabama Press, 1963.

Reynolds, Clark G. "MacArthur as Maritime Strategist." *Naval War College Review* 33 (March–April 1980): 79–90.

Richmond, Adm. Sir Herbert. "Immediate Problems of Naval Reduction." *Foreign Affairs* 9 (April 1931): 371–88.

———. "Naval Problems of 1935." *Foreign Affairs* 13 (October 1934): 45–58.

Rodgers, William L. "The Relations of the War College to the Navy Department." *U.S. Naval Institute Proceedings* 38 (September 1912): 835–50.

Schaffer, Ronald. "General Stanley D. Embick: Military Dissenter." *Military Affairs* 373 (October 1973): 89–95.

Sontag, Raymond J. "The Last Months of Peace, 1939." *Foreign Affairs* 35 (April 1957): 507–24.

Stoler, Mark A. "The 'Pacific-First' Alternative in American World War II Strategy." *International History Review* 2 (July 1980): 432–52.

Thompson, Dorothy. "National Socialism: Theory and Practice." *Foreign Affairs* 13 (July 1935): 557–73.

Utley, Freda. "Germany and Japan." *Political Quarterly* 8 (January 1937): 51–65.

Vagts, Alfred. "Hopes and Fears of an American-German War, 1870–1915, I." *Political Science Quarterly* 54 (December 1939): 514–35.

———. "Hopes and Fears of an American-German War, 1870–1915, II." *Political Science Quarterly* 55 (March 1940): 53–76.

Vlahos, Michael E. "The Naval War College and the Origins of War Planning against Japan." *Naval War College Review* 33 (July–August 1980): 23–41.

Wainwright, Richard. "The General Board." *U.S. Naval Institute Proceedings* 48 (February 1922): 189–201.

Watson, Mark. "First Vigorous Steps in Re-arming, 1938–39." *Military Affairs* 12 (Summer 1948): 65–78.

Weigley, Russell F. "The Elihu Root Reforms and the Progressive Era." In *Command and Commanders in Modern Warfare,* edited by William Geffen. Proceedings of the Second Military History Symposium, USAF Academy, 1980.

———. "Military Strategy and Civilian Leadership." In *Historical Dimensions of National Security Problems,* edited by Klaus Knorr, 38–77. Lawrence: University Press of Kansas, 1976.

———. "To the Crossing of the Rhine: American Strategic Thought to World War II." *Armed Forces and Society* 5 (February 1979): 302–20.

Wheeler, Gerald E. "National Policy Planning between the World Wars: Conflict between Ends and Means." *Naval War College Review* 21 (February 1969): 54–69.

Williams, William A. "The Legend of Isolationism in the 1920's." *Science and Society* 18 (Winter 1954): 1–20.

# Index

United States Army: assessment of, 55–56,
    85–86; constraints on, 157; cooperation
    with Navy, 140–41; and hemispheric
    defense, 34, 68; mobilization, 116;
    nonmilitary functions, 5; officer corps,
    122–23; purpose, 4; readiness, 16, 71–72,
    84, 135, 145
United States Army Air Corps, 5, 130
United States Army Air Service, 6
United States Army Chemical Warfare
    Service, 6
United States Army Corps of Engineers, 5
United States Army Finance Department, 6
United States Army Tank Corps, 6
United States Congress, 6
United States Marine Corps, 4, 12–13
United States Navy: assessment of, 56–57,
    85–86; in Atlantic Ocean, 62; cooperation
    with Army, 140–41; expenditures, 3–4, 6;
    human resources, 64; in Mediterranean
    Sea, 70, 71; at Midway, 115; and Orange
    (Japan), 25, 33, 68, 88–89, 100, 119; and
    Pacific Ocean, 24–25; on Purple (Brazil),
    102; readiness, 13, 71, 99; responsibility
    of, 11–12, 57; two-ocean program, 14–15;
    in War Plans Division, 130
Upston, John E., 134

Vandenberg, Hoyt S., 125
Versailles, Treaty of, 9, 10, 52, 151

Wainwright, Jonathan M., 40, 87, 125, 133
Wake, 12
war aims, 60–61
War College Division of the General Staff, 18
War College Group, 142–43
war colleges, 8
war debts, 9, 60–61
War Department, 3, 5
War Department General Staff: and Army

War College, 17–19, 25, 67, 126–27, 129,
    148–49, 152, 156, 158; establishment, 17;
    functions, 25; inadequacies, 28–29; and
    Manchu Act, 141; officer corps, 113,
    122–23, 125–26; on Philippines, 20; on
    Purple (Brazil), 91–92; reorganization of,
    31; and war-planning process, 35. *See also*
    War Plans Division
war-planning process, 32–36, 139
War Plans Course (1937), 67
War Plans Division: cooperation with Army
    War College, 29, 31–32, 128, 148;
    expansion of, 31; Handy in, 134;
    Lawrence in, 142–43; members, 66,
    77–78, 92–93; officer corps, 113, 122–23,
    125–26, 131, 138; reestablishment by
    Simonds, 130; responsibilities, 25, 29–31,
    158. *See also* Operations Division; War
    Department General Staff
War Plans Period (1936), 59
War Plans Period (1938), 81
Washington Armament Conference, 9, 52
Washington, D.C., 123
weapons, 64
Wedemeyer, Albert C., 137
Weigley, Russell F., 145
West Africa, 91
Wheeler, Gerald E., 136
Wilhelm, Kaiser II, 25
Wilson, Woodrow, 8
Wood, Leonard, 42
World War I, 44, 63
Wuest, Jacob W. S., 138

Yarnell, Harry E., 42
Yellow. *See* China
Yugoslavia, 49, 60, 69, 75

Zhukov, Georgi K., 69

# About the Author

Col. Henry G. Gole, USA (Ret.), served during the Korean War as a rifleman, BAR (Browning automatic rifle) man, and sergeant, and served two tours during the Vietnam War as a Special Forces officer. He served four tours in Germany, including Special Forces, infantry, staff jobs, and as the assistant army attaché in the American Embassy, Bonn. He also worked for the U.S. Army War College's Strategic Studies Institute as a research analyst, and at the Pentagon as a staff officer. Colonel Gole earned a doctorate in history at Temple University and has taught at the University of Maryland, the United States Military Academy, Franklin and Marshall College, Dickinson College, and in the Department of National Security and Strategy at the U.S. Army War College.

Colonel Gole has published over thirty articles and numerous book reviews. Since 1998 he has given papers at academic conferences sponsored by the University of North Texas, the U.S. Marine Corps, Virginia Military Institute, the Inter-University Seminar for Armed Forces and Society, the Society for Military History, and a conference on the Korean War in the Cantigny Conference Series co-sponsored by the McCormick Foundation and the U.S. Naval Institute. Gole resides in Mechanicsburg, Pennsylvania, where he writes, consults, and teaches.